WORKPLACE INDU̶S̶T̶R̶I̶ ̶
AUSTRALIAN CASE STUDIES

General Editor: Gerard Griffin
Other books in the series:
Foundations of Arbitration: The Origins and Effects of State Compulsory Arbitration, 1890–1914—Stuart Macintyre and Richard Mitchell (eds)
Unions at the Workplace: Shop Steward Leadership and Ideology—John Benson

AUSTRALIAN STUDIES
IN LABOUR RELATIONS

WORKPLACE
INDUSTRIAL
RELATIONS

Australian Case Studies

Edited by
Russell Lansbury and
Duncan Macdonald

DAMAGED

Melbourne

OXFORD UNIVERSITY PRESS

Oxford   Auckland   New York

OXFORD UNIVERSITY PRESS AUSTRALIA
Oxford   New York   Toronto
Delhi   Bombay   Calcutta   Madras   Karachi
Kuala Lumpur   Singapore   Hong Kong   Tokyo
Nairobi   Dar es Salaam   Cape Town
Melbourne   Auckland

and associated companies in
Berlin   Ibadan

OXFORD is a trade mark of Oxford University Press

National Library of Australia
Cataloguing-in-Publication data:

Lansbury, Russell D. (Russell Duncan), 1945–
   Workplace industrial relations: Australian case studies.
   Bibliography.
   Includes index.
   ISBN 0 19 553275 9.
   1. Industrial relations in Australia. I. Macdonald,
   Duncan. II. Title. (Series: Australian studies in labour relations; 3).
331.0994

Cover illustration by Josie Ryan
Cover design by Jennifer Johnston
Edited by Kerry Herbstreit
Typeset by Syarikat Seng Teik Sdn. Bhd.
Printed in Singapore
Published by Oxford University Press,
253 Normanby Road, South Melbourne, Australia

Foreword

This is the third book in the series of monographs titled Australian Studies in Labour Relations. The series consists of books written and edited by staff and associates of the Centre for Industrial Relations and Labour Studies at the University of Melbourne.

In 1946 the University of Melbourne offered the first tertiary-level course in industrial relations within Australia. Today it is a major centre for research and teaching in labour studies, offering a masters degree in industrial relations, a graduate diploma in industrial relations, and an undergraduate specialisation in labour studies. The Centre for Industrial Relations and Labour Studies co-ordinates research and teaching in the labour area at the University. The general philosophy of the Centre is to regard labour studies as a multi-disciplinary area of study which is based on knowledge and methods developed in a number of traditional areas of study, including economics, law, sociology, politics, psychology and history.

This book reports the findings of a series of case studies on industrial relations at the workplace level, an area of research hitherto largely ignored in Australian industrial relations. The research focuses on five main issues: the influence of the arbitral systems on workplace industrial relations, the nature of unionism at the plant level, the extent of management control at the workplace, the degree of incorporation of employees by management, and the extent and impact of recent attempts by management to increase efficiency on the shop-floor. The research was specifically designed to complement and to build on the questionnaire-based data contained in the Australian Workplace Industrial Relations Survey (AWIRS); indeed, most of the case study authors were actively involved in designing the AWIRS questionnaire. The case studies contribute significantly towards an understanding of the practice of industrial relations at the individual workplace level. Increasingly, this is an area of profound importance for our evolving industrial relations system.

Gerard Griffin

Centre for Industrial Relations and Labour Studies
University of Melbourne

Contents

List of tables and figures

Abbreviations

ACAC	Australian Conciliation and Arbitration Commission (pre-1988)
ACIRRT	Australian Centre for Industrial Relations Research and Teaching
ACTU	Australian Council of Trade Unions
ADO	allocated day off
ADSTE	Association of Draughting, Supervisory and Technical Employees
AHA	Australian Hotels Association
AIM	Australian Institute of Management
AIRC	Australian Industrial Relations Commission (post-1988)
AMWU	Amalgamated Metal Workers' Union (pre 1991)
APEA	Association of Professional Engineers (Australia)
ARC	Australian Research Council
ASE	Australasian Society of Engineers (pre 1991)
AWIRS	Australian Workplace Industrial Relations Survey
BCA	Business Council of Australia
CAI	Confederation of Australian Industry
CC	Consultative Committee
CEO	Chief Executive Officer
CIP	Common Interest Programme
DCA	Distribution Centre A
DCB	Distribution Centre B
EFT	Electronic Funds Transfer
EI	employee involvement
ER	employee relations
ETU	Electrical Trades Union of Australia
EWU	Electronic Workers Union (pseudonym)
FCU	Federated Clerks' Union (of Australia)

FEDFA	Federated Engine Drivers and Firemen's Association
FIA	Federated Ironworkers Association (pre 1991)
FIMEE	Federation of Industrial, Manufacturing and Engineering Employees (since 1991)
FLAIEU	Federated Liquor and Allied Industries Employees' Union
FMWU	Federated Miscellaneous Workers' Union
HRM	human resource management
IR	industrial relations
JIT	'Just In Time' stock minimisation plan
MEWU	Metal and Engineering Workers Union (since 1991)
MTIA	Metal Trades Industry Association
NUW	National Union of Workers
OHSC	Occupational Health and Safety Committee
ppph	pick per person hour
QWL	'Quality of Worklife' program
RDO	rostered day off
SDA	Shop, Distributive and Allied Employees' Association
TQC	'Total Quality Control'
TUTA	Trade Union Training Authority
TWU	Transport Workers' Union of Australia
VAMG	Value Added Management (Pilot) Group
VBEF	Vehicle Builders Employees Federation

Preface

While there have been previous studies of particular aspects of workplace industrial relations, this volume contains the first comprehensive set of case studies which enable the dynamics of industrial relations in the Australian workplace to be systematically analysed. Each of the cases is structured around five questions concerning the reasons for the emergence of certain patterns of industrial relations. These questions seek to clarify whether or not the arbitration system creates a vacuum in workplace industrial relations; who determines the level, content and direction of workplace industrial relations; and the nature, extent and impact of attempts by management to increase efficiency in the workplace.

Case studies were undertaken using the AWIRS questionnaire as a starting point but went into greater depth on particular areas of interest. In each case, the researchers spent considerable time in individual workplaces interviewing representatives of management, unions and the workforce. Company and union records were scrutinised, meetings of consultative councils were attended and representatives outside the workforce were interviewed. The research techniques in different workplaces varied due to local circumstances, but certain standard information was collected in order that valid comparisons could be made.

The case studies are drawn from Melbourne, Sydney and Brisbane. Most of the workplaces are large with multiple union coverage and are representative of organisations in which a significant proportion of Australians are employed. While it is acknowledged that care must be taken in drawing inferences from case studies, every effort has been made in this study to ensure that conclusions have been reached only after careful consideration of all the available data. Indeed, one of the benefits of working as a team in order to produce this volume is that the final conclusions have been the subject of vigorous debate between the researchers.

The study could not have been undertaken without the generosity of the management, employees and unions associated with each of the workplaces. The anonymity of participating employers has been preserved as one of the conditions on which access was given. With one exception, however, the unions involved with each of the case studies have been identified.

We also wish to acknowledge the financial support of the Australian Research Council which provided a grant for the project, and support of various kinds provided by the Departments from which the researchers were drawn. The Centre for Industrial Relations and Labour Studies at the University of Melbourne and the Australian Centre for Industrial Relations Research and Teaching (ACIRRT) at the University of Sydney were the initial sponsors of the project and hosted numerous meetings of the research group.

Russell D. Lansbury and Duncan Macdonald
September 1991

Part I:
Introduction

Russell Lansbury and Duncan Macdonald

1   Issues in workplace industrial relations

Introduction

In a review of the industrial relations literature in the period 1970–86, Blain and Plowman (1987) noted that 'one distinguishing feature of the literature is that a major gap still exists in the area of shop floor industrial relations'. Drawing on Isaac (1985) they cited particular aspects of workplace industrial relations about which our knowledge is deficient. These include: 'why conciliation procedures sometimes fail, why grievance procedures are often ineffective, and how far work methods based on union demarcation are a serious impediment'. These views have been reiterated in more recent surveys of research on workplace industrial relations (see Zappala 1991a; Littler *et al.* 1989) highlighting the fact that this lack of workplace studies is still evident. While there has been some literature devoted to specific aspects of workplace industrial relations (e.g. Frenkel 1980; Bray and Taylor 1986 and Davis and Lansbury 1986), this book is the first to examine the dynamics of workplace industrial relations in Australia through detailed, integrated case studies.

Traditionally, the focus of industrial relations research in this country has been upon the structures and processes that exist beyond the workplace. The existence of a system of state intervention, very different from that in most industrialised countries, has been at least partly responsible for a preoccupation with industrial tribunals, trade unions and, to a lesser extent, employer associations. Not until the mid-1980s was the workplace to become a more important focus of attention. At that time the New Right mounted a vigorous and well publicised campaign against restrictive work practices.[1] The labour movement subsequently took up the issue of workplace efficiency as part of its general campaign for the revitalisation of Australian manufacturing (ACTU/TDC 1987) and its concerns were manifested ultimately in the two-tier and award restructuring National Wage decisions and in the Government's campaigns for microeconomic reform.

In 1989 the Business Council of Australia (BCA) made a substantial contribution to the debate with its report *Enterprise-Based Bargaining Units: A Better Way of Working*, arguing that if Australian business was to compete successfully in world markets, an enterprise-based, employee relations approach was required. Such an approach, it was claimed, would ensure that most matters relating to the terms and conditions of work would be settled directly by employers and employees (or at least enterprise-based unions) within the organisation and, furthermore, it 'must progressively become an alternative to the current, centrally driven, industrial relations approach' (BCA 1989, vii).

The BCA argument was supported by selected results of a survey of more than 300 workplaces covering nearly 200 000 employees as well as sixteen case studies in Australia and overseas. While the BCA survey provided a wealth of data on workplace matters and focused considerable attention on plant-level industrial relations, the Australian Workplace Industrial Relations Survey (AWIRS) data reveal that its sample was not representative of Australian workplaces, being heavily biased towards the larger plants. One finding highlighted in the BCA report was the fragmented structure of bargaining units in large workplaces. One or more unions were present in 95 per cent of the sites surveyed, it was claimed, while in more than 50 per cent of workplaces there were four or more unions and 29 per cent had between six and ten unions. Furthermore, these unions were seen as predominantly craft and occupational in focus, spreading across many workplaces and industry sectors. The report argued that the interaction of such a union structure and a system of multi-employer awards shifted the bargaining process away from the enterprise to the award and national level more than is the case in most other countries.

The BCA report has been criticised on the grounds that 'neither the survey analysis nor the case studies were able to show convincingly that multi-unionism, award complexity and a lack of union workplace focus were major barriers to productivity growth' (Frenkel and Peetz 1990, 94). Considerable doubt has also been cast upon the methodology used in both the survey and the case studies (Dabscheck 1990), and no empirical justification was found for the BCA's claim that productivity would increase in relevant firms by about 25 per cent if enterprise bargaining were introduced.[2] Thus, while the BCA report has reinforced the importance of workplace industrial relations, it has not gone very far towards filling the void which still remains in this area.

The research project on which this book is based evolved from a series of discussions, conferences and a series of working papers which was initiated by the Centre for Industrial Relations Research (now the Australian Centre for Industrial Relations Research and Teaching) at the University of Sydney and the Centre for Industrial Relations and Labour Studies at the University of Melbourne. These initiatives drew together researchers from a range of institutions throughout Australia who were interested in promoting research into workplace industrial relations. Most of the contributors to this volume were members of this original group.[3] The project, for which funds were obtained from the Australian Research Council (ARC), envisaged a pilot questionnaire survey of workplace industrial relations and a series of detailed case studies. Subsequently, the Federal Department of Industrial Relations undertook the Australian Workplace Industrial Relations Survey (AWIRS). The research group assisted with the formulation of the AWIRS questionnaire and used the funds obtained from the ARC grant to undertake a small number of case studies, which were based on the AWIRS questionnaire but went into more depth on particular areas of interest. Indeed, in addition to interviews with the plant manager, the manager with responsibility for industrial relations and the senior delegate from the largest union, researchers interviewed other managers including some beyond the workplace, full-time union officials and members of the workforce. Considerable time was also devoted to combing company records and other documents and attending meetings of consultative committees and working parties.

With respect to definitions and terminology an attempt has been made to ensure consistency with those used in AWIRS. Kelly (1990) draws attention to the confusion that exists in the Australian literature over the definition of a workplace. Drawing on the work of R. K. Brown (1973) and Hill (1981) she defines the workplace as 'the specific work area defined by the production processes and geographical situation as separate from other workplaces, and with its own managerial organisation' (p. 4). She goes on to suggest that the term is often used incorrectly in Australia because the unit under analysis is something larger than an actual workplace and incorporates higher levels of activity.

Using the example of the steelmaking department at BHP's Port Kembla works, Kelly demonstrates the very significant differences that exist in the pattern of industrial relations exhibited by the different workplaces, so defined, that make up that unit. There is a danger that these differences and the important analytical insights associated with them may be lost in the studies that make up this collection. While the terms 'plant', 'site' and 'workplace' are used interchangeably, in at least some there is more than one 'workplace'; according to Kelly's definition. However the units of analysis in our case studies are comparable to the units used by AWIRS in that they are an 'establishment' or 'locality' all of which could be part of a larger 'enterprise' (see Callus *et al.* 1991).

A further point about the focus and scope of our study concerns the section of the workforce that is examined. In all our cases, relatively little attention is devoted to managerial and ancillary staff; the main focus is on the operatives. Given the nature of the production processes under review, this has meant that, in general, white-collar workers do not figure prominently in the study. Given the nature of the Australian workforce and the relative growth in the white-collar workforce, this is rather unfortunate.

In addition to the AWIRS questionnaire, the researchers were guided by several broad questions concerning the reasons for the emergence of certain patterns of industrial relations at the workplace level. These include:

- the extent to which systems of conciliation and arbitration influence and shape the processes and outcomes of industrial regulation at the workplace;
- management control of industrial relations at the workplace, especially the degree of plant-level autonomy from head office;
- management attempts to 'incorporate' the workforce and its organisations, and whether this is related to the emphasis of productivity growth over cost minimisation;
- the nature of unionism at the plant level and the extent to which union organisation constrains managerial decision-making;
- the nature, extent and impact of recent attempts by management to increase efficiency: such attempts being perhaps related to second tier negotiations or award restructuring, or being quite independent of them.

While this ordering of questions may appear somewhat arbitrary, there are important reasons for it. First, there is the advantage of avoiding the prosaic, stereotyped approach, with its 'systems' overtones, wherein the reader must laboriously digest descriptions of the contexts and the actors before being challenged by any of the interesting issues.

Second, our argument depends upon considering these issues in their given order.

The starting point in debates on Australian workplace industrial relations must be the long-standing view that compulsory arbitration creates an 'updraft' effect and chills collective bargaining (Niland 1978). This has been conventional wisdom for many years and remains the main debating point in the Australian literature upon the workplace. It is not, however, an issue that can be settled without empirical study. Our case studies can partially fill this gap.

Whether or not arbitration creates a vacuum in workplace industrial relations, three further questions must be put about the locus of power and the way it is exercised. First, most large Australian firms (where one might expect workplace bargaining) are multi-plant or multi-site organisations. Do corporate head offices also contribute an 'updraft' effect of their own, or conversely, as current fashion supposes, do they insist on devolution to the shop-floor? Second, management may look beyond workplace negotiation to the issue of employee incorporation. Should they choose to attempt this, their efforts must take effect at the workplace level. By its nature, such activity must be devolved. However, regardless of management's preferences with respect to negotiation or incorporation, there is an alternative, significant locus of power, in unionism, that can force management to negotiate at the shop-floor level. Do unions achieve this, and can they constrain management decision-making? These three questions focus attention upon two sides of a core question: who makes the running in determining the level, content and direction of workplace relations—management or unions?

The final question is concerned with policy. Much attention has been given to raising productivity at workplaces by union–management negotiations (the second tier and award restructuring). Our case studies provide an opportunity for us to assess efforts to achieve this goal. Specifically, we have an opportunity to tell whether or not management and unions have the power to function effectively at the workplace level, whether they chose to focus on improving productivity, and how this may relate to the gains available through alternative 'incorporation' strategies.

Our questions are thus sequenced to proceed from a test of received wisdom to a direct appraisal of management and unions, to an assessment of a significant policy issue. In our view, assessing the policy issue of productivity improvements is contingent upon a full understanding of the four preceding issues.

In the following section, each of the questions is considered in relation to the literature. Then the case studies are introduced and the characteristics of each workplace are described.

The research questions

The impact of the arbitration systems on the workplace

The first question is: to what extent do systems of conciliation and arbitration influence and shape the processes and outcomes of industrial regulation within each of the workplaces under review? Milton Derber recommended attention to this question when discussing areas for further research into metalworking plant relations (Derber 1977). He suggested that researchers should investigate the significance of the role of 'federal and state conciliation and arbitration commissioners in resolving plant problems [and] can governmental (or private) intervention be improved?' (p. 23).

The impact of the compulsory arbitration system has been widely debated for many years in Australia. The conventional wisdom emphasises the pervasive influence of the compulsory arbitration system upon all facets of industrial relations in Australia. Indeed it is claimed that '(in) Australia the tribunals dominate to such a degree that the system of compulsory arbitration is often incorrectly equated with the industrial relations system as a whole' (Dufty and Fells 1989, 248).

The focus of earlier debate has been on the merits of compulsory arbitration *vis-à-vis* collective bargaining systems. Although this debate was conducted in reference to industrial relations in general, much of the argument was relevant to the workplace. The debate actually began in the late fifties (Foenander 1957; Laffer 1958; Isaac 1958), and continued in the 1960s (see, for example, Isaac, Hancock and Laffer in Isaac and Ford 1971). It emerged again in the 1970s,[4] was stimulated by the Hancock Committee of Review in the mid eighties and is still very much alive today, having been revived by advocates of unregulated enterprise bargaining. This is seen as a preferable alternative to the existing system which is depicted as being based on 'the outmoded assumption of conflict' and as leading to 'regulation of outcomes as well as process ... (with) often enforced uniformity of work practices, conditions and pay' (BCA 1989, p. 5 and see also Niland 1989. For critiques of this position see Guille 1989; Quinlan and Rimmer 1989; Littler *et al.* 1989; Frenkel and Peetz 1990 and Dabscheck 1990). Thus the recent writings have focused more specifically on the workplace and on the repercussions of compulsory arbitration for the quality of industrial relations and labour productivity at that level. Littler *et al.*, addressing this question, suggested five direct, and two indirect, effects that arbitration can have on the pattern of workplace industrial relations. These include the centralisation of negotiations, the mandatory recognition of trade unions and the regulation of work practices. While many of these effects are not dealt with in this discussion of arbitration's impact, they do receive attention elsewhere, for example, in the sections concerning workplace unionism and the attempts to improve productivity.

John Niland, a long-time critic of the compulsory arbitration system, has consistently bemoaned the lack of 'effective' plant-level institutions in Australia. This situation, argues Niland, results from the tribunals rather than the workplace being the centre of gravity in the industrial relations system (Niland 1976, 1978, 1989). Fells (1987) supports this stance: 'It is a recognised feature of the industrial relations system in Australia that it does not encourage the development of effective plant level relationships.' (p. 350). However Isaac and others have been critical of this view, claiming that the influence of compulsory arbitration is not so all-pervasive and that there is sufficient evidence of independent bargaining and negotiation to justify the system being described as a hybrid or as 'arbitrated bargaining' (Yerbury and Isaac 1971; Isaac 1979, 1989). There are also the traditional 'pockets' of bargaining such as the waterfront, the airlines and metalliferous mining that have been well documented in the past (Perlman 1953; de Vyver 1959, 1970; Blain 1972; Hotchkiss 1970; Deery 1977, 1978; Howard 1985).

Niland also identifies other influences that the system exerts on the processes of bargaining and negotiation. He cites North American evidence regarding the 'narcotic' effect and the 'chilling' effect that compulsory arbitration exerts on bargaining (Niland 1976); effects which lead Niland to recommend the necessity for parties to be able to pursue the bargaining process free of the influence of these effects (Niland 1978). This line of reasoning is supported by Brown and Rowe (1986) but is questioned by Isaac (1979, 1989) and Hancock (1987).

In Dufty's study of firefighters (Dufty 1979) it was claimed that while collective bargaining had been the norm for some time, the arbitration system exerted a significant influence in several ways. The state arbitration system set the framework within which bargaining took place and compulsory arbitration was always there in the background as the alternative means of resolution should negotiations break down. However, little indication is given by Dufty that this background presence of compulsory arbitration exerted either a 'chilling' or a 'narcotic' effect. He refers in the concluding chapter to a 'ghost at the bargaining table' role in one particular instance, but concludes elsewhere that 'even though compulsory arbitration hovering in the background exerts an influence, it certainly does not prevent meaningful bargaining taking place with results seen as broadly satisfactory to both parties' (p. 279).

The traditional system of conciliation and arbitration, however, has also been criticised strongly by the BCA. While the provision for Certified Agreements under Section 115 of the 1988 Commonwealth Industrial Relations Act was appreciated as a step in the right direction, it was seen as only 'tentative'. The BCA's recommendation is for a completely separate 'second stream' of regulation to allow 'individual employers and employees at the enterprise or workplace level to enter into fixed-term enterprise agreements as an alternative to award coverage.' (BCA, 1989, 15). Thus there is a need, according to the BCA report, for the parties to be able to escape entirely the influence of the compulsory arbitration system in order that enterprises in Australia are able to achieve relationships with their employees that are flexible and amicable enough to enable the companies to become internationally competitive.

Fells (1987) describes a contrary situation where the existence of the compulsory arbitration system acted as an inducement for the parties to achieve a negotiated settlement. Anxious to avoid the involvement of those higher up on both the management and union sides, the local managers and union representatives at the Kwinana (BP) plant worked hard to achieve a negotiated settlement because they both knew that going to arbitration would take the matter out of their hands or at best reduce their autonomy and discretion.[5]

Some writers have been ambivalent about the impact of the arbitration system. Lumley (1983)[6] found a variety of institutions within the workplace and various degrees of dependence upon the system. His study identified how workplaces and processes can vary despite the existence of a common macro-level institutional framework which others have perceived as highly influential at lower levels. Obviously, however, if this influence does exist, it is modified by other significant factors.

The arbitration system has long been seen as resulting in relatively underdeveloped mechanisms for the conduct of workplace industrial relations because it has encouraged both management and unions to depend on the external system of arbitration to resolve disputes and set wages and conditions. (See, for example, Howard and Fox 1988.) Thus, management does not seek to develop an industrial relations function beyond that necessary to participate in the arbitration system. Smaller employers, in particular, rely upon their employers' association to provide the necessary information and representation services. Furthermore the external system is seen as lacking the ability to deal with plant-level industrial relations problems. Walker (1970) found the tribunals unwilling and ill-equipped to deal with matters of disputation within the workplace and, according to Fisher (1972), the system contributes to the existence of a vacuum at this level.

In this book, attention will be focused not so much on the debate concerning the merits of the compulsory arbitration system *vis-à-vis* collective bargaining, but on the extent to which the arbitration system influences and, in particular, restrains the actions of the parties at the workplace level. Evidence from the cases will cast light on the questions of whether the development of effective workplace institutions and processes has been prevented by the existence of the arbitration system, as well as whether the degree and quality of workplace bargaining depends on factors other than the presence of compulsory arbitration.

Management control of industrial relations at the workplace

The second question, management control of industrial relations at the workplace, is a very broad one to which considerable literature has been devoted, especially in recent years.[7] Rather than explore, in detail, the whole question of management and control, this study will focus on one particular aspect: the extent to which head office controls industrial relations at the workplace level; that is, how much autonomy is enjoyed by local management and what means are employed by head office to exert control. Given that all the case studies in this book involve multi-plant organisations, and to that extent they are representative of the larger Australian plants,[8] these are highly pertinent questions.

While there has been only one major Australian study concerning the question of head office control (Deery and Purcell 1989), the overseas literature is fairly substantial. Head office control, it seems, may be direct or indirect with direct control involving strict lines of reporting and limited autonomy for individual plant managers, while indirect control may take the form of financial and other means of regulation with plants being designated as autonomous business units or cost centres (Edwards 1987). In the latter case greater freedom may be available to plant managers to formulate and implement industrial relations strategies. Marginson *et al.* (1988) suggested that there were three means by which corporate head office could attempt to control management at the plant level: first, 'power of internal audit and performance'; second, 'financial control, through the allocation of capital funds' and third, 'the design of appropriate managerial incentives' (p. 262).

In *Managing the Factory*, Edwards (1987) used his survey of production managers in medium to large British manufacturing plants to reveal the nature and extent of controls that were exerted by corporate head office. He also gave consideration to the question of relative productivity and how it is influenced by certain management characteristics including the relationship with more senior managers. His main conclusion was that: 'Plants were given a good deal of autonomy in managing their own internal arrangements, but the results of the exercise of this autonomy were carefully monitored by companies' (p. 111). This he found to be reasonably consistent with the conclusions of Peters and Waterman (1982) that successful firms utilised a simultaneous 'loose–tight' relationship with their constituent plants.

Marginson *et al.* (1988) examined head office or corporate control of plants in multi-establishment enterprises. Questions raised included the impact of the internal organisation of companies on industrial relations arrangements, the prevalence of consistent approaches to labour management, the nature of decentralisation (mentioned above) and the extent to which perceptions of autonomy vary across different organisational levels (p. 258). In their concluding chapter they conclude that the traditional dichotomy between strategic and operational decisions (whereby 'strategic' decisions were the concern of corporate head office while the 'operational' decisions were made at plant level) is weaker than originally thought. In brief, Marginson *et al.* found that 'the extent of head office involvement in non-strategic matters was considerably more than the literature had led us to expect' (p. 260). Considerable differences were found in the extent of involvement in the management of industrial relations at the plant level. Factors pertinent to this appeared to be product market environment, structure and financial performance. Size, somewhat surprisingly, was found to be largely irrelevant.

The relative merits of centralisation and decentralisation in the control strategies of multi-plant organisations in Australia have been discussed earlier. Frenkel (1980) referred to the potential influence of the degree of centralisation of corporate decision-making on how employers deal with industrial issues (p. 17). However the case studies in his collection do not provide any definitive answers on these matters.

Following the approach of Marginson *et al.*, Deery and Purcell (1989) surveyed 142 organisations and found a pronounced tendency for large firms to decentralise control, with the responsibility for profit and many operational aspects, including industrial relations, being devolved to local management. They concluded that

> companies will seek to structure industrial relations to fit their overall strategy and organisational structure. Responsibility for the industrial relations function will be placed in the hands of operational management with head offices adopting a more discreet role of monitoring and advising. (p. 476)

However they warn that both trade union strategy and national wage decisions would influence the ability of organisations to devolve the responsibility for industrial relations management in this fashion. Also Gilmour and Lansbury (1977, 1984) have found first-line supervisors possess a low level of managerial skills and this may compound the difficulty of devolving the management of industrial relations.[9]

Focusing as they do on multi-plant enterprises, the case studies in this book provide an excellent opportunity to shed some light on the nature and extent of head office control of industrial relations at the workplace level.

Incorporation of employees by management

The third question actually has two parts: to what extent do managers attempt to incorporate the workforce and its organisations; and, is this related to the degree to which productivity growth, rather than cost minimisation, is emphasised as the major goal? Curtain and Mathews (1990) suggest two models of award restructuring; a 'Cost Minimisation Approach' and a 'Productivity Enhancement Approach'. As the names suggest, the first is a short-term approach with as little investment in the process as possible, while the second is a long-term approach and necessitates considerable commitment by all parties and considerable investment on the part of the employers. To a large extent the 'productivity growth' goal approximates the 'productivity enhancement approach' suggested by Curtain and Mathews, while 'cost minimisation' as a goal relates closely to their 'cost minimisation approach'.

Involved with this question of incorporation is the issue of human resource management (HRM) versus industrial relations (IR) strategies; i.e., to what extent does management attempt to reduce the importance of the industrial relations function by emphasising a broader role of human resource management? An HRM strategy (sometimes also referred to as an employee relations strategy) and its associated techniques are often regarded as lessening the 'adversarial' relationships between employees and management (epitomised by the presence of unions as representative bodies which negotiate on behalf of the workforce) and emphasising the cooperative or collaborative aspects of employee–management relations. Techniques of this kind include programs encouraging employee involvement or common interest, which emphasise the need for winning employee commitment and developing mutual understanding (but not necessarily power sharing) between employees and management.

The origins of incorporation attempts, which often involve the use of HRM techniques, lie ultimately in the basic ideology underpinning managerial attitudes and, according to at least one recent assessment, '[t]he prevailing management ideology in Australia—of both organisations and managers—is the unitarist one' (Dufty and Fells 1989, 78). Thus, it is not surprising to find that most managers want their employees to see their interests as coinciding with those of the organisation and thus adopt strategies to strengthen this view. In other words, incorporation seeks to develop the links between employees and the organisation while at the same time reducing the extent to which employees look to outside bodies, particularly trade unions, for protection and improvement in wages and conditions.

The nature of employee incorporation varies considerably but ultimately involves some means by which employees participate in decision-making or at least exercise some greater control over their work lives. The managerial critiques of Taylorism have been based on the need both to improve the quality of work life and to provide increased worker participation: goals which reinforce one another. The ability to exercise some discretion over the various aspects of their working lives is crucial to the improvement in employees' job satisfaction and work life quality and a vast literature, mainly North American, has been devoted to the topic (see, for example, Beer and Spector 1985; Champagne and McAfee 1989). Although much of this writing has been widely challenged, if not discredited (see Bamber and Lansbury 1989), it is often adopted uncritically, even fervently, by Australian management.

Blandy *et al.* (1985) discuss a number of cases in Australia where attempts have been made to secure increases in productivity by giving employees the chance to obtain greater job satisfaction; this is based on the work of Herzberg. These include Citibank, where large productivity increases flowed from extensive job redesign, and other well known examples such as Philips and Simpson Pope.

Edwards (1987), looking at British companies, also questions how far management has tried to bring about worker commitment especially to do with the introduction of more flexible work arrangements. He concluded that there was impressive evidence of attempts to involve workers in work change on an ongoing basis in some areas. Yet, in other areas such as the public sector and the services sector, managements have pursued increased flexibility with the aid of more coercive measures and, 'do not appear to have made worker commitment a major priority' (p. 192). Edwards found that workers in larger, more prosperous, workplaces were more likely to become committed to the firm.

In relation to unionism, formal mechanisms of worker participation are important because such procedures may mean that unions are by-passed or are made to appear less relevant. Instances of worker participation and its stronger variation, industrial democracy, take on varieties of forms and various schema for their classification have been suggested (see, for example, Lansbury and Davis 1990). In the main, where such mechanisms are introduced by management with the intention of incorporating the workforce, it is likely that they will take the form of worker participation rather than industrial democracy. Employers have been traditionally reluctant to embrace the latter with its connotations of power sharing. Preferred instead are participatory schemes where worker representatives have some involvement in decision-making processes but do not necessarily affect outcomes (e.g. worker directors).

Cutcher-Gershenfeld, Kochan and Verma (1987) distinguish between two types of employee participation schemes: those which are *self-contained* and are not accompanied by any major changes in organisational structure, and those which are *highly-integrated* with the rest of the organisation. They conclude that the former 'stand alone' approach is less likely to last for a long period of time, while the 'integrated' approach is more likely to survive because it is not an independent or isolated phenomenon. They also argue that if the unions are supportive and involved in an 'integrated' approach, employee participation will be more likely to have a longer-term positive outcome.

Gardner *et al.* (1986) cite British and Australian evidence to support the contention that management was not interested, in most cases, in schemes that involved genuine power sharing. They point out that certain types of schemes such as quality circles, improved managerial communication or job redesign, were really 'the most advanced current techniques for enhancing company loyalty ... ' (p. 150). Ramsay (1986) supports this in discussing the motivations behind the introduction of particular mechanisms: 'employees may gain a sense of ''belonging'' which entails their being more deferential to control from above' (p. 53). This sentiment captures, very accurately, the underlying intentions of many managers when 'participation' is placed on the agenda for discussion.

Management may also try to restructure the union presence to make it more consistent with the objectives of the enterprise. These attempts include the fostering of enterprise-based bargaining units or, at least, single union coverage. Some overlap with the first question concerning the impact of compulsory arbitration becomes obvious in that certain proposals for enterprise bargaining to replace centralised arbitration include a significant restructuring of the union presence at the plant level (see Niland 1989 and BCA 1989). Management's ability to have employees identify with the corporation is strengthened by the development of enterprise unionism. Also *de facto* enterprise unions, by definition, should assist greatly in redirecting the focus of employee loyalty.

The case studies in this volume provide an opportunity to identify and analyse various forms of incorporation strategies and to ascertain whether any such attempts are related to particular organisational goals; i.e. productivity growth or cost minimisation.

The role of unions at the workplace

The fourth question is: what is the nature of unionism at the plant level? To what extent does the union organisation constrain managerial decision-making? Recent reform proposals, especially those aimed at the reduction of union power at the workplace, assume that the decisions of plant-level managers are seriously restrained by the presence and activities of trade unions at that level (e.g. BCA 1989). While in some industries such as the railways, power generation and metal trades there have been well-established traditions of active workplace unionism, there are many other areas where workplace unionism has been, at best, limited and sporadic (see Rimmer 1989).

Certainly in various white-collar and semi-professional areas workplace unionism is non-existent beyond the presence of a nominal union representative or delegate and perhaps a noticeboard. Even in those instances where high levels of union density and even militant leadership at the state or national levels prevail, this is not always translated into an active workplace presence, and plant-level management decision-making may remain largely unconstrained by unionism. The situation in many NSW state schools provides an excellent example of this phenomenon. The Teachers' Federation is regarded as a highly active, militant union yet at the level of the individual school there is often little evidence of a union presence and school principals enjoy almost unlimited power in decision-making (Macdonald 1985a). Thus, for certain areas of industry, at least, the claims of dramatic productivity gains to be made by removing workplace union power bases such as the closed shop (e.g. by the BCA) may prove to be unrealistic. Rimmer (1989) lists a number of factors favourable to a resurgence of workplace unionism in the 1980s, such as the increased popularity of grievance procedures, the advent of occupational health and safety committees and the two-tier wage determination system.[10] However Rimmer cautions that workplace industrial relations can develop without there necessarily being any expanded role for unionism. The employer decision as to the extent of union involvement will be critical, he warns, to the future of workplace unionism (p. 142).

In a study of changes in plant relations in metalworking during the 1970s, Derber (1977) found that union influence on managerial decision-making had increased considerably. Moreover he found that unions had a more sophisticated presence at the workplace; delegates and stewards received more education than they had earlier.[11] However his study was somewhat limited in depth and was restricted to metalworking within a rather brief period. With this industry employing a decreasing proportion of the total workforce, it is necessary to look beyond it. While there are several studies considering the role of stewards or delegates in Australia (see Benson 1988), very little specific attention has been given to the question of the degree to which managerial discretion is limited by workplace unionism. Both Benson (1988) and Rimmer (1989), in substantiating the levels of Australian shopfloor union activity across industries and over time, provide some evidence of its impact upon management.[12] Also Benson (1988) mentions the degree of management–employer support as a factor suggested by the literature which influences the nature of shopfloor union organisation. However neither of these studies nor most other Australian literature is specifically concerned with the impact of shopfloor unionism on management. Frenkel and Coolican's work (1984) is somewhat an exception in that this question is at least addressed, although not in much detail. The two unions which provide the focus of that study, the Building Workers Industrial Union and the Amalgamated Metals Foundry and Shipwrights Union (now the Metal and Engineering Workers Union) are regarded as industrially active and, especially in the case of the latter, supportive of workplace unionism. However the picture that emerged was one of 'comparatively weak workplace organisation' (p. 105) with management not consulting stewards on several important issues. For example, it was found that

> in 40% of the workplaces there was no consultation over dismissals and in over half of these workplaces (51.3%) no consultation took place over the distribution of overtime. In relation to the organisation of work there was even less consultation: nearly two-thirds (65.0%) of the workplaces reported no consultation over this issue. (ibid.)

There is of course a significant body of literature, almost exclusively originating from overseas, that considers the impact of unionism on productivity; the best-known contribution being Freeman and Medoff (1984) (see Edwards 1987 for a review of this literature). Arguing that the conventional wisdom is wrong concerning the impact of trade unions on productivity, Freeman and Medoff contend that the presence of active unionism forces management to devote more resources to the management of employees and this, in combination with the 'exit–voice trade-off', results in an improvement in productivity. Combining this thesis with the findings of Frenkel and Coolican, it could perhaps be argued that Australia's unions are not sufficiently militant at the workplace level to force the changes that would lead to productivity gains.

The case studies in this book will provide the opportunity to consider the question of the extent to which management is constrained by unionism at the workplace, along with more general issues such as the nature of workplace unionism. More specifically, attention will be directed to the significance to managers of factors such as:

(a)   the numbers of unions at the workplace,
(b)   the extent of union workplace organisation,
(c)   the ideology of the unions involved, and
(d)   the existence of inter-union bodies or shop committees.

These issues, always considered to be important, have been highlighted in recent times by the claims of various conservative commentators concerning the adverse effects of unionism and union influence on the productivity of Australian industry.

Improving efficiency in the workplace

The final question concerns the nature, extent and impact of recent attempts by management to increase efficiency. Some such attempts have been related to National Wage decisions while others have been quite independent of them. Nevertheless, the pace of change or reform has quickened in recent years and there are various perspectives from which this change can be viewed. Firstly, management is continually attempting to make changes at the workplace in the interests of increased efficiency. However, the intensity of these attempts will depend upon the intensity of pressures such as product market competition or budgetary constraints (Macdonald 1985b). Furthermore, the relative success of these attempts will be affected by the relative power positions of the unions and the workforce and their degree of opposition to management. Secondly, there are perspectives such as the 'second industrial divide' (Piore and Sabel 1984) and 'post-Fordism' (Mathews 1989; Badham and Mathews 1989) which emphasise dramatic changes to the product market as being an important catalyst for a revolution in workplace organisation and in the status and role of employees. Thirdly, there is the more sceptical or pessimistic perspective labelled by some as 'neo-Fordist'. This depicts management utilising an increased power base to secure higher profits through increased work intensity and significantly poorer working conditions for a large proportion of the workforce (for reviews of the debate see Macdonald 1989 and Bramble and Fieldes 1990).

At a more specific or concrete level, workplace change or reform, as driven in Australia by the two-tier and award restructuring national wage decisions, has been analysed with the aid of various schema and typologies. Rimmer and Zappala (1988), drawing to some extent on flexibility categorisations devised overseas, utilised a five-category typology for the analysis of changes that occurred under the second tier in twelve separate awards. They found that the greatest changes occurred with respect to 'internal numerical flexibility' and 'functional flexibility' and that the extent of change therein was 'impressive and valuable' (p. 588). Furthermore, Rimmer and Zappala concluded that the Australian industrial relations system could be made considerably more flexible. Thus they felt that the calls for decentralisation and deregulation that were to reach a peak with the publication of the BCA Report were unjustified.

Rimmer followed up this research with a wide-ranging empirical study commissioned by the BCA and conducted in conjunction with the Industrial Relations Research Centre at the University of New South Wales (Rimmer and Verevis 1990). This involved sixteen case studies that encompassed both the second tier and award restructuring although they were primarily concerned with the latter and with the progress therein. They assessed the extent of the changes that had been implemented and attempted to isolate the factors that had been influential. Of these, the most important were found to be the degree of managerial motivation and the level of management skills and organisation. Also very important was the ability to stop flow-ons from elsewhere (these greatly reduce employee-union incentive) and shopfloor union support. Significantly, the enthusiasm for the results of the second tier exercise that was expressed in the earlier study (i.e. Rimmer and Zappala 1988) was not repeated in the later study. In several cases it was found that the experience of the second tier had soured relations and created unfavourable attitudes towards the reform of work practices, while in others it made more difficult the task of finding sufficient offsets to satisfy the Structural Efficiency Principle.

In this collection of case studies attention is devoted to a range of work reforms that have been attempted in the interests of greater efficiency and higher productivity during recent years. These reforms are analysed to determine their motivation and impact, especially on the workforce, and the factors that have been associated with their degree of successful implementation. To some extent there is overlap with the previous question in the sense that incorporation is often associated with attempts to introduce change in the workplace. Thus it is appropriate, especially in the light of the framework utilised by Rimmer and Verevis (1990), to consider the extent to which change has been driven from within, rather than beyond, the workplace and whether this is significantly associated with the degree of successful implementation.

The case studies

The strengths and weaknesses of the case study method have long been debated in both the behavioural and social sciences (see, for example, Queen 1928; Stouffer 1962; Crombie 1969; Walton 1972; Mitchell 1983). One of the benefits of case studies is the opportunity to gain an in-depth knowledge of the dynamics and texture of workplace industrial relations. This has been achieved in the current project by the researchers, who were able to spend considerable time in each workplace, interviewing a wide range of people and examining documentary material. This process made it possible for the researchers to obtain the relevant facts and at the same time gain a 'feeling' for the relationships which existed between the various parties involved. By utilising the questions in the Australian Workplace Industrial Relations Survey (AWIRS), a common data base and approach was established, but each of the case studies tended to highlight different aspects of workplace industrial relations, especially in drawing conclusions. In the Automakers case, for example, attention was focused on the effects of a centralised approach to industrial relations by corporate head office. By contrast, another multinational enterprise, Paintco, provided an example where the corporate headquarters sought to devolve decision-making on industrial relations matters to the plant level.

Limitations of the case study approach should also be acknowledged. Although most of the studies were conducted over twelve months and involved a number of visits to the plants, they are not longitudinal studies and therefore represent only an account of what was happening during a relatively short period of time. In all cases there have been subsequent developments which may have changed the way in which workplace industrial relations would now be described. Furthermore, the case studies were undertaken during a period when the process of award restructuring had only just begun. Industrial relations in the workplace are also affected by broader political and economic circumstances. Nevertheless, the case studies provide a useful and accurate account of the situation in the late 1980s and early 1990s.

The case studies were drawn from Melbourne (4), Sydney (3) and Brisbane (1). Their selection was influenced by a desire to provide a wide cross-section of Australian workplaces in which various patterns of industrial relations could be analysed; it also depended on the willingness of employers and unions to cooperate with the project. Most of the workplaces were relatively large with multiple union coverage enabling a broad representation of unions.

The characteristics of the various workplaces chosen are shown in Table 1.1 (see pp. 22–23). It should be noted that in two of the case studies, two separate plants within the same company were studied. This had the advantage of demonstrating the diversity of industrial relations practices and experience which can be found within a single enterprise even when the corporate policies governing the different workplaces are similar. The anonymity of participating organisations has been preserved, as this was one of the conditions on which access was granted to the researchers but, with one exception, the unions involved in each study have been identified.

The workplaces studied vary in size from 105 employees in the case of the metals manufacturer to 4200 employees in one of the two automobile assembly plants, with a median of approximately 550 employees. Given that 75 per cent of Australian workplaces have less than 20 employees (see Callus, *et al.* 1991) the plants in this study are far larger than is typical. However the AWIRS data also shows that 25 per cent of the Australian workforce is employed in organisations with 500 or more employees even though these comprise only one per cent of the total of workplaces. Thus, while the workplaces may be atypical in terms of size, they are representative of the organisations in which a significant proportion of Australians are employed. Only two of the organisations are wholly or partly Australian-owned with the majority being subsidiaries of firms based in Britain, New Zealand or the US. This again is atypical of Australian workplaces generally but not so much of larger workplaces, as the AWIRS data shows that both partial foreign equity and the existence of foreign head offices increased markedly with size. While most of the workplaces are located in the same city as their Australian head office their ages vary from three to fifty-three years old.

Most of the workplaces have some form of 'closed shop' arrangement with their principal unions[13] which is again fairly common in larger organisations although the prevalence is not uniform across industrial sectors (Callus *et al.* 1991). The number of unions covering the workforce varies from three to eight, with a median of four unions. This statistic coincides closely with the AWIRS results which show that organisations with 500 or more employees have, on average, 6.1 unions and those employing between 200 and 500 have an average of 3.6. In all of the workplaces there is one dominant union which covers the majority of employees. Union coverage of non-managerial and administrative staff varies from 50 to 100 per cent, with a median of 90 per cent.

The number of union delegates varies considerably from one to fifty-six, as does the ratio of delegates to employees. In the metal manufacturing plant, where the dominant union was the Federation of Industrial, Manufacturing and Engineering Employees (FIMEE), there is one union delegate for every fifteen employees, while in the hotel

Table 1.1   Characteristics of the Case Studies

	Receptacles	PaintCo	Hotel International	Comel	Automakers Plant A	Automakers Plant B	FoodCo Plant A	FoodCo Plant B
Type of Industry	Metal manufacturing	Paint manufacturing	Hospitality industry	Electronic communication manufacturing	Automobile manufacturing	Automobile manufacturing	Retail storage and distribution	Retail storage and distribution
Number of employees in the workplace	105	503	575	561	927	4200	425	231
Number of unions	3	6	3	7	4	8	4	4
Level of unionisation*	100%	100%	80%	90%	100%	100%	99%	98%
Name of the dominant union	FIMEE	FMWU	FLAIU	EWU◆	VBEF	VBEF	NUW	SDA
Coverage of the workforce by the dominant union	90%	50%	90%	65%	90%	70%	95%	95%
Number of union delegates	7	7	1	14	11	56	6	7
Ratio of union delegates to employees in the workplace	1:15	1:72	1:575	1:40	1:84	1:75	1:71	1:33

	Receptacles	PaintCo	Hotel International	Comel	Automakers Plant A	Automakers Plant B	FoodCo Plant A	FoodCo Plant B
Type of Industry	Metal manufacturing	Paint manufacturing	Hospitality industry	Electronic communication manufacturing	Automobile manufacturing		Retail storage and distribution	
Comparative level of over-award payments in the workplace	High	High	Medium	Nil	Low	Low	Medium	Low
Level of industrial disputation in the previous twelve months	Low	Medium	Low	Medium	Low	Medium	Medium	Low
Age of the workplace in years	13	30	16	3	53	31	9	7
Location of the workplace	Sydney	Melbourne	Melbourne	Melbourne	Sydney	Melbourne	Sydney	Brisbane
Location of corporate head office in Australia	Sydney	Melbourne	Sydney	Melbourne	Melbourne	Melbourne	Sydney	Sydney
Dominant country of ownership	UK	UK	UK	Australia	US	US	Aust./NZ	Aust./NZ

* Excluding managerial, professional and administrative employees

◆ EWU = Electronic Workers Union (a pseudonym)

there is only one delegate (from the Liquor Trades Union) for the entire workforce of 575 people. The median ratio of union delegates to employees, however, is one to seventy-two. Again there is consistency with AWIRS in that workplaces with 500 or more employees were found to average one delegate to every ninety-eight members.

The level of over-award wages received by employees at each workplace varies considerably. Although the measures used are approximate, in only two of the workplaces in the study are employees paid significantly above the award. In three workplaces, medium to low over-award payments are made, while in one workplace the employees receive no over-award payments. Again the size of the workplaces in this study would appear to be reasonably representative. The frequency and levels of over-award payments were found by AWIRS to be negatively correlated with the size of the organisation.

In the twelve months prior to the studies, which were conducted in 1989/90, the level of industrial disputation, including strikes and other forms of disruption, was low to medium. In some workplaces there have been major industrial disputes in the past, but these had decreased in recent times, partly as a result of particular economic and political circumstances. This is again representative of the situation Australia-wide as reflected in the AWIRS data. They show that while 88 000 workplaces have never had any industrial action another 12 000 have experienced no action for two years or more.

The picture which emerges from the general description of the case studies is of a general absence of much explicit industrial conflict, even though the workforces are highly unionised and the workplaces are medium- to large-scale by Australian standards. While the dominant unions representing the employees include some of the more moderate or conservative factions of the labour movement, other more militant unions are also represented. These are prepared to exercise their influence, through industrial action, when necessary. In general, however, most of the time lost through industrial disputes was related to national campaigns around issues such as second-tier wage negotiations or changes in the awards. There were very few protracted disputes at the workplace level. Thus while exhibiting characteristics of the AWIRS 'active bargainer' category, on closer inspection these workplaces could, more accurately, be depicted as 'reactive bargainers', a proposition to be explored in the concluding chapter.

A brief introduction to each of the case studies follows with much greater detail provided in the chapters dealing with the individual case studies.

Receptacles

Receptacles is a metal-processing operation of 105 employees located in an outer western suburb of Sydney. It is part of a large British-based conglomerate, Steadfast Pty Ltd, which has sixty plants and more than 4000 employees in Australia. Receptacles is a highly efficient and profitable plant which, at the time of the study, exported approximately 50 per cent of its production, with Japan taking a significant share. The eighty-five production workers are employed under a post-entry closed shop arrangement which has operated since the plant opened some thirteen years ago. There are three unions: the Federation of Industrial, Manufacturing and Engineering Employees (FIMEE), Australian Society of Engineers (ASE) and Electrical Trades Union (ETU), with the FIMEE representing all but eight employees in the plant. Although there is a relatively large number of union delegates (seven in a plant of 105 employees), there is no delegates' committee on site and the senior FIMEE delegate appears to exercise considerable influence in the local negotiations. While there has been an occasional industrial dispute, labour–management relations are generally harmonious. The company is regarded as a 'good payer' and considerable emphasis is placed on employee communications and participative schemes, such as a Common Interest Programme and Consultative Committee Systems.

Paintco

Paintco is a large paint manufacturing and warehouse facility located in Melbourne. It has 503 employees, 40 per cent of whom are from non-English-speaking backgrounds and most of whom are semi-skilled. The plant is thirty years old but has been substantially remodelled in places. It is a fully-owned subsidiary of a major overseas company which employs some 12 000 people throughout Australia in a large number of work sites. Paintco has a large share of the product market and has a range of specialised products for which no substitute is readily available. There are six unions in the plant, the largest being the Federated Miscellaneous Workers' Union (FMWU) which has 205 members and covers virtually all the production workers, and the National Union of Workers (NUW) which covers the sixty-two store persons. The blue-collar workforce is covered by an informal closed shop. The workforce has been periodically militant with a known capacity to sustain long strikes, particularly on issues such as wages, job security and working conditions. The plant is regarded as a 'pacesetter' and is frequently at the leading edge of national negotiations and wider union campaigns. In recent years, however, there has been a more harmonious industrial relations climate. This has coincided with a period in which corporate management has sought to devolve more authority and responsibility to management at the plant level. The company is also seeking to establish more enterprise-based bargaining structures. Several consultative arrangements have also been introduced to change the culture of the workplace. These have included a Customer First program, an employee share ownership scheme and a health and safety bonus scheme. These appear to have generated a more peaceful and cooperative industrial relations climate at the workplace.

Hotel International

Hotel International is a leading five-star residential hotel in Melbourne which opened in the 1970s. It was acquired by a British-based company with substantial interests in the hospitality and retail industries, in 1987. The hotel has 637 employees, of whom 51 per cent work on a casual basis. More than half of the workforce are in sales and personal service positions. The Federated Liquor and Allied Industries Employees' Union (FLAIEU) covers approximately 80 per cent of the workforce. There is only one elected union delegate and a small non-elected shop committee. The weakness of union organisation at the hotel is partly a product of the nature of the workforce, which has many female and younger workers employed on a casual basis. Hotel management, however, is also vigorous in its efforts to inculcate the workforce with a corporate culture which stresses 'client service' and a strong identification with the employer. At the same time, Hotel International management has been active in the Australian Hotels Association and has been influential in shaping the negotiations concerning award restructuring. Management stresses the importance of keeping wages low and maintaining flexibility of employment to ensure that the industry remains competitive. Hotel International has had few industrial disputes and appears to have high employee morale, as measured by low levels of absenteeism and labour turnover. However, the union is seeking to raise its profile and strengthen its presence in the hotel through the introduction of a new delegate structure.

Comel

Comel is one of five regional establishments of a large firm in the electronic communications manufacturing industry. The plant is in a

Melbourne suburb, and was established in 1987 from the merger of three workshops and a few small stores in the inner metropolitan area. The activities of the plant are wide-ranging but include reconditioning, servicing, designing and manufacturing equipment and parts for the parent company. There are 561 employees, of whom 350 are in the production area. Most of the production workers are female from non-English speaking backgrounds. There are seven unions, the main union being the Electronic Workers Union (a pseudonym) which covers 80 per cent of all non-managerial and administrative employees. A Combined Union Shop Committee which was very active in earlier times had, over the previous two or three years, gone into decline, and comes to life only spasmodically when particular local issues arise which are of concern to employees in the plant. There is a high turnover among delegates and positions are rarely contested. Management has sought to emphasise the importance of direct communications with the workforce and, in line with the BCA Report, seeks to promote the importance of 'employee relations' over 'industrial relations'. Some emphasis has been given to team-building and total quality management (TQM) techniques, despite lack of union support for these measures. Yet the low incidence of industrial disputes would appear to indicate that employees are willing, at this stage, to follow management's leadership in these matters.

Automakers

Automakers is a major vehicle manufacturer which employs 12 000 people at four main locations in Australia. The case study focused on the Sydney plant (with 927 employees) and the Melbourne plant (with 4200 employees). These provided interesting contrasts in terms of industrial relations. The small Sydney plant has a history of industrial harmony and is often cited as a model of labour–management relations. Although there are four unions in the plant, the Vehicle Builders Employees Federation (VBEF) covers all production and maintenance workers. By contrast, the Melbourne plant has a turbulent industrial relations history and has often been the focus for union campaigns to improve wages and conditions. It also has a reputation for independent and militant shop steward activity. There are eight unions in the Melbourne plant with fifty-six union delegates. Although the VBEF is the largest union, the Metal and Engineering Workers Union (MEWU) exercises considerable influence within the plant. The level of industrial conflict has fallen in recent years particularly in the Melbourne plant but it is difficult to determine the extent to which this is due to internal rather than external factors. The management of Automakers has a highly centralised approach to industrial relations and, since the early 1980s, prominence has been given to the development of an Employee Involvement (EI) program. Both management and the VBEF claim this has contributed to higher levels of quality in automobile production as well as improved employee relations. Automakers has also introduced innovative methods of production, including a greater emphasis on group work, in the assembly of a new export model at its Melbourne plant.

FoodCo

FoodCo is one of Australia's largest retail grocery chains. The case study focused on two of the company's major distribution centres (DCs) in Sydney (with 404 employees) and Brisbane (with 261 employees). As with Automakers, this provided the opportunity to compare two different industrial relations outcomes within similar workplaces in the same company. The Sydney DC was established in 1981 and has suffered from high levels of industrial unrest. FoodCo's corporate headquarters launched a range of initiatives to improve the situation, including contracting out Sydney DC to an independent operator, but this was not a long-term success. The National Union of Workers has total coverage of the employees in the Sydney DC. The workforce there has a history of militant action, sometimes in defiance of the official leadership of its own union. By contrast, the Brisbane DC has a record of labour–management cooperation and little strike activity. The Shop, Distributive and Allied Employees' Association (SDA) has total coverage of employees and is regarded as a moderate union. Indeed, some of the workforce at the Brisbane DC complained that the union had been slow to act on their behalf. Yet the Brisbane management also has a consistent record of attending to problems as they arise and creating a positive work environment. The result of these contrasting situations is that the Brisbane DC has achieved much higher levels of productivity than its Sydney counterpart. The recent negotiations over the second tier and award restructuring, nevertheless, have created problems at both DCs. It would appear the FoodCo corporate management may recently have been intruding more into industrial relations at the Brisbane DC, particularly in regard to negotiations about the second tier, with negative consequences. Nevertheless, Brisbane remains well ahead of Sydney on all performance criteria. This case is interesting in the light of the BCA's arguments about single union coverage enhancing productivity. In effect, both of these sites are covered by a single union but one has much higher productivity levels than the other. This reminds us that there are other more powerful determinants of productivity than the number of unions on site.

Summary and overview

The motivation for this collection of studies arose from the recent growth of interest in the workplace by industrial relations practitioners and researchers. This growth of interest has, in turn, been generated by the greater role attributed to microeconomic activity by those responsible for planning and directing the Australian economy. While there is an extensive collection of literature of general relevance to the Australian workplace, very little research has been devoted exclusively to the specific analysis of structures, processes and outcomes of industrial relations at this level.

To complement the large-scale survey recently undertaken (AWIRS), it was thought appropriate to provide some more intensive workplace research. Thus a series of case studies has been undertaken and brought together in a volume designed to assist the understanding of workplace industrial relations in Australia both through the insights revealed by the individual cases and through the findings that emerge from their comparative analysis.

Extreme care must be taken in drawing inferences from case studies. The workplaces under consideration have shown to be reasonably representative *vis-à-vis* the AWIRS findings for similar sized workplaces and on that basis it could be argued that drawing inferences from them is quite valid. However Mitchell (1983) makes the point that it is the 'validity of the analysis rather than the representativeness of the events' that determines whether or not inferences can be drawn (p. 190). We believe that our analysis meets this criterion.

Each of the following six chapters is devoted to a factual account of an individual case study. The final chapter attempts to bring together the main findings from each; especially with respect to the five questions that were posed earlier in this chapter. The six case studies are presented in an essentially descriptive fashion and a conscious attempt has been made to avoid references to the literature. The relevance of previous research to this study and the links between the findings that emerge from this research and conclusions reached elsewhere are explored in the first and final chapters. Thus, the case study chapters are not intended to 'stand alone' but must be read in conjunction with both the Introduction and the Conclusion.

Part II:
The case studies

2 Receptacles

Background to the case

Workplace case study research represents an almost anthropological facet of industrial relations study. It is quite impossible to draw generalisations, but the richness of the data often provides stimulation to examine many more ideas raised. Here, time and resources limited the number of matters that could be examined in some detail, and no doubt there are many aspects of work life at the plant in question which would reward further probing. Nevertheless, the relationships and be-haviours explored do provide some useful insights and pose some interesting questions for others to explore.

The workplace concerned is in many ways representative of one set of 'typical' Australian plants. It is in the metal manufacturing industry, and in employment terms it is of average size. It has a strong local product market position, one built upon internal company trans-actions, and has acquired an enviable Japanese export outlet in recent years. More relevantly, the plant is part of a large publicly-listed, vertically-integrated, Australian-based company which is itself predominantly owned by a large overseas corporation. Over the years a continuing theme and emphasis of the Australian parent company's senior management has been productivity enhancement through the approach taken to labour management. For the purposes of this analysis we shall designate the Australian parent the Steadfast Corporation and the focal workplace Receptacles Ltd.

By way of overview, industrial relations at Receptacles appears closer to a management approach based upon consent rather than one based upon coercion. Human relations ideas are strongly evident but so too is an acceptance of unionism. In general, management regarded the approach that it took towards labour as a 'reasonable' one, and that in return unions were expected to display 'sensible' unionism. In practice, this largely meant that management rationale and logic should predominate; 'sensible' unionists would subscribe to this line and adopt such a logic in consultation and negotiation where work organisation and other matters were discussed. Yet it could be argued that at a deeper level there are definite traces of the hegemonic style to which Burawoy (1985) refers in his discussion of factory regimes.

The style of accommodation processes within the Receptacles workplace at the time of this study was somewhere between consultation and bargaining. While the system of conciliation and arbitration exerted some influence over events and outcomes it was not a dominant and constricting influence. The parties at Receptacles enjoyed considerable autonomy in the management of industrial relations and indeed management usually was able to achieve the outcomes that it preferred. These themes will become clearer and some reasons for them will emerge in the sections which follow. The methodological characteristics of the underlying research will first be briefly sketched.

The research material on which this study is based was gathered over a period of six months from August 1989 to February 1990. Data were obtained by means of semi-structured interviews with plant and headquarters management within Receptacles and Steadfast and with local union representatives. In addition, copies of a variety of documents were obtained and minutes of the meetings of a number of joint bodies operating in the plant were made available for perusal. Moreover, several times the researcher was able to explore in detail, and at close quarters, the entire production process at the plant. This revealed the complexity of the labour process and helped to clarify the various job requirements expected of the workforce.

The Receptacles plant

Receptacles was opened in 1977 in an industrially-zoned strip of an outer western suburb of Sydney. It produces a range of very similar products which are essential inputs for the storage of one of Steadfast's main end products. Initially the whole of the output of Receptacles was supplied only to other Steadfast companies. In the last five years however, marketing initiatives have been undertaken and now approximately 50 per cent of production is exported, with Japan taking a significant share; 20 per cent is sold on the domestic market to non-Steadfast buyers, with the remaining 30 per cent sold internally.

This is the only plant producing such specialist 'receptacles' in Australia. Some minimal measure of protection is afforded by the general import tariff, but technological know-how and productive efficiency have ensured that domestic competition is almost absent. On a worldwide basis there are very few 'receptacle' producers. Japan has two, and according to the general manager, both had higher unit costs than his plant. Despite this he was emphatic that in the last financial year the net rate of return on written down capital employed for his plant, which operates as a profit centre, was well over 25 per cent. In short, this is a highly profitable plant.

In the five years leading up to this case study, Receptacles experienced a rapidly rising level of demand for its output, largely as a result of its marketing strategy. Much of this growth came from the Japanese market, but at the time of the research the rate of growth of demand, though still substantial, had eased a little.

In addition to this trend factor, Receptacles also experiences some seasonal patterns in demand, with a peak in the summer and a trough in the winter. Taken as a whole, Receptacles enjoys a very favourable product market situation and this has been the case for some years now. The effect has been to bring capacity utilisation at Receptacles to a high level, perhaps just short of full capacity, according to senior management. This proposition is supported by the fact that the main production facility on the site operated on a three-shift basis, Monday to Friday, with additional shifts worked regularly on Saturdays, and even Sundays at times, while the study was being carried out. The technology in use required little adaptation in response to changes in shifts worked.

Seven basic 'receptacles' are produced on the site, six in the main production facility and the remaining one in a much smaller and less sophisticated unit. Colour and external variations to suit user requirements give some additional variety to the end product, but these are simply minor modifications to the basic specifications of the seven different-sized products.

Viewed in production terms Receptacles is fundamentally a metal processing operation. The process entailed is best regarded as an amalgam of large batch and process technologies with its centrepiece being an extrusion operation. Around this core activity there are firstly several preparatory activities necessary to ensure that the prepared metal blanks meet required standards and that they are free of surface contaminants.

Secondly, there are some post-extrusion processes of varying degrees of technical complexity and sophistication. Together these 'finish' and transform the extruded blank according to rigorous specifications with regard to legally required tolerances and capacity measures. Because of these requirements specific quality checks are made at a number of points in the whole process and these tasks are performed by specialist 'quality viewers' who in effect have a roving role throughout the plant.

Production work tasks requiring varying degrees of skill and experience are arrayed along what might be loosely described as a 'line'. Workers operate specialised machines, metal baths, ovens, and other production apparatus, mostly in ones and twos. The factory building is relatively large for such a small workforce, however the work environment is noisy and in places subject to high temperatures. Normal conversation is difficult except in the paint shop and the packing and storage areas.

In mid-September 1989, there were 105 full-time permanent employees at the Receptacles plant together with one part-time casual. There were eighty-five direct production workers, including two apprentices. The numbers employed varied little over time. More labour was obtained through occasional changes to overtime shifts. Despite the existence of a corporate-level policy on equal employment opportunities in Steadfast there had been only one female production worker employed at the time of this study. Few employees were over fifty years of age and less than 10 per cent had English as their second language. The vast majority of employees had been employed at Receptacles for over a year and it was estimated that about 40 per cent had been employed for over five years. Only eight of the eighty-five production workers were tradespersons.

Management and organisation

Corporate level

As a publicly listed company Steadfast is one of the largest 100 such organisations in Australia. It has a long history in Australia. Its corporate existence of over fifty years was preceded by activities undertaken in Australia by its overseas-located controlling owner. This overseas parent has always held a major slice of equity in the corporation and at the end of the eighties increased its interest from just short of 60 per cent of share capital to a little below 90 per cent. Steadfast is quite clearly a foreign-controlled organisation and this is reflected in the fact that the overseas parent plays an active role in senior executive appointments, with short-listed candidates often interviewed at international headquarters.

The eighties have seen two rounds of corporate restructuring within Steadfast with the later effort still under way while this study proceeded. These moves have seen much greater emphasis given to the 'core' business of the corporation and future expansion is seen to lie more in this direction than in that of greater diversity. Increasing attention is to be given to the development of operations and exports in the Asia-Pacific region with Australian headquarters playing a leading role.

In late 1989 Steadfast had around 4000 employees located in over sixty workplaces, of which Receptacles is one. The vast majority of these workplaces have a small number of employees. In addition, Steadfast has responsibility for a range of subsidiary operations in Asia and the Pacific, as well as Australia.

Financially, Steadfast has been an even performer according to its published figures. It is by far the most influential firm in its core business in Australia, and in most of its operations it holds the substantial market share. This core business is vertically integrated from basic raw materials through to distribution. The worldwide network of its parent permits it to take advantage of research and development, technology, and other transfer arrangements. Internationally, the parent company has a formidable position in its key markets.

A little over twelve months before this case study began, the long-serving chairman and chief executive officer (CEO) retired. A new external chairman was appointed and, at the same time, the CEO post was filled by promotion from within Steadfast. No member of the 1989 board had a professional background in industrial relations or personnel, but the new chairman is a past president of a major Australian employer association.[1] These changes in corporate leadership are consistent with a move from a situation of gradual change to one where more profound organisational change is envisaged. One senior manager interviewed felt that recent changes in top posts within the corporation had been accompanied by a shift from a 'softer' to a 'drier' approach to industrial relations matters. In other words there seemed to be a discernable change in management style appearing around the time of this project.

Corporate headquarters is located in Sydney. Industrial relations matters form part of the responsibilities of the human resource department and its head, the general manager (human resources), reports directly to the managing director of Steadfast. The Department has an establishment of twenty including secretarial support staff. Despite the size of this unit Steadfast's stated policy is to devolve industrial relations matters to operating units. Industrial relations is not considered a major matter at board level but periodic and *ad hoc* reports are prepared.

Though organised along divisional lines for financial reporting purposes, Steadfast does not maintain a divisional human resource management structure between headquarters and operating units. The first step beyond the plant for industrial relations matters is the corporate human resources department.

Corporate communications measures

Considerable effort and resources are put into the employee communications program and strategy of Steadfast and its overseas 'parent'. Communications practices within many business organisations have been revitalised and modernised recently (Townley 1989). There is now growing interest within management circles in pro-active types of communications policies as part of a more integrated and strategic focus taken towards the management of labour. This was traditionally associated with a human relations approach to management. Key objectives now include the 'education' of workers regarding the market and competitive position of the company, and promotion of a sense of commitment, mostly in a 'top–down' style. 'Personal' video messages from chief executives are growing in popularity.

Steadfast practices shared many of these features. Every six months international headquarters of the world-wide group of related companies circulates a professionally-produced short video on the group's developments for the information of the employees. In addition, material for staff notice boards is produced at the same organisational level. In Australia, the Steadfast Corporation's chairman or managing director (or both) provide the 'talking head' for a regular Australian-focused video production. A quarterly corporation newspaper is distributed to all employees. This places great store on productivity improvements and personal achievements. An annual financial report for employees has been produced for some years. The Australian operation produces local notice board material to complement the international material distributed by its overseas majority owner.

In the past the former managing director made annual visits to most of the larger Steadfast workplaces where he addressed gatherings of workers and plant managers. This is expected to be resumed by the new CEO after a settling-in period.

There are two benefit schemes designed to bolster commitment among employees: a competitive children's overseas scholarship scheme, and an individual, voluntary, employee share scheme.

Altogether these elements of the group's communications strategy are more than a set of *ad hoc* measures. They indicate the development of a desired corporate identity among the workforce and reflect a longstanding and continuing human relations theme in the underlying philosophy of senior management. No doubt this strategy was begun by former senior executives, but the use of video techniques for dissemination of messages clearly indicates a desire to continue in a more sophisticated way the original top–down communications program to enhance unitarist sentiments within the organisation.

Plant-level management

Management of industrial relations and personnel at the Receptacles plant is primarily the responsibility of the production manager. He is assisted by a personnel supervisor who looks after payroll, leave, and other records. When the study commenced, the production manager had held the post for only six months. His predecessor was still employed at the site (as technical manager) so there was scope for helpful advice. The production manager estimated that about 40 per cent of his time was spent on personnel and industrial relations matters. In a separate interview the general manager of Receptacles estimated that he, too, spent almost the same proportion of his time on such matters. While neither of these managers had tertiary-level industrial relations education, both had participated in specialist in-house training programs provided by Steadfast headquarters' human resources department.

There are several reasons for the apparently large amounts of time spent on labour management matters by these two managers. First, as is elaborated on below, Receptacles has some joint structures which operate on a regular basis and demand significant management involvement. These are the Common Interest Programme (CIP) Representative Meeting, the Consultative Committee (CC), the Occupational Health and Safety Committee (OHSC) and the Value Added Management (Pilot) Group (VAMG). Second, there have recently been considerable industrial relations innovations and management has willingly devoted time to second tier, award restructuring and superannuation matters to ensure benefits were attained. In addition, Steadfast corporate human resources has promoted an Annual Wages Review (see below) for production staff, and negotiations on this have absorbed further managerial time. Third, during 1989 two matters arose which resulted in industrial action, with one stoppage lasting five working days requiring conciliation and arbitration by the Industrial Relations Commission. Finally, the limited experience of the production manager in 1989 is likely to have been a compounding factor in absorbing his, and the general manager's, time.

Receptacles is a member of the Metal Trades Industry Association (MTIA) in its own right but makes only limited use of the Association's services; for example, it seeks occasional advice on award standards. In the matter which resulted in a work stoppage, management rejected the advice of the Association and obtained representation in subsequent conciliation and arbitration proceedings from the Australian Chamber of Manufactures, of which Steadfast is a corporate member. Steadfast is also a member of the Business Council of Australia.

Union organisation

Manual workers at Receptacles have been employed under a post-entry closed shop understanding since the opening of the plant. This has been Steadfast company policy for all its manual workers throughout Australia for many years. (No present managers were fully aware of the reasons for the introduction of this measure.) Senior managers at both headquarters and the plant were adamant that they thought there were net benefits in the arrangement because it ensured that union representation became only a peripheral issue. On the other hand, unionisation had never been encouraged among clerical staff and there was no knowledge of their membership numbers. There is then a distinct difference between the union membership status of the two groups of employees in the Steadfast Corporation. A now common check-off arrangement is also in place at the Receptacles plant.

Two unions represent production labour at Receptacles—the Federation of Industrial, Manufacturing and Engineering Employees (FIMEE) and the Electrical Trades Union (ETU). The last union had only eight members in the plant, while the FIMEE had the remainder. Each of the two craft unions has one delegate, while the FIMEE has five: a senior delegate, one for each shift in the main production unit and one for the smaller production unit. Delegates do not meet on the site either as a single union committee, or jointly. The links that they do have are informal and the senior FIMEE delegate appears to exercise considerable influence over the direction taken by the delegates in local negotiations. Some difficulties are experienced when the senior delegate is rostered on to night shift since the various joint committees meet during day shift times.

Delegates are given paid time off to attend to approved union business (or are paid to attend if they are off shift). They also have access to a phone and have a notice board for union materials. There is, however, no independent union accommodation on the site.

It was not surprising to find that the FIMEE organiser is by far the most significant full-time union official for the plant. He also has responsibility for another larger Steadfast plant in the region as well as Receptacles and so is able to monitor practices at both sites. He works from a district office near the plant which is shared with the ASE.

The organiser visits Receptacles at least monthly and he estimated that during 1989 he had attended the plant more than twenty times. These visits are either regular 'housekeeping' calls, or in response to phone requests from delegates, or for scheduled negotiations. To maximise contact with membership, he arranges meetings around morning or afternoon shift changeovers.

Some difficulties arose at Receptacles during this case study which required his involvement. One matter concerned the union membership status of contract labour used to carry out specialist work on site. The second concerned moves to eliminate a leading hand position which had been seen by the union, and the delegates, as a traditional promotion expectation for shop-floor workers. This matter, which resulted in a work stoppage of five days and proceedings in the Industrial Relations Commission, is considered further in a later section of this chapter.

While the plant (and the company more generally) was seen as a 'good payer' by delegates and the organiser, some difficulties could be identified. One of the more immediate problems noted was the limited industrial relations experience of plant management. The organiser felt this became obvious where explanations of management rejection of union (delegates') requests were either not given, or were unconvincing. The organiser also advocated a grievance procedure that worked on the site to ensure that matters did not get out of hand prematurely. He considered senior Steadfast management seemed to have become more conciliatory towards the workforce. He was also aware that some companies, especially Business Council members, were pursuing a 'white ant' (incorporation) strategy against unions at the workplace, but was confident that this would not happen at the Receptacles plant.

The organiser clearly felt confident that any attempt by management to weaken the labour force's union loyalty would fail because of the competence and independence of job delegates. Certainly, at the time of the study this appeared likely to be true. But much hinged upon the experienced senior delegate, upon his continuation in that position, and upon how he perceived management initiatives. It was clear that the few industrial tensions that had occurred led all the senior managers interviewed to conclude that, from their point of view, things could be better at Receptacles. They wanted more cohesion in attitudes between the workforce and management.

As we shall see in the discussion of industrial regulation at the plant, a central bargaining role is played by job delegates. Full-time union officials, and especially the FIMEE organiser, play a relatively limited coordinating part in the process, particularly over effort-related questions, but even in wage related issues they did not dominate.

Plant management was happy with the existing external union structure that existed. The general manager felt the potential costs of trying to convert the plant to a single union site would far exceed any possible benefits. In any case, he thought these benefits would be minimal, or non-existent, given the present climate of industrial relations at the site. Management was concerned however, to modify the internal structures within which delegates operated, and this was seen as a priority issue for 1990.

A detailed discussion of negotiation and participative machinery in existence at Receptacles comes later, but it is worth briefly noting management's wish to streamline existing internal joint structures during 1990. They hope to consolidate the Common Interest Programme Representative Committee and the Consultative Committee into one body, simply termed the Site Committee. Though still being thought through, this proposed Site Committee would become a joint negotiating body and leave only one other joint body—the Safety Committee, which is required under New South Wales State legislation.

Job regulation through negotiation

Production workers at Receptacles are formally covered by the Federal Metal Industry Award 1984—Part 1. In practice, limited use is made of the Award and a number of unregistered and quasi-formal plant-level agreements actually address current job conditions. These arrangements have led to consultative structures being formed which have performed bargaining and consultative roles.

In the following two sub-sections the key matters of wage determination practices and the nature of the second tier agreement are discussed. These are the two most significant recent areas of formal bargaining within the plant, but there are some less evident and less formal aspects of job regulation which should be mentioned first.

There are some minor local agreements and understandings to be noted. Overtime working arrangements are under frequent review as changes occur in requirements, and as different problems are identified by both labour and management. Another example of such agreements is the rather informal understanding about the scheduling of annual leave at the time of a seasonal dip in demand. These are typical non-wage matters that were settled through the consultative mechanisms discussed later in the chapter.

Non-production workers do not engage in negotiations. They work under terms and conditions of employment set by the company. Formally the common rule provisions in New South Wales mean that the Clerks' Award (NSW) applies to them. However, management thought the prevailing wages and conditions at Steadfast largely outstripped the minimum standards in this award.

Wage determination

Until the end of 1988 wages paid to blue-collar workers at Receptacles reflected a rather complex history. Payment conceptually included the base award rate for each classification together with an appropriate supplementary payment which added from 6.4 per cent to 10.8 per cent. On top of these rates were two 'company margins', or over-award components. The first of these largely reflected the differing historical market positions of the various categories of labour. The second, more recent, 'company margin' added a further 2.5 per cent to the sum of the other components (the award rate, the supplementary payment, and the first 'company margin').

To these universal elements were added award allowances and site allowances. The former comprise leading hand and similar allowances, the latter included, up to the end of 1988, allowances for twelve designated situations, together with two company service payments applying at the site. Under these arrangements there were five ironworker classifications, along with fitter and electrician positions.

Regular overtime and shift premiums are added, where necessary, to these various components. It should be stressed here that it was common practice at Receptacles for two or even three weekend overtime shifts to be worked by production employees so that many workers came to expect to work a sixth shift. Also, the regular dividend (or bonus) from the Common Interest Programme (see below) also needs to be added to give the total remuneration paid to the blue-collar group. Taken as a whole, the weekly earnings of manual workers at Receptacles were quite high, and in the words of the FIMEE organiser, the employer was a 'good payer'.

From January 1989, these wage components were significantly modified as a result of the negotiation on site of what is known as the Broadbanding Agreement. This agreement was in effect the award restructuring exercise for the Receptacles plant and was negotiated over much of 1988 by FIMEE union delegates with some assistance from their organiser. The agreement has resulted in the consolidation into a single rate of the previous award, supplementary and company margins components; the reduction in the number of effective ironworker classifications to two (an inexperienced operator effectively has a six-week probation period while in the lower band operator position); and the elimination of six special site allowances. Under the new arrangements the various tasks to be performed on the site have been analysed in terms of their skill content, and assigned a points rating, according to complexity, on a 1-to-7 scale. The relevant clause in the Agreement explains the link between pay and skill:

> Employees will receive a payment of $2.50 for each point of skill rating learnt up to a maximum of 20 points or $50.00. Points accumulated beyond 20 will have no value. This payment will form part of the permanent all purpose wage rate.

During their six-week probationary period new employees are expected to acquire at least two lower level skills to justify the extra $5.00 paid to them from the end of that time.

All employees covered by the agreement are to be provided with the opportunity to achieve the maximum twenty points over a three-year period from the date of implementation, or from when they begin employment. Furthermore, those employees who, after a two-year phasing-in period, cannot achieve enough points to keep a skill loading equivalent to their pre-agreement permanent allowances, will be able to seek a review of their wage by the Consultative Committee.

Skill formation is to be on-site and provided by existing staff. When training is given by an employee that person is to be paid a training allowance, on a shift basis, equivalent to the lowest leading hand rate in the Award. The skill credentialling process now rests upon agreement between the trainee, the trainer and the company that competency has been achieved. Payment is on a 'skills acquired' rather than 'skills utilised' basis, and the company can now move individual workers to any part of the work process that their skill inventory permits.

Thus the Broadbanding Agreement has created scope for more flexibility and variation in work than in the past. More significantly it provides a way in which workers at Receptacles can steadily increase their pay apart from wage increases flowing from national wage case decisions and other sources.

A further aspect of wage determination at Receptacles is the Annual Wage Review. Considering national wage setting arrangements at the time this was a somewhat novel practice initiated by Steadfast head-quarters in 1988 for its plants. The central idea has been to negotiate with local union representatives an annual company-wide wage increase which is timed to be paid from the start of each new year. Corporate management sees a number of advantages in such a scheme. First, the wage increase is seen to come from the company rather than from the industrial tribunals. Second, employees receive what the company an-ticipate as the likely increase coming from a national wage case decision some time before that decision. Third, employees may receive a larger increase than that awarded by the tribunals if the Annual Wage Review offers more than the tribunal grants. Any shortfalls are to be made up under agreements signed so far. Fourth, it sets in place a company- and plant-level pay-setting structure capable of greater utilisation should the Australian system move to a more decentralised pattern of wage determination.

Late in 1988 the first such agreement was reached. It provided for a 4 per cent pay rise from early January 1989, in effect yielding a 1 per cent margin over the nationally-determined figure of 3 per cent. A second round of negotiations commenced towards the end of 1989 with Steadfast again offering workers a 4 per cent increase, or a 1 per cent margin once more. This time, Receptacles job delegates rejected the offer, refusing the condition imposed by management that they agree to a written grievance procedure designed by management. In the estimation of the delegates, this seriously impeded their rights to take action. Their view was not shared by the FIMEE organiser, who con-sidered that the package was acceptable in its original form.

Second-tier agreement

A workplace-level Second-Tier Agreement was concluded towards the end of July 1987. All manual unions at Receptacles are party to this agreement, though the only union official to sign it, other than site job delegates, was again the FIA district organiser. This was a little earlier than the formal effective date of implementation (1.9.87) of the 4 per cent pay increase ratified in the then Conciliation and Arbitration Commission following submission of local agreements made by parties to the Metal Industry Award 1984—Part I.

The key restructuring and efficiency improvements reflected concerns at Receptacles' local plant level. They included:

(a) *Rostered day off* (RDO)—flexible arrangements to apply in order to provide increased operating time and scope for preventative maintenance.

(b) *Demarcation*—commitment given by unions to undertake a 'reasonable approach to demarcation'.

(c) *Consultative Committee*—to be formed and to meet monthly.

(d) *Modified overtime allocation rules*—for example, those absent on Fridays must produce a doctor's certificate to permit them to work weekend overtime.

(e) *Skill rationalisation*—undertakings given to work further in this direction.

(f) *Absenteeism*—a new warning and counselling system adopted.

(g) *Operator quality checking*—the intention is to work towards this arrangement.

(h) *Work practices*—changes to shift starting time arrangements, to reworking, and to stock systems.

(i) *Management restraint*—entertainment of visitors on the site will reflect spending constraint.

Neither management nor the unions saw the Second-Tier Agreement as a source of significant change in itself. Instead it assisted by setting in place structures and preconditions for later changes, especially through 'climate creation'. The Consultative Committee arrangements fast acquired significance at Receptacles and the foreshadowed changes to skills created the basis for the Broadbanding Agreement. On the other hand overtime allocation and requirements have remained a difficulty. Management's need to operate a number of weekend overtime shifts for extended periods has placed pressures on workers' domestic lives, yet at other times the occasional fall-off in requirements has generated some tension among in those who have come to rely on the additional earnings derived from overtime.

Perhaps what was even more notable about the second tier, according to informants, was the role played by local delegates in negotiations on the one hand, and the limited impact provided by union officials on the other. At Receptacles, negotiations over the past three years have created a procedural basis for workplace bargaining. Moreover, because of continuity of service, the group of delegates has become more experienced as negotiators. But this is only one side of bargaining. Whether such changes mark any shift in the bargaining power of labour at this plant remains an unanswerable question. The continuing buoyancy of the product market has ensured that management are themselves not pressing hard for cost cutting, which might be the case in tougher market circumstances. Up to and including the period of this study, growth in demand has been a constant ingredient in labour–management relations. It remains a hypothetical question whether the emerging workplace bargaining arrangements would have the strength, without greater support from the wider union community, to withstand pressures for substantial concessions to management in a more difficult market setting.

Taken as a whole, therefore, the formal external system of Australian industrial relations does cast a shadow of sorts over the processes of job regulation at Receptacles, but that shadow is very hazy. Over the years management has sought, and obtained, a pay scale and payment system which enables it to attract and retain high quality labour in a local labour market region where supply persistently outstrips demand. Through initiatives of both the local plant and headquarters, pay has been maintained at relatively high levels, and increases have been paid either soon after national wage decisions, or before them. To a large extent the capacity of the company to sustain such a labour market position rests upon its particularly strong product market where it is by far the most significant supplier, and the sole producer in Australia, and upon its ability to sustain its export sales to Japan.

Job regulation through consultation

The Common Interest Programme (CIP)

The origins of what is known as the CIP, a value-added bonus scheme, are in the late seventies. Two main reasons account for the introduction of the CIP into the Receptacles plant and other Steadfast units. First, at that time, during the period of wage indexation of 1975–81, the company came under significant union pressure to lift its over-award payments at some of its sites. In response, the then corporate personnel manager proposed introduction of the CIP on a company-wide basis as a way of increasing the pay of manual workers, but in a manner which would be effectively self funding because of its productivity-oriented characteristics. Second, the then CEO of Steadfast was a strong public advocate of participative arrangements in the workplace and also a visible public figure in the productivity enhancement institutions which had been established and promoted in Australia. This parallelled the policy being developed by the coalition Federal Government of the day. A Department of Productivity had been created and a number of well publicised policy statements on participation were prepared by the National Employee Participation Steering Committee and issued by the Minister.[2] Both of these factors therefore gave impetus to the CIP proposal being considered by Steadfast.

The CIP scheme is marketed by a consultancy organisation led by a former union official. This firm briefed Steadfast headquarters and operating unit managers on the philosophy and form of the program, and on possible strategies for implementation at Steadfast. The Board supported the CIP concept, but decisions on its introduction were to be left to site management. The Receptacles plant, being one of the newest in the company, was seen as an appropriate test site, and local management agreed to its introduction early in 1981. Implementation took more time as the scheme had to be adapted to the specific production characteristics of the plant, and base figures established. More importantly, the concept had to be explained and sold to the workforce, and the institutional structure shaped and put in place. The first dividend flowing from the CIP at Receptacles was paid on 1st April 1982 and the scheme has continued to operate since then.

In essence the CIP at Receptacles is a productivity-related plant-wide bonus scheme paid over a monthly cycle, or over a longer period when Christmas and Easter periods are involved. A weighted base production figure is established and specified in unit manhour terms with adjustments made for standard reject rates for each product. Conversion to a monetary figure is made by use of an average hourly wage for the plant as a whole. Bonus is made or increased by reducing the unit manhour requirement, or the reject rate, or both, below the base level. Dividends are reported to the Representatives' Meeting and are divided equally among all participants. Thus the dispatch worker and general manager of the plant are both paid the same monthly bonus. It should be pointed out that only half the productivity gains made in any one cycle are paid out to employees as a bonus. The actual 'pool' created is first split on a 50/50 basis with the organisation leaving only half of the productivity benefits for the workforce. Should an individual participate in strike activity, or take unpaid sick leave, their entitlement would be adjusted on a pro-rata basis.

Employees can participate indirectly in the CIP through the monthly Representatives' Meeting. The constitution agreed when the scheme was introduced provides for up to twelve participants, half elected by employees and half appointed by management. Though this constitution does not recognise unions, in practice union delegates are often elected as representatives. For most of its life the Representatives' Meeting has comprised only eight members, reflecting the size of the plant.

Meetings are held in work time and commonly run for up to two hours. They bear some similarity to a plant-wide quality circle with proposals for productivity improvement seen as the key agenda items. The minutes revealed many such items being raised, but two main concerns were also evident. Workforce representatives expressed periodic frustration over the lack of action on proposed changes designed to raise productivity, and management representatives regularly aired their concerns that the meeting was considering matters which they felt were industrial. For example, in 1987 the representative of one group of workers informed the meeting that those he represented wanted no new business raised until outstanding matters were cleared up, while later in the same year management representatives reiterated that the meeting could only consider 'genuine' CIP matters.

Despite these concerns the CIP has provided a substantial boost to incomes for workers at the plant. During the first forty-one weeks of 1989 the average gross weekly payout had been $70.00, ranging from a high of $108.59 in one cycle to a low of $43.51 in another. The size of the bonus and its effect on the financial performance of the plant has recently led to a review of the scheme with a change in the base figure to apply from 1990. Management's key concern has been that the effects of capital expenditure and gradual improvements to technology had significantly eroded the historical base figures. A further concern of management has been that the pay increases that will flow from the Broadbanding Agreement, as skill points are accumulated by the workforce, could be considered to be double counting, given the impact on productivity and growth in the CIP dividend. The effects of this review, approved by the Representatives' Meeting in return for a one-off lump sum payment, will become clearer during 1990.

Thus the CIP is a long-standing participative mechanism in the Receptacles plant. As a structure it has thrown up some of the traditional 'jurisdictional' issues between bargaining and consultative processes common in such bodies, and when this study was completed management hoped that they would be able to streamline participative structures during 1990 so that the Representatives' Meeting would disappear as such, and the CIP become simply an agenda item for the revamped Consultative Committee, renamed the Site Committee.

The Consultative Committee

This Committee was established in 1987 as part of the Second Tier Agreement. It consists of union delegates from each area of the plant and has representation from each of the three unions on site. On the management side there are four representatives—the production manager, the operations manager, the personnel supervisor and one foreman. The charter of the Committee, according to the Second Tier Agreement is:

> ... to provide a communication forum for such matters as technology change, TQC [Total Quality Control], JIT [Just-In-Time] (and similar programmes), discussion of policies on grievance procedures.

It meets monthly, or as required. Membership overlap is evident on both employee and management sides between this Committee and the CIP Representatives' Meeting.

In practice the Consultative Committee has gone well beyond its intended scope. Many of the matters it has considered are clearly traditional bargaining matters. A continual issue has been the procedure relating to overtime rostering and notice. Another has been arrangement for rostered days off (RDOs), and during 1988 this body spent considerable time on the development of the Broadbanding proposal which culminated in the agreement signed with the unions early in 1989. After the Broadbanding Agreement was reached the Consultative Committee spent some of its time discussing the associated training arrangements, and it has been recognised as the appropriate body to review difficulties which might arise in the transition period from the old system of skill allowances to the new points-based model.

As might be expected the career of the Committee has not been entirely smooth. In July 1989, following a week-long work stoppage, union delegates presented a unanimous vote of no confidence in the production manager and the personnel supervisor to the meeting and requested alternative management representatives. FIMEE delegates also notified management that the shop-floor workers wished to abandon the mechanism. No meeting was held in August 1989, but one was held in September, preceded by an address from the production manager concerning his vision of the role of the Committee and its future.

New procedures are now in place for the Committee. Union delegates are entitled to meet as a caucus for thirty minutes before the Committee commences its business. Draft minutes are to be provided to delegates for comment before being posted on notice boards, and better advance notice of agenda items is to be provided. The frequency of meetings has been discussed, with a proposal being put that they be held on a 'needs' basis rather than monthly. The abovementioned rationalisation of participative/bargaining structures contemplated for 1990 by Receptacles management seemed to be a sensible proposal designed to rectify some of the frustrations arising under prevailing arrangements. Except for the Safety Committee which operates under State legislation, the newly-proposed Site Committee would become the recognised bargaining body.

In effect the Consultative Committee has become a *de facto* site level negotiating committee. Both the unions and management believe that it has merit and provides a very useful forum to explore issues. As it has evolved, union delegates appear to have loosened the firm control that management had hoped to retain. Management thinks this is more a product of the personalities of the delegates rather than a reflection of shop floor pressures. Equally, the tensions evident in mid-1989 in the operation of the Committee were attributed by the union to management personality and inexperience. To an outsider they reflected more the dynamics of a bargaining process in action.

Other participative institutions

It should already be evident that Receptacles management is concerned to create and maintain a strong participative milieu at the plant, based on the presence of the institutions already considered above. However, there are other bodies on the site. In keeping with recent statutory requirements, a Safety Committee meets monthly during work time for periods of up to two and a half hours. This Committee is comprised of five union delegates and three management representatives. Management expressed two main concerns over the regulation of safety through this process. First, they felt that matters raised in the Committee go well beyond health and safety. They feel they intrude on maintenance and requisition policies. Second, management considered that the meetings take up too much time with the agendas expanding to fill the allotted time. A review of the Committee is planned for 1990.

A recent initiative quietly introduced in Receptacles is a Value Added Management (VAM) pilot project. In the past two years this has been a relatively low-key exercise involving an informal study group. The general manager considers that despite this style the pilot project has generated some very significant results. Productivity improvements are believed to be much greater than both those flowing from the CIP and those likely to arise out of the Broadbanding Agreement. In practice the VAM pilot embraces TQC and JIT concepts as well. It is likely that the plant will soon embark on a second phase of VAM with much greater attention being given to promotion of the underlying philosophy. To ensure that the momentum desired by management is built up around the ideas of VAM/TQC/JIT the production manager saw it as crucial that a participative style and structure takes root.

It was of some concern that the VAM initiative, like the Broadbanding exercise, can 'contaminate' the CIP scheme. Indeed one of the reasons for the 'blow-out' in CIP bonuses was the success of the VAM pilot project. It remains to be seen exactly how this problem will be confronted if productivity continues to improve based on these new management techniques in the future.

Management believes that a 'rational' workforce—one which is involved in the process of change through suitably structured institutions, and 'sensible' unionism, will provide the commitment needed to achieve organisational goals. This has led management to adopt a logic of continual productivity improvements. A sentiment which emerged often in interviews with management was that any lack of commitment shown by a worker in the face of 'reasonable expectations' was most likely to be the product of individual personality problems, rather than structural conflict.

Industrial action

This plant has experienced industrial action recently. Despite this, it is not regarded as a conflict-prone site by either union officials or senior Steadfast management. The matters which have arisen at the site in these years have all been domestic rather than wider issues. This fact has led to both plant management and the FIMEE organiser maintaining interest in the development of an acceptable grievance procedure. The rejection of the 1990 Annual Wage Review proposals put by management occurred because the delegates on the site were not prepared to forgo their right to take action and endorse the procedure sought. In particular, concern arose over a part of the procedure which stated that:

> It is the spirit of this Agreement that industrial action or interruptions to normal production must be avoided to ensure a continuation of operations to enable the Company's continued competitiveness in the marketplace.

So the issue of a grievance procedure persists.

The most common form of action taken by workers at the plant is the stop-work meeting. A recent example of this was a cessation of work in late September 1989, an hour before the end of day shift, to consider the question of non-union labour being allegedly used by contractors on the site. Work resumed with the commencement of the afternoon shift.

Strike action also took place in July 1989. Work stopped for about five days over the question of an appointment to a leading hand position. When the FIMEE delegates protested against the proposed company nominee for the post on the grounds that the person concerned did not have the seniority considered traditional, the company decided to abolish that leading hand position, and incorporate the duties into other positions, as it claimed it was entitled to do under the Second Tier Agreement. This action resulted first in a stop-work meeting, then a strike.

Receptacles' management notified the Industrial Relations Commission of the dispute under the standard Section 99 procedure. Conciliation proceedings followed and these resulted in a return to work followed by inspections at the plant and a recommendation. In the decision the Commission recommended retaining the leading hand position 'at this stage', and a reasonable trial with appropriate training for the union-preferred candidate. A conference of the parties was also planned for early 1990 to review the matter.

It would be accurate to say that these two matters, occurring so close together, did have the effect of slightly souring the industrial relations climate at Receptacles. Reference has already been made to the boycott on the Consultative Committee initiated at this time. The rejection of the 1990 Annual Wage Review might also be interpreted in a similar light.

These events and the reported patchy history of industrial action at the site suggest that workers are generally committed to company objectives, but the cultivation of an industrially passive workforce at

Receptacles and the by-passing of union mechanisms at the local level cannot be considered viable policies at Receptacles.

Relationships between plant management and headquarters

One of the more contentious issues to arise within the industrial relations literature in recent years has been how much decision-making autonomy workplace management have in industrial relations (Marginson *et al.* 1988). Most empirical research has been undertaken overseas and the area is fraught with methodological difficulties, but despite these an attempt was made in this study to assess the balance of influence between the factory-based Receptacles management, and Steadfast corporate management.

It should be noted that the overseas parent of Steadfast appears to have no direct input into Australian industrial relations policy development. However, it would be surprising if the 'culture' of the parent did not find some reflection in the 'style' adopted. Given the limited canvas of this research it was impossible to verify this proposition one way or the other. Much more scope existed for an examination of the relationship of control between Steadfast and its plants in Australia, such as Receptacles.

It is clear, first of all, that Steadfast's corporate-level management closely monitors the financial health of the Receptacles plant. As a profit centre Receptacles' management provides detailed and regular financial reports on profit (or loss), labour and other costs, labour productivity, sales revenues and orders, and can provide many of these for each of the production units, and according to individual product type. Reject rates are also recorded as part of the accounting system required for the CIP. With regard to investment decisions the general manager of the plant indicated that for projects above a certain unspecified level he was required to seek corporate approval but had not experienced any refusals in his time at Receptacles. Lower level managers at the workplace have only a limited right to approve capital expenditures. Most must be referred to the general manager.

With regard to reporting on employment and industrial relations matters, constituent workplaces of Steadfast are required to provide their corporate counterparts with only limited regular data. This is seen to be consistent with the company's espoused policy of decentralising labour matters. Thus, while data on aggregate numbers employed are gathered monthly by head office, as is information on strikes, bans and other forms of industrial action, no regular data are obtained for matters such as absenteeism, turnover, and overtime working. However, *ad hoc* reports on labour matters are requested from plants. For example, the human resources department recently requested a report from Receptacles on CIP payments when fears arose that the base had been eroded with a resultant excessive growth in monthly payouts. Similarly, when strikes occur there will be a request for an *ad hoc* report from the plant on details and, typically, corporate staff become directly involved.

As well as written reports, links between Steadfast corporate staff and those with industrial relations responsibilities at the plant are maintained through two-day in-house human resource conferences held three or four times per year. These meetings permit contact to be made with those having 'front line' industrial relations responsibilities, and they also provide an opportunity for plant managers to build up an informal network among themselves. Unfortunately, the focus of this study did not permit an examination of any network hypothesis, but in the context of the debate concerning the locus of industrial relations decision making, it does seem to be an area that warrants future attention.

An attempt was made through parallel interviewing to further assess the extent and areas of autonomy left to plant management. Corporate management formed the view that the autonomous decentralised approach taken with the second tier negotiations left much to be desired in Steadfast. Though not directly involved in subsequent negotiations, head office adopted a firm hand-holding approach for plants in the subsequent round of structural efficiency discussions. These negotiations have been centrally supervised, and an internal company consultant analysed tasks to prepare for local award restructuring negotiations. Interestingly, the only approach made in recent years to Steadfast management by the main union at Receptacles, the FIMEE, was in relation to award restructuring, and this was only in general terms, on a company-wide basis, by national officials. Apart from this contact there have been no approaches made to Steadfast executives over the past two to three years by the national union.

Corporate human resources executives had introduced the Annual Wage Review. However, some discussions were held with ACTU officials over details before the idea was put to plant-level management as a proposal that could be placed before job delegates and local union organisers in 1988. In the case of both award restructuring and the Annual Wage Review it is clear that corporate staff played a key role in shaping the parameters for plant-level negotiations without itself having a direct presence at the negotiation table. A similar situation may well be characteristic of other industrial relations and employment issues.

This issue was also pursued in interviews. Areas considered by the interviewees included reference of matters to industrial tribunals, dismissals, setting of staffing levels, and handling of work stoppages. On almost all matters, except regular events such as level of overtime working and scheduling of leave, the general manager, human resources said that his department would *advise* the plant, and under more difficult circumstances he would *instruct* local management. On the other hand, the manager with responsibility for industrial relations in the plant, while concurring in part about advice, held the view that ultimately he would decide such matters on his own, or perhaps consult with other managers at the site. Because it was not possible to explore the specifics of particular events it was difficult to resolve this apparent contradiction concerning the degree of influence exerted by head office over plant-level decisions, through its advisory role. In any case, the ephemeral nature of much decision-making renders it extremely difficult to decide whether the corporate managers or the plant managers have the final say. Nevertheless, it would appear that head office views on most matters are well known to plant staff and it would be surprising if there was not considerable agreement. In short, the nurturing of a Steadfast industrial relations style, well understood by operating managers, would assist a high degree of 'fit' between courses of action favoured by corporate managers and those taken at plant level.

This is certainly not indicative of an autonomous arrangement for industrial relations management at the local level. Broad ideas and initiatives are typically the product of head office, and many industrial matters are monitored centrally. 'Autonomy' is much more evident in the implementation of measures and proposed changes, and around questions of work organisation. Similar findings have been reported by Kinnie (1989) in his recent examination of practices in a number of British organisations. Thus the current managerial vogue for devolution of industrial relations to workplace and operational levels seems more likely to occur in the form of the decentralisation of execution, rather than the conception of managerial industrial relations work.

Conclusions

Crucial to an understanding of industrial relations within the Receptacles plant in the late 1980s is first an awareness of the character of the plant itself and the product market that it serves. It is a small specialist plant and in financial terms an exceptional performer by most standards. This success has been built upon a steadily expanding product market, and especially its export component. Over time this growing demand has approached full capacity utilisation. As things stand the use of weekend overtime shifts has lifted the marginal cost of recent increases in orders, and under existing production arrangements any further growth will also be at this higher cost.

As a consequence of these developments since the mid-eighties, management's primary concern has been the introduction of productivity enhancement measures, and an associated mentality among employees. Greater labour productivity growth would in effect reduce the level of capacity utilisation for a given volume of production, and lower costs at the margin if fewer weekend overtime shifts needed to be worked to achieve the existing, or even an increased, output. Thus work organisation and productive efficiency have been central concerns for management. In this context the high wages/earnings strategy of management can be interpreted in instrumental terms. It constitutes perhaps the key factor used to promote increased efficiency. High earnings assist the recruitment and retention of better quality labour and arguably are designed to motivate the workforce towards greater effort and the maintenance of low reject rates.

Until very recently management has emphasised consultative procedures. This was consistent with the traditional human relations style of the corporate entity, Steadfast. Shop floor union representatives were willing to play this game up to a point. What management expected to gain through the maturing CIP, the Consultative Committee, and the new Value Added Management Study Group, was an increasing level of commitment from the delegates and the workforce they represented, together with clear increases in productivity through improved work organisation. Moreover, the new Annual Wage Review can also be interpreted as an arrangement designed to promote commitment, as can the increasingly sophisticated and co-ordinated communications program.

This proliferation of industrial relations developments in recent years at Receptacles, especially those of a procedural kind, has had some contradictory effects. The consultative mechanisms aimed at improving production have increasingly absorbed blocs of non-productive time from both delegates and managers concerned. Not only that, these mechanisms have also provoked an increased bargaining awareness among union representatives, so that these internal company institutions have tended much closer to a bargaining role rather than the intended consultative role. Management's response to this emerging contradiction, so it seems, will be to promote consolidation of a number of the consultative bodies into a Site Committee which will have a more overt negotiation function. Paradoxically the 'sensible' unionism originally sought through a human relations style of consultative mechanism may now emerge in a bargaining framework.

Another dilemma which has emerged in recent times is the problem of double counting in productivity-related wage and earnings payments. The longstanding CIP bonus system which rewards productivity performance over the established (and recently modified) base, presumably will reflect any benefits which flow from the new Broadbanding Agreement. But the Agreement itself also provides for payments to be made according to the enhanced skill inventories of individual workers, in recognition of their greater functional flexibility and productivity.

For the workforce there is a further contradiction embedded in current moves relating to more productive efficiency. Unless demand continues to grow it is possible that increased productivity will result in less need for overtime work; overtime earnings, then, will drop for those affected. Under arrangements in place in the late eighties overtime earnings were almost an institution, with many workers relying strongly on this element of earnings. It was hardly surprising, in these circumstances, to find considerable tension evident around overtime issues.

What influence do institutions and elements beyond the plant exert over industrial relations within Receptacles? So far as the industrial tribunals are concerned, their role is hardly more than marginal. It is true that the National Wage two-tier wage decision of March 1987 did result in some procedural developments within the plant, but there had been a much longer interest in participative forms of productivity improvement at Receptacles through the Common Interest Programme and its associated Representatives' Meeting. The Broadbanding Agreement was certainly different, foreshadowing as it did the structural efficiency principle introduced later by the National Wage Bench. This agreement did introduce some modifications to classification and skill formation, but in a sense this was not a revolutionary change. On-the-job training had long been the informal practice at Receptacles, and the Broadbanding Agreement has formalised much of this. But it did introduce a new wage element into the plant, one which, as we have noted, has the capacity in the future to erode the bonus system associated with the Common Interest Programme through an element of double counting.

Ultimately there was no strong reliance on the tribunal system at Receptacles, nor did the system appear to seriously restrict management and unions except at the margins around certain idiosyncratic disputed decisions, where tribunal assistance was occasionally sought.

The wider union movement likewise could not boast a high visibility at Receptacles. Here the key figure has been the FIMEE through its local organiser, but successive occupants of this role perceived that their members appeared to be considerably satisfied with the pay and conditions. Plainly, there were occasional disputes but the situation was fundamentally more than suitable to the unions. Implicitly, if not explicitly, the organiser's role had come to be seen as one of responding to members' concerns over matters arising from management decisions, along with some assistance in negotiations. There was certainly very little evidence of national union office activity, and virtually no sign of strategic initiatives arising from outside union sources.

Employers' associations were even less visible than the wider union movement. Very limited use was made of Receptacles' MTIA membership, and when strike action led to hearings within the Industrial Relations Commission, advocacy services were sought from the Chamber of Manufactures, to which Steadfast belonged. The influence of the Business Council was also limited with neither Receptacles nor Steadfast senior executives supporting the single union model being advocated by the Council at the time of this study.

Steadfast corporate management provides a distinct contrast in terms of involvement. Historically it had provided the initial endorsement of the Common Interest Programme and support for the unofficial closed shop. In addition, its influence and support was evident around the introduction of the over-award or company margins components of wages, though clearly local union pressure also played some part here. The recently introduced Annual Wage Review was initiated by head office, and moreover its guiding hand was in evidence around the wage parameters of the Broadbanding Agreement, though many of the details were quite obviously determined through negotiations at the workplace level. This was less the case for the Second Tier Agreement which appears to be an example of high local autonomy. But there are other considerations which need to be taken into account in any evaluation of the relationship between the workplace and its corporate headquarters.

There is little doubt that Steadfast corporate management was able to shape some of the underlying parameters of industrial relations at Receptacles. First there was a tacit, if not stronger, endorsement of the high wage/earnings policy for the plant. Second, though there is a little room for debate over this matter, it did seem clear that on the more significant issues and questions head office advice, and at times their instructions, were key determinants of decisions made by local management at Receptacles. Third, the contacts created through in-house courses and conferences set in place an extra source of corporate influence and an associated network for those managers with industrial relations responsibilities. Finally, the corporate communications program was concerned to promote a culture of productivity growth and commitment throughout the corporation as a whole.

Knights and Collinson (1984), in their discussion of control versus consent approaches adopted by management towards labour, note that those firms, like Receptacles, who are able to escape the rigours of highly competitive markets tend to veer towards consent strategies, and away from what Burawoy (1985) terms 'despotic factory regimes'. In the Receptacles plant, management was convinced that a rational workforce would strongly endorse the corporate culture, and support consent-based participative institutions. The evidence of this case study suggests, however, that this endorsement was at best only partial and spasmodic. Sources of conflict and tension persisted not so much because of individual attitudes and other common psychological explanations, nor because of interfering industrial tribunals, but because the historical dynamics of industrial relations played out at a reasonably unconstrained micro-level continued to throw up contradictory situations to which labour and management, at both plant and corporate levels, have continued to respond.

3 Paintco

Background to the case

This case study deals with a large paint manufacturing and warehouse facility which we will call Paintco. It is one of several plants and distribution centres throughout Australia that make up a paint operating group. This group was once an independent company. However, it now belongs to the largest of four divisions which comprise one of Australia's biggest and most diversified manufacturing corporations. The paint operating group accounts for approximately 50 per cent of sales within its corporate division. Thus the corporation, despite its wide product range, depends heavily upon its paint business.

The paint operating group holds a large share of the Australian paint market compared with its two chief competitors and more than 110 other lesser producers. Given this market strength, profitability is usually strong, although this dipped in 1988 following some market dislocation and redundancy costs arising from the acquisition of another firm. To ensure future viability the operating group underwent considerable rationalisation which included reducing the number of paint factories within the group and concentrating product lines at particular sites. Since then profitability has recovered to consolidate the paint operating group's position as a strong profit centre within the corporation.

Rationalisation has had a marked impact upon Paintco. For almost thirty years this site produced both technical (industrial) and decorative (household) paints. The production of decorative paint was discontinued and production transferred to interstate factories. All technical paint production was then relocated to Paintco, securing for it a vital role within the group. Other developments testify to the operating group's long-term commitment to this site. Notable here are the construction of a new warehouse and a resin plant. The site also houses the main laboratory and head office for the operating group.

Production of technical paints is far more complex than decorator or household paints primarily because of the special ingredients used, stricter quality requirements, and small-scale product batches. The principal ingredients of technical paint are resin, pigment, and solvent. Of these, only resin is manufactured on site, although a few additional resins must still be brought in from outside. Production is undertaken on a batch basis using relatively simple technology. Chemists list the paint formulae for a specific product mix on computer. Pigments are then drawn from stores, weighed, sent to 'make-up' and ground (if powder or grits). The 'make-up' centre is the heart of the manufacturing plant. It comprises several specialised machines to mix resin and pigment (including sand grinders and a ball mill), and twenty mixing tanks where solvent is added. These tanks are positioned on the second storey of the building directly above the filling floor. After mixing, samples are sent to a laboratory for analysis. The tanks are filtered into 40-litre drums on the filling floor. Drums are then removed to the warehouse.

The most complex and vital parts of the production process are tinting and testing which can take up to seven days to complete. Linked to this is a production cycle which tends to run through the working week. In this cycle material dispersal, make-up, and tinting work is done primarily at the start of the week and then slackens, while filling and testing accelerate toward Friday and Saturday. Up to 300 different products are made in this way, the main differences lying in the pigment (colour) and resin (which determines special paint qualities such as hardness and drying speed).

Several features of technical paint production must be made clear at this point because of their importance for industrial relations. First, Paintco has a large market share, and its products are not readily substituted by customers. This allows 'cost-plus' pricing, making the company relatively insensitive to labour cost increases. Second, the operation of the production cycle requires or permits tasks to be performed outside normal working hours. Thus, earnings can be inflated through shiftwork and overtime.

Employment

Employment in Paintco's primary production centre is relatively small. It is made up as shown in Table 3.1.

Table 3.1 Employees at 1.2.90, Excluding Workers Absent on Worker's Compensation Payments

Manufacturing service	17
Ingredients dispersal	8
Make-up	39
Tinters	11
Thinners	6
Protective coats	22
Laboratory tester	15
Filling room	36
Heavy duty paints	7
Maintenance/site serv.	23
Resin plant	20
Waste treatment plan	5
Total	209

Elsewhere on site are employed sixty-four warehouse employees, 130 research and development workers (laboratory), and 100 head office workers plus a small number of ancillary staff (groundkeepers and gatekeepers). This case study is concerned solely with industrial relations among the manufacturing plant and warehouse employees. We do not deal with research laboratory, head office, or ancillary staff.

While Paintco is the largest employer within the operating group, in 1989 it accounted for only about 300 out of 1200 award employees. The remainder were dispersed in manufacturing and distribution centres elsewhere in Australia. Employment in the operating group also includes 1300 non-award staff and 300 employees in trade centres (regional wholesale distribution), giving a total of 2800 employees. Although the 300 manufacturing and warehouse workers at Paintco constitute only 11 per cent of operating group employment, they are, as we will see, an especially important group in terms of industrial relations.

The factory and warehouse employees with whom we are concerned are mainly semi-skilled or unskilled. With the exception of maintenance and laboratory workers, employees are hired without prior qualifications and experience, and are taught on the job. Job training is brief. A new employee spends one day with the training manager, one week being directed and watched by a leading hand, and remains on probation for three months. Most jobs are learnt simply and quickly. However there are some tasks which require a special aptitude that may take years to develop. Notable here is tinting, which is done by a small, stable and highly experienced group of so-called semi-skilled workers.

A job hierarchy and internal promotion system exists based upon advertising within the factory. However, until the advent of award restructuring, the career structure tended to be rather flat. Only the high-status tinters were drawn from production employees, while other senior workers such as supervisors, laboratory workers, and maintenance workers were recruited directly from the external labour market. Opportunities for advancement are beginning to improve. Supervisors are now promoted from within the plant.

Approximately 40 per cent of the semi-skilled workers are from non-English speaking backgrounds. These employees are dispersed fairly evenly through the plant. There is also a very small minority of female employees in the main production areas and a significant proportion in the laboratory. Casual employment is small (seven or eight in total), and confined to one or two sections of the plant. An industrial agreement limits the job tenure of these employees to a maximum of three months. Management has little need to make use of casual employees. Since demand for technical paint tends to be fairly steady it is not necessary to structure the workforce to compensate for fluctuations in production. Paintco's workforce tends to be fairly stable, growing slowly with plant expansion.

Awards and earnings

We have chosen to give a detailed account of the way award base rates are supplemented to make up earnings at Paintco. There are several reasons for doing so. Pay, of course, governs the living standards of employees. Analysis of its composition can inform us about the methods employees use, both individually and collectively, to improve those standards. It follows that we can learn much about what is, for many unionists, the central activity of unions at the workplace. On the other hand, pay represents to management a major component in production costs. Analysis of its composition and determination can tell us how they control those costs. Indirectly, we can then learn much about how management deals with its workforce in response to product market and other influences. Thus, pay is a vital concern of management and workers and a key indicator of the central activities in workplace industrial relations.

A total of six awards and registered agreements apply to Paintco. Four of these cover employees in the factory and warehouse—the

Australian Paint Industry Manufacturing Award (1986), the *Australian Paint Industry (Storemen and Packers) Agreement (1976)*, the *Metal Industry Award (1984)*, and the *Australian Paint Industry (Superannuation) Award (1986)*. The first of these covers production employees, the second storepersons, the third applies to maintenance workers, and the fourth deals with superannuation for all these groups. The remaining two awards are the *Australian Paint Industry Manufacturing (Clerical Officers) Consolidated Award (1984)* (which applies to clerks), and the *Australian Paint Industry (Association of Draughting, Supervisory and Technical Employees Laboratories) Agreement (1976)*. These do not apply in the production or warehouse areas. All of these are federal awards or agreements. In the past, paint production workers were covered by state awards but these were consolidated into a federal award.

The main award (Paint Industry Manufacturing Award) had thirty task-based classifications for production workers, broad-banded into five wage groups. Before award restructuring took place, Paintco used a maximum of thirteen of these classifications and three of the wage groups (2, 3, and 4) which gave a wage dispersion of only $9.50. This award also included a separate eight-point salary structure for laboratory assistants (now reduced to seven salary points). Paintco used three of these salary points, paying between $18.50 and $46.50 above the Group 2 production workers. The Storemen and Packers agreement had four rates of pay based on experience and equipment operated. All four of these were used. Again there was a flat pay structure with a wage dispersion of only $14.90 prior to award restructuring. Awards with a flat pay ladder and short career path were common for blue-collar workers. They have been widely condemned as a disincentive to skill formation; award restructuring came about, in part, as a remedy for this.

Award restructuring has changed the paint industry classification/wage structure. A new training classification has been introduced. The five wage grades remain although associated task classifications have been eliminated to allow multi-skilling. Wage dispersion has increased to reflect skill differences, the new award spanning $63.60 from top to bottom compared with $36.90 under the old award. A new classification of 'team leader' has been added for employees exercising special responsibility in performance appraisal, quality control, production control, training, and safety management. Also warehouse and factory wage rates have been matched to discourage demarcation.

The old and new classification rates are shown in Table 3.2.

Table 3.2   Old and New Classification Rates

Classification	Award Rate* March, 1989	Award Rate November, 1989
Group 1	332.10	399.00 (Trainee)
Group 2	338.00	403.30
Group 3	342.30	419.70
Group 4	347.50	435.60
Group 5	363.50	462.60 (Team Leader)

* There is a lower rate for a 3-month trainee in each grade

The main awards are all 'paid rates' awards which are intended to set a maximum wage and thus prohibit over-award payments. However, small individual over-award payments are paid to most tinters ($4.60 to $13.60), to some Group 2 production workers ($3.60 to $6.90), to some laboratory workers ($1.10), and to most Group 2 warehouse workers ($0.70). Maintenance workers under the Metal Industry Award (a minimum rates award) receive substantial over-award payments (up to $132.85). Base rates for all groups incorporate an industry allowance ($13.00 in 1986 and now $13.90) which compensates for disability and other rates which are not paid. In addition base rates for all workers at Paintco were fixed approximately $41.00 above award base rates in spite of the paid rates award. Finally there is a 'safety incentive' scheme which yields a periodic payment of up to $90.00 per annum.

The new award rates introduced by award restructuring represent a substantial increase of from $66.90 to $99.10 on the base rate formally applicable eight months earlier. However, the base rates currently used to calculate earnings at Paintco have not risen by this entire amount. The new base rates absorbed the old industry allowance of $13.90 (originally the 'Workplace Allowance' of $15.00 for men and $11.50 for women—averaged to $13.90 and extended to the whole industry) and they included the 3 per cent first stage adjustment, and classification increments for higher groups. There remains a discrepancy of some $40.00 which does not constitute a net addition to the workplace base rate. This element appears to absorb the earlier over-award payment. It should be noted that actual earnings in the plant had not been calculated from award rates since the introduction of an operating agreement in 1982 granting more than $40.00 in an over-award payment.

Actual earnings are also made up well in excess of award minima by a number of award-based extras. These additional payments are closely associated with work patterns. First, a significant proportion of workers undertake shift work (a shift loading of 17.5 per cent is paid for afternoon shifts, and 20 per cent for night shifts). The number of shift workers in production at any one time is shown in Table 3.3.

Table 3.3   Number of Shift Workers in Production at One Time

Day shift	114
Afternoon	62
Night	13
24-hour shift pattern (Resin Plant)	20
Total	209

Not all sections work shifts. It depends upon the nature of technology and work organisation. Thus resin plants must be operated continuously, while tinting work and most maintenance are only done in normal day shift. However, the nature of paint manufacture requires continuous crewing at a low level in most areas of the plant.

Second, a high proportion of workers work overtime. In the last pay period of January 1990, of 387 workers on site (including warehouse, head office, laboratory and ancillary workers on weekly pay), 37.8 per cent did no overtime, 25.0 per cent did from one to seven hours, and 37.2 per cent did eight or more hours. The number doing no overtime is inflated by approximately 100 secretarial and other staff from head office. In contrast almost all factory and warehouse employees do some overtime and a significant proportion do at least one shift or more. In the warehouse, overtime levels of sixteen to twenty hours are not uncommon. Much of this overtime is systematic and linked to work flow. In 1982 a 35-hour week was introduced, the reduced hours to be taken in an allocated day off (ADO) which is often taken on a Monday. This corresponds to a slack workpace at the beginning of each week. Work intensifies towards the end of the week, and a half or full shift at overtime rates is normal on Saturday to complete the weekly work cycle in the factory.

Other minor award-based additions to earnings include a first-aid allowance (normally $9.95 earned by approximately 10 per cent of employees), meal allowance, tinting allowance, Saturday morning allowance, safety officer allowance, and tool and clothing allowances. A number of these allowances are built into the individual worker's base rate, while others are paid irregularly as justified. Most of these additions are quite small and confined to a few workers. Nevertheless, they add to the diverse methods by which time rates are pumped up to make the plant a high-paying employer of semi-skilled and unskilled labour.

Table 3.4 shows the composition of earnings in the last week of January 1990 for a random sample of workers in five important production, warehouse and laboratory groups. Three points are clearly established by this data. First, average weekly earnings for all these groups of semi-skilled workers are quite high ($600.51 in the 'Make-up' department to $718.15 in the warehouse). Second, overtime is the main constituent lifting earnings above base rates (which are calculated to include over-award and personal allowance components in some cases).

Table 3.4 Weekly Earnings: 5 Key Groups—Week Ending 1.2.90

	Base Rate (incl. personal over-award payments)	Over-time	Shift allowance	Other (mainly meal allow.)	Gross earnings
Tinting (n = 7)					
Highest paid indiv.	515.59	268.11	—	14.30	798.00
Average for group	451.09	172.74	—	12.25	636.11
Lowest paid indiv.	419.70	—	—	—	419.70
Make-up (n = 10)					
Highest paid indiv.	439.27	305.27	—	14.30	758.84
Average for group	420.56	140.03	25.20	7.15	600.51
Lowest paid indiv.	419.72	—	—	—	419.72
Fill & label (n = 10)					
Highest paid indiv.	447.51	246.64	62.64	7.15	763.94
Average for group	417.56	103.65	26.67	5.05	613.84
Lowest paid indiv.	408.31	—	—	—	408.31
Warehouse (n = 10)					
Highest paid indiv.	419.86	439.68	—	21.45	880.99
Average for group	427.03	267.76	11.91	11.44	718.15
Lowest paid indiv.	419.72	8.99	—	—	428.71
Laboratory (n = 10)					
Highest paid indiv.	419.72	393.71	58.72	14.30	886.45
Average for group	424.70	164.71	30.02	5.85	618.08
Lowest paid indiv.	420.80	—	—	—	420.80

Note: Data for the highest and lowest earnings of individuals in a group need not show the highest and lowest specific components of earnings—especially Shift Allowance and 'Other' Earnings.

Third, there is a dispersion of earnings within each group, depending almost exclusively upon the amount of overtime worked.

Since overtime is such an important component of earnings it is useful to look at its distribution. There are some groups (notably in the warehouse) where high overtime (over twelve hours) is widespread and regular. There are others such as clerical workers who do little or no overtime. The pattern in the production centre is more complex. In some sections, such as the laboratory, individuals who work heavy overtime do so because it is associated with shift work. Elsewhere the pattern tends to vary, with individuals in make-up and filling experiencing fluctuating overtime levels.

The distribution of overtime is associated with the allocation of ADOs. Rules have grown up and are partially honoured to discourage Saturday overtime for those rostered to take ADOs adjacent to the week-end. But for the most part overtime allocation is a flexible blend of employee choice and employer selection. Other factors influencing overtime levels at the time the case study was conducted were the high level of industry demand for technical paint (this has been consistently strong since 1982), and the intensified workload arising from the transfer of product lines.

It has been noted that certain market and technical characteristics make Paintco insensitive to labour costs, and amenable to working patterns which inflate earnings. First, Paintco holds a large share of technical paint production, a characteristic which has strengthened following industry rationalisation. Second, most of the products are highly specialised, comprising resins and pigments combined to meet customers' unique requirements. Third, the pattern of work organisation is linked, partly because of technology, to a weekly production cycle in which the pace of work intensifies for particular groups at non-standard times. The evidence cited above demonstrates that Paintco has allowed earnings to grow to very high levels (for semi-skilled workers) through the use of overtime, shift working, and, in the past, lax control over allowances and over-award payments. Notwithstanding this, Paintco remains highly profitable.

Management

The parent corporation to which Paintco belongs is known for a philosophy which places considerable emphasis upon devolving industrial relations decision-making to the enterprise level, and fixing wages and employment conditions on an enterprise basis. This approach has born fruit at several plants which have rationalised all aspects of bargaining structure (management decision-making, union organisation, and formal awards/agreements) around the unit of the enterprise. As far as Paintco is concerned, this corporate philosophy is relatively novel and is, in most respects, still to be implemented. Leaving aside, therefore, corporate philosophy, how has general and industrial relations management been conducted in relation to this site?

Beginning at the top of the organisation, the corporation now has a complex structure organised around both a number of operating groups (of which Paint is one) and a number of corporate units (including Finance, Planning, Research and Personnel). Each operating group and corporate unit is headed by a general manager responsible, via the chief executive officer, to the Board of Directors. The paint operating group is headed by an operating group general manager who is a member of the enterprise's Panel which also comprises the chief executive officer and an executive director with responsibility for Paint.[1] For practical purposes, the management structure most relevant to the plant lies below the Panel. Beneath the operating group general manager lie five managers of whom two are line managers (the general manager technical paints, and the general manager decorative paints— not at this site) and three staff managers (finance, personnel, and planning).

The general manager technical paints runs Paintco operations while the three staff managers are housed in a neighbouring head office building, but hold responsibilities for other factories throughout Australia. These staff managers are answerable to both corporate unit general managers (in personnel, finance, and so on) and to the operating group manager. This dualism carries on below. Thus the personnel manager for the site (and for other Victorian plants) is answerable to superiors in both specialist staff and (indirectly) general line positions. Also the national employee relations manager is answerable to superiors in personnel and (indirectly) the operating group. Since both the state personnel and the national employee relations managers are located on site, they have considerable day-to-day involvement in Paintco which is considered to be more closely watched by head office than plants in other states. On the operations side, there is an operations manager, with five divisions under him: production, distribution, engineering, quality control, and material control. These align closely with divisions in the plant layout and workforce. Beneath this tier lie a few specialist staff positions, with that of training manager being most relevant to industrial relations. There are also a number of first-line supervisors and forepersons followed by leading hands.

This management team is top heavy, or at least appears so to the Paintco shop floor which is close to the complex head office structure. It also contains scope for a contentious division between line and staff managers, exemplified by line management passing industrial relations problems on to either a direct superior or the personnel manager in an inconsistent manner. This workplace has undergone some changes in that regard. Industrial relations were traditionally handled by line management, chiefly the operations manager who had most dealings with union organisers and delegates over plant-level issues. Attempts were made to strengthen the direct responsibility of staff positions with the appointment of a state personnel manager (dealing almost exclusively with the site) but responsible primarily to the upper staff hierarchy. This experiment has been abandoned, and the incoming arrangement is for a technical paints personnel manager to answer to the general manager technical paints. Meanwhile, day-to-day industrial relations has been pushed back to line management in operations and production.

Senior management have, until quite recently, exhibited considerable stability, in spite of the transformation of the operation from a partly-owned subsidiary to a 100 per cent owned operating group. Formal position titles have changed, for example the managing director becoming the operating group manager. But for the most part personnel did not. However in the last two or three years both the management structure and personnel have been transformed. The operating group manager transferred to Europe. A new general manager technical paints was brought in from the higher group level. The operations manager retired. Also the removal of decorative paints eliminated a number of line positions. These changes do not appear to have adversely affected industrial relations.

Managing the industrial relations function

The same stability is not found among specialist industrial relations and personnel management. There was a long record of instability here. Of most concern was the position of industrial relations manager. No less than five incumbents have left this position in the past five years. Few of these departures have arisen from internal promotion. More often they reflect difficulties experienced in the area. The effects of this turnover have been to dilute experience and introduce inexperience into the plant's operations, to breed mistrust on the shopfloor, and to dislocate authority since new incumbents sometimes proved reluctant to take decisions. Union delegates spoke of the incapacity of staff managers to make decisions, which created low trust between management and union delegates.

A new status quo in industrial relations management emerged out of this state of disorganisation. First, in 1988, an industrial relations specialist was employed in the position of national employee relations manager to take responsibility for national issues, award matters, tribunal hearings, and to advise upon plant negotiations. This development is important since the paint operating group is seeking consistency between its sites throughout Australia after experiencing some pay leapfrogging between them in the past. In addition technical industrial relations competence is, paradoxically, necessary to translate corporate philosophy about enterprise bargaining units into practice. (Some of the work associated with establishing enterprise bargaining units proceeds in industrial tribunals.) This position also strengthens the hand of management in two other ways. It reduces dependence upon officials of the NSW Employers' Federation, which handles formal tribunal proceedings—increasingly with assistance from this specialist manager. Also it provides back-up for plant production management when dealing with any site negotiations which carry national significance or require specialist industrial relations competence.

What, then, is the residual role for the state personnel manager in the management structure? In theory, the position adopted in the late 1980s required line management to take more active responsibility for site industrial relations, reducing personnel to an advisory and monitoring role. In practice, the personnel role appears to have been almost redundant. In addition to routine personnel work (records, payroll, counselling, workers' compensation, health care etc.) the personnel manager claimed to devote 50 per cent of his time to industrial relations issues such as interpreting awards, communicating award changes, negotiating with full-time union officers, initiating enterprise policies to eliminate anomalies in pay and conditions, and performance appraisal. These functions constituted an unstable role, easily absorbed elsewhere in the organisation (specialised industrial relations, line management, or clerical work). As a result the personnel role seems to have been a light one in practice, and not highly regarded.

Especially significant was the way the personnel manager could be by-passed on plant industrial relations matters. The operations manager would go straight to the national employee relations manager for advice and would only pass minor issues to personnel. Also, most site issues would be dealt with at the level below the operations manager, although this varied according to the capacities and wishes of management at this level. Thus the production manager tended to be independent (doing much routine personnel work herself), while the warehouse manager relied heavily on the personnel manager to assist with minor matters such as worker queries on overtime rates. Perhaps because of these difficulties, when the position of state personnel manager fell vacant, it was not filled.

One is left with the impression of a complex formal management structure that left little for personnel to do. An informal system existed resting upon personalities and individual preference. The actual management responsibility for industrial relations had little to do with formal group policy or structure (which was changeable, and at times unworkable). Capable individuals tended to absorb responsibility irrespective of their formal roles and duties, and there was often (due to management turnover and re-organisation) a dearth of such people.

The clearest evidence of capable managers taking over industrial relations is to be found in the policies and activities of the long-serving operations manager and the younger production manager. Facing a situation of mistrust and tension following a dispute over the 35-hour week in 1982, the operations manager decided to assume a high profile in site industrial relations. This attitude was also assumed by the new production manager appointed in 1988. Between them they shouldered the bulk of site industrial relations in the production area, including negotiations and consultation with the site committee and individual union delegates, dealings with individual employees upon discipline and dismissal, transfer, promotions, safety, some aspects of hiring, induction, union training, and major matters such as negotiation upon the 'second tier'. There are several reasons why so much responsibility rested with these two line managers. These included formal company policy (intermittently), their physical proximity to union delegates resulting in a strong mutual trust, their grasp of shop-floor custom and practice (with which staff management were generally unfamiliar), and their location as a key step in the award grievance procedure (a procedure which worked largely because of them).

The power exercised by production management close to the shop floor—much of it assumed as a practical way of dealing with shop-floor power—created a high degree of informality in the operation of management. For example, communications with union delegates were entirely verbal. Agreements tended to be spoken, not written. (In fact there were very few written agreements in the plant, and those were extremely rudimentary.) While production management could maintain consistent policies and treatment of workers in their area of responsibility, these were not necessarily in line with company policy. In this respect the plant tended to operate as a law unto itself, a situation which was difficult to reconcile with the proximity of head office and with attempts by senior corporate management to impose structures and policies upon a rather pragmatic and personalised management system lower down. Several examples can be found of higher level company initiatives which fitted badly with plant production management and the workforce, and which occasionally led to disputes and tension with the unions. These included contracting out canteen work (which led to a strike by canteen workers), and using an agency to hire casual workers in breach of an unwritten agreement.

Central to the conduct of industrial relations and personnel management at Paintco is the changing relationship between corporate and plant management. This is a dynamic relationship governed by a range of influences. These include changes in the formal status of the plant from a partly-owned subsidiary to a fully-owned operating group, changes in corporate policy to introduce a devolution philosophy, and attempts to rein in a somewhat indulgent and loose local management style by co-ordinating industrial relations throughout the operating group.

There appears to be a paradoxical or contradictory character to these developments. Paintco traditionally possessed a devolved style arising from its legal independence and the *de facto* decision-making power of local production management. Yet the modern philosophy of the corporation is to encourage precisely this kind of devolution, ostensibly a characteristic already evident in the conduct of industrial relations. Is this workplace attempting changes which amount to re-affirming the traditional way? The answer to this question is probably in the negative. The old devolution style was indulgent. Local management made concessions, many of them covert and inconsistent with practices at other group plants and with formal undertakings (such as the paid rates award). The new devolution style is intended to permit greater consistency and scrutiny, while allowing responsibility to be exercised by shop-floor management.

Much corporate-level involvement in Paintco may be transitory. The intention seems to be to use specialist expertise to formalise the shift toward enterprise structures by, for example, a site appendix to the industry award which may ultimately be a formula for genuine plant independence. However, there are conditions which can militate both for and against such independence. One factor favouring the authority of shop-floor management is the long-standing (by now) strength of their working relationships with union delegates, and their capacity to deal with actual shop-floor custom and practice. Against this is the geographical proximity of group head office, which can easily be pulled into plant affairs to suit the vagaries both of central policy, and of shop-floor politics.

Uncertainty pervades the actualities of devolved authority within Paintco's industrial relations and personnel management. Much of this arises from the intervention of the parent company, which, amongst other things, may have done much to destabilise settled managerial personnel, as well as policies and structures, and in the process introduce novelty, uncertainty and weakness. On the last point, there seems little doubt that despite the resources of corporate and plant management, there is some degree of competition over power, disorganisation over roles, and ultimately division and weakness in dealing with unions.

Trade union organisation and action

Employees are covered by six unions.[2] The Federated Miscellaneous Workers' Union (FMWU) of Australia covers production workers and has 205 members; the National Union of Workers (NUW) has sixty-two storepersons; the Association of Draughting, Supervisory and Technical Employees (ADSTE) has approximately 130 members in the laboratories and research and development area attached to the head office; there are fifteen Amalgamated Metal Workers' Union (AMWU) members and one Electrical Trades Union of Australia (ETU) member in maintenance; and the Federated Clerks' Union (FCU) of Australia nominally covers clerical staff. These are all occupational unions, with the arguable exception of the FMWU which could be classified as either a 'general' union or a 'multi-occupational' union.

There are a number of non-unionists in the maintenance area (mainly electricians), in plant ancillary tasks such as health care, and in white-collar areas. However the FMWU, NUW, and AMWU maintain an informal closed shop and have 100 per cent membership. This is supported by payroll deductions of union dues. The company is willing to support union organisation in this and other ways, including the provision of extensive facilities for union delegates such as STD telephone, offices, conference rooms, and travel facilities (coaches) for union members to attend mass meetings.

Job delegates and committees

Within the plant and warehouse there are several job delegates (four NUW and three FMWU). Four of these hold long service both as employees and as delegates. The two senior FMWU delegates have more than seventeen years employment service each and at least eight years continuous service as delegates. The two senior NUW delegates have been employed for a similar period and have been delegates for eleven and fourteen years respectively. By any standards, these four are very experienced both in the technical workings of the plant and in the performance of job delegate duties. The remaining three delegates are relatively new, and only service special shifts. All the four senior delegates were elected, and have been opposed for re-election on at least one occasion, although the outcome of re-election was no formality. Delegates have in the past been defeated at elections. The two FMWU delegates deposed an earlier group in 1982 when there was rank-and-file dissatisfaction over the negotiations on the 35-hour week.

Only the four senior delegates spend a significant amount of time on union duties. They form the backbone of delegate organisation in the plant and warehouse, spending a variable amount of time away from their jobs, although as a matter of routine this can be up to $1\frac{1}{2}$ hours a day, mostly involving visiting members' work stations. Amongst the delegates' longer absences from their work stations would be periodic major negotiations, attendance at paint industry delegates' conferences (up to three a year), and attendance at training courses (both FMWU and NUW delegates have attended approximately six courses, including three at the Trade Union Training Authority and two safety courses). Their routine duties as delegates include signing up new members, dealing with problems and grievances, attendance at safety committee meetings, and a number of other tasks.

The activities of individual union delegates are supplemented in several ways. There exists a Site Committee for the plant, comprising eight to ten members, including the FMWU and NUW delegates plus additional representatives from residual work areas. It was established in 1982 following a dispute over the 35-hour week, and only meets periodically when a major site problem occurs: it has dealt with the introduction of night shift, start-up of the resin plant, changes in ADOs at Christmas, second-tier negotiations, and other major plant-wide matters of this kind. While the two major unions, the FMWU and NUW, clearly use the Site Committee to consult on site issues, they tend to take up different approaches and do not work together closely. The Site

Committee was deemed important and valuable by the plant operations manager, who remarked that 'most issues are resolved at this level' without the need for mass meetings. Communication with members took the form of Site Committee representatives reporting back to each section. The Site Committee is clearly a negotiating body of some importance. However, it is a formal body, and its activities should be kept in perspective. Most communication between the four key union delegates and between these and other delegates, section representatives, and members, is informal. On occasion, there is a need for formal communication through mass meetings. These do not appear to occur often, but certainly take place to ratify major decisions such as the outcome of 35-hour or second-tier negotiations.

Unions outside the workplace

Contact between the wider unions and plant organisation is strong, and is maintained in several ways. First, there are visits every two or three months by state union organisers. These may be courtesy visits, or arise from specific problems in industry or enterprise negotiations. The NUW delegates appear more willing to involve organisers in plant issues than the FMWU delegates, the latter preferring to handle everything themselves. The NUW delegates use an electronic paging system to contact their officials. Second, on occasions national union officers visit the plant. The nature of these visits tends to be somewhat different. They are called in very infrequently to break an impasse in negotiations. The second tier is a case in point. On this occasion, the FMWU brought in a national official to explain the second tier, and to persuade local members to participate in negotiations. Third, delegates are frequently involved in union paint industry conferences. The FMWU in particular plays a very active role orchestrating and co-ordinating the activities of delegates in different paint plants. These meetings are frequent and important, keeping the delegates well informed on major issues and campaigns. Delegates also use these meetings as an opportunity to maintain contact with other company plants, obtaining information about concessions made elsewhere by management which might be of advantage in their own workplace. This flow of information does not depend solely on the FMWU paint industry conferences. Frequent telephone contact exists between delegates throughout the operating group. Fourth, the delegates utilise other union services, the most important being training courses. These were highly valued by the senior delegates.

Management also initiates contact with union officials. This has been done on several occasions, usually for important negotiations over, for example, redundancies or award restructuring. This is consistent with the general pattern of full-time union official involvement in the plant. Most non-routine visits arise when one side or the other at Paintco sees a tactical advantage in calling upon a professional outsider. Management, as well as the delegates, use union officials to legitimise or strengthen their hand in plant negotiations, or to relieve them of responsibility in dealing with a difficult issue. The treatment of dismissals and redundancies illustrates this point. Both union delegates and management respectively have called upon union officials to deliver this bad news to the employees concerned. Although union officials are used extensively in these ways, this should not be taken to signify lack of expertise or weakness on the part of delegates who appear to be capable of handling most issues themselves, and usually prefer to do so. The plant organisation of the two major unions is extremely strong and usually self-reliant. Delegates utilise the services of officials knowledgeably and to advantage, rather than depending upon them to compensate for shop-floor weakness.

A contrast may be drawn between the weakness and instability of the plant's management, referred to above, and to the strength and stability of union shop-floor organisation. The latter depend upon the experience and ability of four long-standing delegates in the two major unions, backed up by powerful membership which has demonstrated a willingness to take industrial action. These four delegates hold a pivotal position in workplace industrial relations, mediating between their members and management. Some of the managers welcome the activities of delegates and offer full recognition and extremely extensive facilities. Management generally hold confidence in the capacities of these delegates, seeing them as able to nip disputes in the bud and able to sustain the established pattern of devolved negotiation and dispute settlement. Very close relations exist between production management and the FMWU delegates, obviating the need to involve either higher or corporate management or external union officials, except on rare and difficult occasions.

Negotiations, disputes, and workforce incorporation

The strength of Paintco's union organisation is evident in its involvement in negotiations. It is necessary here to distinguish two types of issues, those that arise within the workplace and those that originate outside. Vigorous and frequent negotiations take place within the plant upon both kinds of matters. The union delegates are active in raising purely domestic issues, and because the plant (indeed the industry) is a pacesetter, it is frequently at the leading edge of negotiations arising out of Industrial Relations Commission national decisions or wider union campaigns.

Bargaining on workplace issues

The scope of the domestic issues dealt with in negotiation is extremely wide. Managers and delegates were asked if they had bargained in recent times over fifteen broad areas. Their agreed responses are shown in Table 3.5.

Table 3.5   Bargaining Areas

Issue	Recent domestic negotiations have occurred	Management decision only	Management restrained from unilateral decisions	Established practice—no active negotiations
Pay	*			
Conditions	*			
Work practices	*		*	
Work scheduling	*			
New technology		*		
Organisational change		*		
Demarcation	*			
Grievance proc.				*
Discipline	*			
Quality circles		*		
Health & safety	*			
Social security		*		
Training leave		*		
Union rights				*
Union security				*

Note: Since these issues are defined broadly, specific sub-issues may be treated differently, and so entered in different columns.

It is apparent from Table 3.5 that union delegates do negotiate and consult upon a wide array of issues, that management has in the past been restrained from acting independently and been drawn into negotiations, and that there are numerous matters where negotiations could arise but both sides are content with a long-settled status quo or custom and practice. The residual domain of management prerogative is correspondingly narrow. Management will initiate decisions upon new product lines, equipment, plant rationalisation, and so on. But whenever these decisions touch upon worker interests, discussions and negotiations in some form are likely to occur.

Pay negotiations may be considered surprising given that the main awards are paid rates awards, and should not be added to locally. However, money matters are negotiated infrequently. Thus when a 24-hour shift operation was introduced for the new resin plant, negotiations occurred for an allowance to attract shift workers (even though Cl. 23 of the Paint Industry Manufacturing Award provides special conditions for 24-hour shifts). Also problems relating to award application are handled in negotiations, particularly when there are anomalies between awards. For instance, a special agreement was negotiated specifying that all Sunday work be paid at the highest rate in any award to maintain plant-wide consistency. Pay issues are negotiated by the senior delegates and not union officials. They usually deal with Paintco production management, although plant and head office personnel or industrial relations specialists tend to become involved in award interpretation.

There have not been any significant stoppages recently over pay, although in the past over-award payments gave rise to difficulties. Before the workplace allowance was absorbed in the award, there were infrequent negotiations over it. One such episode led to the FMWU applying overtime bans on alternate days to the decorator and industrial paint lines, and sticking rigidly to the 35-hour week. The company responded with threats to stand down employees, which provoked an early-morning strike meeting. This was aborted following the intervention of the factory manager. The factory manager asked the delegates to defer the meeting, whilst he succeeded in organising the relocation of a production manager who stood in the way of a settlement.

Physical working conditions are the second most frequent item in plant bargaining. One illustrative case concerns warehouse employees who demanded the provision of a full wardrobe of warm clothing following the opening of the new and inadequately heated warehouse in 1988. Management's failure to respond over a period of two months led to a stop-work meeting in the canteen. This was followed by successful negotiations in which management conceded nine of the ten disputed clothing item. Again, a union delegate handled the matter with the national employees relations manager. A union organiser was summoned but did not turn up to deal with the dispute. Smaller episodes of this kind occur fairly often, although work stoppages are uncommon.

Work practices (manning, multi-skilling, contract labour, temporary labour, and so on) also give rise to frequent negotiations and occasional stoppages. There is, for example, an unwritten agreement governing the use of contract labour, forbidding hiring through contract agencies and requiring that award standards be upheld. An unwitting breach of this agreement occurred when contract fitters working on the resin plant were paid a different rate from plant fitters. This dispute was only settled with the aid of two full-time union organisers. Similar disputes have occurred over the use of contract labour in the warehouse and temporary labour. In at least one instance there has been a serious stoppage over contract labour. This particular dispute concerned the transfer of canteen work from company employees to a contracting system. In this case the female canteen workers picketed the plant, stopped its operations, and achieved guarantees of employment and wage security. The personnel manager responsible for the disputed innovation in catering subsequently left.

Work scheduling (overtime rosters, allocated days off, shift starting times, and so on) are the most frequent subject of domestic negotiations. Awards authorise bargaining on matters of this kind (for example Cl. 23 of the Paint Industry Manufacturing Award), a necessary provision since work scheduling generally, and shift time in particular, may need to be varied due to the state of preparation of paint. The broad framework of agreements governing standard hours and the ADO was negotiated and re-negotiated for the plant, but during two wider campaigns over the 35-hour week and second tier. They shall be dealt with below. However the administration of these agreements and other work scheduling issues requires almost constant piecemeal bargaining. For example, *ad hoc* arrangements usually have to be settled about the coincidence of ADO rosters with public holidays such as Christmas and Australia Day. Further, the application of rosters to individuals requires the frequent involvement of delegates.

Demarcation is another significant matter in negotiations. The primary issue here used to be demarcation between the warehouse and factory, embodied in a 'yellow line' between the two areas. Since the warehouse has been moved to some distance from the factory, it is claimed that demarcation problems arise less frequently. Thus, there is an agreement in force that FMWU members drive completed stock to the warehouse on a small train comprising three carriages. NUW members must unload this train and relocate stock to the warehouse.

However, management claims that demarcations still lead to significant over-manning. In the long term, management would like to move towards one union covering the entire site. In the interim, demarcation has arisen in negotiations, under both the second tier and award restructuring. Some difficulties between the FMWU and NUW have been removed, although not all. Demarcation is also based on job classifications in the production area, again a matter which might be dealt with under award restructuring. Demarcation issues used to arise between Transport Workers' Union of Australia (TWU) and NUW members in the warehouse, an issue not entirely resolved by putting TWU work out to contract. A local written agreement has to be enforced as to who loads and unloads delivery trucks. This does not entirely settle the matter since the contract transport firm itself is expected not to breach demarcation standards in its own work site. A ban was placed at the Paintco warehouse upon trucks from the contractor when it was found that TWU members off-site were doing NUW work. Such industrial action is rare, in part because management is sensitive to union opinion on demarcation, and is anxious not to antagonise the unions. The persistence of managerial concern over demarcation is made evident by repeated attempts to negotiate its removal.

Negotiations over discipline are also significant. These arise from a long-standing written agreement, now partly incorporated in the award (Cl. 39 of the Paint Industry Manufacturing Award). This agreement allows for summary terminations to be halted for ten days while management/union discussions proceed. During this time the suspended employee is paid. In practice, the union delegate is informed of disciplinary action. In minor cases he is informed at the second stage (written warning) of the company's procedure. In cases warranting instant dismissal (fighting, theft, wilful damage) the delegate is invariably involved. Since the production manager (who handles discipline) and the delegates have a close working relationship, disputes arise infrequently. Union officials are sometimes brought in on difficult cases, or those concerning the dismissal of groups of employees. One such instance concerned several employees suspected of stealing paint drums, an unproven allegation which resulted in the employees' transfer rather than termination.

Health and safety issues lead to extensive and time consuming consultation and negotiation. Much of this is formalised through health and safety committees which meet monthly. These operate at two levels:

the section and the site. Issues not resolved in three months at the section level must go to the Site Health and Safety Committee. Production management has considerable authority on health and safety issues, including substantial power to initiate expenditure upon factory equipment. Fire and toxicity are considerable hazards, given the chemicals used in paint manufacture, and considerable discussion takes place over fire prevention and associated issues. In addition, a large part of induction or training procedure concerns safety, although union delegates are not involved in this. Furthermore, the enterprise has applied considerable resources to accident reporting and monitoring as a way to keep track of safety performance in general and identifying trouble spots for remedy.[3] Again delegates are not directly involved in this. One area where bargaining pressures can arise is the Safety Incentive Scheme introduced in 1986 at the initiative of the operations manager. Under this scheme, work groups with a clear safety record are paid up to $90.00 per annum. The group nature of this scheme creates several pressures: upon careless employees, on the accident reporting system, and on management who must administer it consistently, a difficult task towards the end of a twelve-month period when expectations of imminent payment are high.

These are the most important matters on which domestic negotiations take place. It will be apparent that the procedures governing domestic bargaining are varied and flexible. At times these procedures involve different levels of management and unions (although external union and employer association officials are called upon quite rarely), and they also exhibit varying degrees of formality (some issues such as safety and discipline being confined to a relatively strict procedure while others are dealt with in an *ad hoc* way). The procedure governing workplace grievances in general is set out formally in awards (for example: Cl. 39 of the Paint Industry Award). Both union delegates and management commented that this procedure is observed flexibly, that is, steps in it will be jumped if necessary. It is apparent too that the procedure does not prevent all stoppages and bans over domestic grievances. Also significant is the fact that the final stage in the procedure, reference of disputes to the Industrial Relations Commission, has never been successfully invoked. On only one occasion has action been taken to refer a matter to the Industrial Relations Commission— the dispute over wage rates for fitters in the Resin Plant. This action was at the initiative of an employer association which has almost nothing to do with the industry (the Metal Trades Industry Association), and the Commissioner referred the dispute back for plant settlement.

This does not mean that bargaining at the plant is not influenced by tribunals. Rather it reinforces the distinction between domestic issues (which are not taken to the Industrial Relations Commission) and issues which arise from general campaigns on which the Commission does play a role.

Bargaining upon wider campaigns

Turning to general union campaigns, five of these deserve mention. These were a wages dispute arising out of the breakdown of wage indexation around 1979, the 35-hour week campaign in 1982, superannuation in 1985, the second tier in 1987, and award restructuring in 1989–90.

The first two matters will be dealt with briefly because they represent an era in plant industrial relations which influences the present, but no longer characterises it. The pay dispute followed managerial rejection of a thirty-two-item log of claims and led to a six-week stoppage by the FMWU, which did much to establish sour union–management relations. The stoppage appears to have been mismanaged badly by both sides. The union applied no pickets for five weeks, permitting adequate paint supplies to interstate customers, and the FMWU failed to seek support from other unions in the plant. The delegates responsible for this have since left. Although management refused the pay claims, thus prompting the stoppage, they continued to negotiate throughout the strike without being able to terminate it. The most effective line manager responsible for industrial relations was temporarily absent from the plant during the period when the dispute took place. This factor too may have contributed to poor handling of the dispute by management. This six-week strike is significant primarily for contributing to a subsequent climate of poor domestic relations, and for the place it still holds in the memories of long-serving union delegates and employees. Workplace unionists are now wary of allowing such mismanaged displays of militancy to recur, while management are still conscious of a workforce with some explosive potential.

The 35-hour week campaign had a worse effect upon the climate of plant industrial relations, even though no actual stoppage took place. In 1980 the factory was a majority-owned subsidiary of a company which had already conceded the 35-hour week at other plants. The company indicated a willingness to negotiate the 35-hour week at its remaining plants, including the paint factory. Negotiations were temporarily suspended following the prohibition of productivity bargaining and working hours in the Australian Conciliation and Arbitration Commission's (ACAC) April 1981 wage guidelines.[4] However, expectations had already been created amongst the workforce. Negotiations between management and the new Site Committee resumed in late 1981 and 1982. In these, the paint factory conceded the 35-hour week with no corresponding cost offsets, as well as granting a substantial over-award payment. The agreement was taken to a member of the ACAC for ratification, which was promptly refused. The Commissioner was clearly annoyed that management had conceded working hours below the 38-hour community standard in place by then. One of the delegates remarked that management had made a 'marvellous mistake'. However the same delegate observed that industrial relations then fell to their lowest level in sixteen years, since management proceeded to close the door upon any further negotiations, allowing small grievances to fester. Since the Commission refused to register the 35-hour agreement, it remains a voluntary agreement to this day, although it is scrupulously honoured by both sides.

The next major campaign arose in September 1985 out of a log of claims served by the NUW on all paint manufacturers seeking the introduction of the union's superannuation scheme as an alternative to the company's scheme. Industrial action in support of the claim began in interstate plants. Attempts by the Commission to resolve the matter failed, and on 23 October bans were imposed on local paint manufacturers, to prohibit interstate shipment and supply of paint to the vehicle industry. These bans were lifted on 30 October, but progressively reimposed from 8 November, remaining in place till the end of the month. Meanwhile, national paint industry negotiations proceeded, by this time encompassing the FMWU and other paint industry unions. During this period, the vehicle industry was gradually closed down, with 2900 Ford Broadmeadows workers being stood down on 20 November, and Nissan, GMH, and Mitsubishi following suit over the next few days. By 26 November, a total of 7300 vehicle workers were out of work. Local paint manufacturers started to stand-down NUW members on 20 November on a 'no work—no pay' basis, affecting approximately 300 unionists for about seven days. On 28 November mass meetings took place to approve a settlement in which the paint industry conceded what was a pace-setting example for the subsequent National Wage Case hearing upon superannuation and productivity. The employers were to fund 3 per cent of wages to superannuation and allow employees the choice between the union fund and the company fund. This peace package was finally formalised by the Commission in

December 1986 after principles governing superannuation were set in June of that year. However, the substance of that settlement was no more than had been conceded under duress by the paint industry twelve months earlier. The role of Paintco in this dispute was a subsidiary one, yet vital. At no stage were negotiations conducted at the plant, since the dispute possessed a national character, with the NUW orchestrating bans throughout the eastern states. However the bans at this plant were especially important since it was a significant supplier to the vehicle industry, and the cessation of supply from it served to escalate the campaign to the point that the combined paint manufacturers conceded the union claims. These bans and stand-downs by NUW members at the paint factory were the last major stoppage on site.

Second-tier negotiations began in 1987 as part of a national process, and contrasted with previous wider campaigns in their freedom from acrimony. The only stoppage took the form of a half day stop-work meeting initiated by federal union officials. The atmosphere that surrounded this event may be judged from the fact that the company supplied buses to take unionists to the city location of the stop-work meeting. The negotiation process, on this occasion, was put firmly in the hands of workplace bargainers. Negotiations were conducted primarily between the Site Committee (although a union official sat in) and the operations manager (the industrial relations manager's position was vacant at the time and a personnel manager had yet to be recruited).

The formal outcome of these negotiations was an impressive list of cost offsets in return for a 4 per cent wage increase. However, the practical value of many of these offsets was quite limited. The offsets are as follows:

(1) It was agreed that shift overlap be reduced from thirty to fifteen minutes; in practice the thirty-minute overlap has carried on.

(2) Employees had to seek the foreman's permission for relief breaks; in practice it was found that this caused production to drop and was informally discontinued.

(3) Personal over-award payments were to be absorbed; in practice this has only occurred when any of the handful of workers who receive such payments resign.

(4) Cash wage payment was to be replaced by Electronic Funds Transfer; many married male workers objected to this, and so this system of payment became voluntary.

(5) Workers were expected to do their own in-line testing of paint quality; this enabled the elimination of one position for a specialist tester.

(6)   Meal and tea breaks were staggered to improve production; this has worked unevenly in different sections of the factory and warehouse.

(7)   Restrictions were placed upon taking weekend overtime when workers' ADOs were rostered on either a Friday or Monday; a compromise has emerged here, with the prohibition on weekend overtime applying only to those taking a Friday ADO.

(8)   A fixed ADO roster system was introduced to be settled in October each year; in practice, flexibility has emerged around the operation of this roster.

(9)   Several areas of demarcation were removed, in one instance with a transfer of members between unions. In most of these cases, the changes have been observed.

It will be apparent that the second-tier package proved less valuable than the formal agreement might suggest. Nevertheless, some small gains were made by management. Many of these changes were unwelcome to employees. Opposition was especially strong to the restrictions upon weekend overtime, although there was a division of shop-floor opinion on this matter between those (especially the delegates) who considered the 35-hour week a valuable gain in leisure time, and those who boosted earnings through heavy overtime. A national union official was called in to instil solidarity on this matter by arguing that a failure to agree would threaten the survival of the unregistered 35-hour week agreement. This intervention had the desired effect and the shop-floor accepted the total second-tier package. The second-tier agreement was ratified by the Commission in October 1987, one of the first to be approved, again testifying to the position of the paint industry as a pacesetter in campaigns of this kind. In this instance the Commission approved an agreement not only covering most plants, but also covering the four main paint industry unions. This was the first occasion when they had successfully collaborated throughout such a campaign.

We have outlined the main changes arising from the award restructuring campaign in the opening section of this chapter. These were primarily directed to new classification structures, broadbanding, the establishment of team leaders, and industry training. The major changes under the first stage adjustment were agreed mainly at the industry level in negotiations between employer association and national union officials, although substantial discussion took place with shop-floor delegates through the union–paint industry conferences. The first stage adjustment was ratified by the Commission on 13 November 1989. The second stage adjustment could proceed six months later, and this was likely to entail enterprise changes more valuable for the company, on demarcation, spread of hours, and other issues. However these further plant negotiations fell outside the fieldwork period.

It will be clear from the outline of these general campaigns that they play an important part in the conduct of plant industrial relations. Plant-level managers and unionists are clearly familiar with personnel and proceedings at the industry and national levels. They are accustomed to Paintco finding itself at the forefront of such campaigns. Also the resultant settlements (at whatever level they are achieved) are usually implemented fairly directly in new workplace rules. It may also be observed that the plant's pacesetter position sometimes results in settlements that are out of step with the community standards that evolve later. The 35-hour week is the most obvious illustration of this. It is also apparent that the character of national campaigns has changed, away from the rather intransigent kind that took place over wages and standard hours in the late 1970s and early 1980s, towards a more cooperative kind exemplified by the second tier and award restructuring. Workplace managers and unionists agreed that a new and more harmonious industrial relations climate was developing at the plant, and some of them attributed this in part to the bargaining episodes that occurred through the second tier and award restructuring rounds. It is unlikely that this is a sufficient explanation for the decline in tension. Domestic factors were also at work, notably the readiness of plant management to implement changes arising out of negotiations on domestic issues. Nevertheless, the conciliation and arbitration systems can influence the processes and outcomes of plant-level regulation, in this case by guiding the local management and unionists towards bargaining issues when there is a higher probability of mutual advantage.

Abutting the areas of negotiation outlined above lie several management initiatives which may be broadly characterised as possessing a consultative character or are to do with transforming the culture of the workforce. Three of these deserve mention: a Customer First program, an employee share ownership scheme, and the health and safety bonus scheme.

The Customer First program originated with the managing director of the operating group in late 1988. It was designed to shorten delivery time to customers and to ensure that orders were accurately filled. Teams of four to eight persons were established throughout the organisation (clerical, laboratory, factory and warehouse employees) along functional lines (and then given distinctive team titles). Team leaders were designated and taken through a short leadership skills training program. Each team then met in work time to iron out operating problems in their work area. Proposed solutions were passed on to the state co-ordinator of the Customer First teams who then approved or disapproved suggestions within seven days. Team incentives took the form of both social and financial rewards. In workplaces that maintained a 90 per cent per annum accuracy rate on delivery time and content, a $1000 bonus was paid to each employee (irrespective of their participation in the scheme, although non-participation was noted by management).

There is anecdotal evidence that these teams won some shop-floor support and functioned effectively. This led, for example, to improvements in drum handling procedures (resulting in a 50 per cent productivity improvement in pigment handling), minimising cross contamination between sprayings, and saving congestion and transmission time for 'pots' by relocating work stations. A monthly national newsletter publicised successful innovations, after noting the payback time—the period in which innovation costs were recovered. One problem with this scheme was that 90 per cent was too high a target, and proved unattainable despite substantial efforts to improve efficiency. To reward workers, some erosion of the 90 per cent standard took place. Other problems also emerged once the novelty had worn off. Some workers tended to resist social pressure to attend meetings. In addition, frustration was experienced amongst teams unable to coin ideas. However as an interim measure the scheme was judged successful. It was established for just twelve months, and intended to be only a forerunner to something like a Quality Circle system. A modified version of it is now in operation.

A more established arrangement is the parent company's employee shareholder scheme. Employees have been encouraged since 1987 to purchase shares in the parent company through the provision of interest-free loans. Just on 25 per cent of manufacturing and warehouse employees currently hold loans acquired for this purpose. The impact of this scheme upon employee attitudes and upon productivity is difficult to isolate, although its operation does coincide with a period of lessening tension between management and unions—a change which clearly has several causes.

Company initiatives to improve health and safety, including the provision of a bonus plan and the mandatory operation of heath and safety committees, have been noted above. These are a significant part of the company's plans to improve employee welfare and involvement. It will be apparent that in most of these areas (especially the Customer

First program and the employee shareholding scheme) unions have had no visible role to play. Two observations may be made about this. First, union silence on these matters can be read as mute compliance. Some of the delegates expressed approval for proposals which may strengthen employee loyalty to the company. Second, union delegates do not regard these forms of employee involvement as a threat to either the union or to their members' economic interests or custom and practice.

Three aspects of negotiation and employee involvement have been discussed in this section. These are negotiation and disputes upon domestic issues, bargaining and stoppages arising from industry or national campaigns, and employer initiatives to enhance employee welfare and involvement in the company's operation. Negotiations can be described as frequent, wide ranging in subject, and utilising a range of procedures depending upon whether issues arise on the shop floor or outside the workplace. Underpinning negotiations across these dimensions is the proven willingness of unionists to take industrial action, the skill and experience of a strong delegate and external union organisation, and a management which is increasingly willing to negotiate freely with unions and involve its employees.

Conclusions

In the preceding sections we have set out the salient features of workplace industrial relations at Paintco. These include background factors such as product markets, technology, employment, awards and earnings. We have also discussed the organisation of management and unions and their interaction in bargaining, consultation and disputes as well as management initiatives to incorporate the workforce into closer identification or cooperation with Paintco. We now turn to consider the five themes of this book. What does the evidence we have assembled about Paintco tell us about them?

First, to what extent have systems of conciliation and arbitration shaped the processes and outcomes of industrial relations at Paintco? It is necessary here to distinguish two types of issue. First are domestic problems and disputes. Industrial tribunals have almost no perceptible influence upon the settlement of such local matters. Second are issues which originate outside the workplace, either through National Wage Case decisions, or through general union campaigns. Tribunals clearly have a role in either setting or responding to these agendas and Paintco has a well-established role as a pacesetter plant, which makes it important in the conduct of these campaigns.

What, then, is the relationship between Paintco and the tribunal? Often it has been a troubled relationship. This may be because workplace management has made concessions locally which the Commission cannot approve since they would constitute unwelcome precedents. Further, the workplace has been involved in major stoppages arising from union campaigns seeking a breakthrough in establishing new standards (in, for example, the superannuation campaign). Notwithstanding the fact that tribunal members are familiar with events at this workplace, the pattern of the past is that it is beyond tribunal control. Strong unions win concessions from management irrespective of the attitude of the Commission.

Nevertheless the character of national campaigns has changed, and as a result, the role of Paintco in these campaigns has altered. The second-tier and award restructuring rounds introduced a new type of bargaining compared with the sharply divisive campaigns of the early to mid 1980s (35-hours, superannuation, and so on). In establishing new wage principles for productivity bargaining, the Commission contributed indirectly to a more cooperative climate in workplace industrial relations.

However, one must be careful not to exaggerate this trend. The plant is still likely to experience frequent and serious stoppages, and the workforce remains suspicious and often opposed to the kinds of changes introduced through the second-tier and award restructuring. Nor should the Commission be credited exclusively with introducing the agenda for productivity bargaining at this workplace. To a large extent the FMWU and management took the initiative upon this. The Commission has played little part in conciliating or arbitrating upon the local application of either the 1987 or 1988 National Wage Case decisions as they apply to this particular workplace. All it has done is frame principles which management and unions have found opportune to use.

Second, to what extent is plant management autonomous from head office? The relationship between plant and head office management is both dynamic and complex. Changes can be linked, in part, to developments in formal ownership and control relations as the plant has become part of a wholly-owned operating group. They may also be linked to innovations in corporate employee relations strategy, emphasising a devolution approach. Paradoxically, head office intervention is needed to install devolution. For both reasons, head office has considerable influence over local management. This type of 'top-down' approach has its roots in both the general policy of the head office, and to a lesser degree, in the perception that industrial relations had been mismanaged in the past. There are two kinds of problems that arise as a result of this approach.

The first is that new corporate policies have little to do with the established pattern of management–delegate relations on the shop floor. These older relationships depended upon the authority of production management to make decisions, informality, mutual trust, and personal compatibility. Such a relationship could clearly be seen as indulgent, given the strength and capacity of the unions within the plant. Nor could it be depended upon to ensure smooth relations since trust was liable to wither when disputes took place (a frequent occurrence). Head office has little knowledge of this delicate fabric of management–delegate relationships and has on occasion interceded and disrupted them by introducing new policies.

The second point is that head office may also intercede by making changes to management structures and personnel, as well as to policy. There has been considerable management staff turnover within this workplace, carrying a heavy cost in terms of management's understanding of how the workplace and its unions and workforce actually operate, and in terms of the continuity of management–delegate relations. This has unsettled industrial relations at the shop floor.

Much recent head office intervention in plant affairs has been directed to developing a devolution approach to industrial relations in which plant management (especially production management) would have greater autonomy. At the time of writing it was too early to see whether this initiative will work as intended—to facilitate an 'island' approach, thus separating the plant from its pacesetter position in the paint industry, and spawning a more harmonious workforce culture. Union strategy has traditionally operated in a contrary fashion, and may exploit plant managers who are granted genuine autonomy from head office.

Third, to what extent have management attempted to incorporate the workforce and delegates, and is this aimed at productivity growth or cost minimisation? Three initiatives can be listed here, the Customer First program, the employee share ownership scheme, and the health and safety bonus scheme. All three are relatively recent innovations, the employee share ownership scheme and the Customer First program both being introduced after 1987 when the company became a wholly-owned subsidiary. It is reasonable to presume that the corporation had much to do with installing or inspiring programs of this kind.

All these measures were apparently aimed at raising productivity. In fact where indices of performance could be operationalised, as with the Customer First program and the health and safety bonus scheme, they concerned cost minimisation. Thus, the Customer First program elicited suggestions from workteams which were almost invariably costed upon savings in time, materials, etc., even though bonus payments were ultimately based upon an aggregate productivity measure for the whole workplace (the speed and accuracy of deliveries to customers). To the workforce this scheme would have been perceived first as a way of making savings for the company, and only second as a way of improving service to customers. Similarly, the health and safety bonus rested upon a visible and significant cost saving to the company in terms of a measure of accident-free days. Cost minimisation, not productivity enhancement, was the most immediate objective of both these schemes. The employee share ownership scheme was qualitatively different, seeking to establish mutual employer–employee bonds in a much looser fashion. Since the scheme was a corporate one, not confined to Paintco, it is difficult to see how it could breed a strong sense of common interest at the shop-floor. The performance of shares depended only very slightly upon workplace performance, let alone individual or group worker performance.

The impact of these schemes upon the culture of the workplace is hard to determine. As it happens, the introduction of the Customer First and employee share ownership plans coincided with a decline in industrial confrontation. However, no causal role can be attributed to these management initiatives. There were other possible explanations, notably the role of the Accord, and of specific wages policies including the second tier and award restructuring.

Fourth, what was the nature of unionism at the plant level, and did it constrain management decision-making? Workplace unionism can be summed up as follows. The blue-collar workforce was covered by a *de facto* closed shop, it was periodically militant with a known capacity to sustain long strikes, it placed heavy demands upon both management and union delegates, and the key delegates at least were skilful and experienced at harnessing this power. Relationships with external union organisers were not always close but the delegates understood how to use the resources and facilities of wider union organisation in their immediate dealings with management.

The purposes to which this power was harnessed tended to be

instrumental. The primary concerns of members and delegates alike were money, job security, and working conditions. Interest in management decision-making was correspondingly incidental to these other purposes. Little attempt was made to constrain management initiatives upon plant re-organisation, new equipment, or any other major changes, except at the point where they touched upon workers' economic interests. At that juncture delegates were likely to bargain actively. The net effect of this was that management decisions could be blocked by workforce resistance. Notable examples of this included changes regarding temporary workers, contract workers and putting canteen services out to contract. Further constraining management was the web of custom and practice rules which operated on the shop floor. Management might break this web in ignorance and at some cost.

Notwithstanding these strictures, the paint plant had clearly undergone extensive re-organisation in recent years. Relevant here were the termination of decorator paint production, the construction of a new warehouse, and the installation of a resin plant. None of these plans were significantly influenced by shop-floor resistance, even though incidental matters (demarcation, the use of contract labour in construction, and so on) had to be settled through negotiation.

Fifth, and finally, what has been the nature and impact of management attempts to improve efficiency? Two types of initiative are relevant here. The first has been dealt with in a previous discussion about incorporation of the workforce. As far as we could judge, two of the policies under this heading proved reasonably successful in achieving measurable improvements: the Customer First program and the health and safety bonus scheme. Second were negotiations under the second tier and the structural efficiency principle. It is possible to draw final conclusions about the second tier, although not upon the structural efficiency principle, which remained to be implemented at the time when case study fieldwork was completed.

The second tier was not a great success at this plant. The FMWU members were opposed to making concessions, and had to be pressed by union organisers to accept them. The plant negotiating machinery, the Site Committee in particular, worked reasonably efficiently in terms of the formal processes of bargaining over offsets in return for the 4 per cent wage increase. Where the exercise fell down was in implementation. Very few of the offsets were adhered to in a way that realised their full value in terms of useful savings. One is left with the impression that the processes of negotiation over efficiency were quite smooth, but the outcomes were of negligible value.

In contrast, the incorporation schemes seemed to have a better pay-off in terms of improving efficiency. The reasons behind these contrasting experiences can only be surmised. First, it is plausible to suggest that the issues raised in the second tier and award restructuring were more threatening to worker interests than those which arose in the health and safety bonus scheme and the Customer First program. Second, in the latter two schemes workers were given more immediate scope to contribute, rather than having to accept and work with imposed solutions (often the handiwork of agencies outside the plant). Third, there was a continuous financial incentive underpinning involvement in the incorporation schemes, whereas there was a once-off wage settlement for the second tier and award restructuring which, once paid, demanded no further necessity for workers to take implementation seriously. Whatever the reasons, there seemed little doubt that incorporation schemes produced better results than negotiations over the second tier and perhaps award restructuring.

We turn now from our review of these five questions to summing up the central features of Paintco's industrial relations. Perhaps the most striking feature of this plant is its product market position. A strong market share, combined with specialised products for which no ready substitute can usually be found, positions the plant strongly in relation to the customers for industrial paints. It follows that there is a degree of market power which has tended to lead to low cost–price sensitivity. It is, at least for the present, capable of a 'cost plus' pricing policy.

In this market context, the presence of a powerful and skilful union organisation is likely to define the conduct of workplace industrial relations. There was no apparent weak link in the chain of union organisation at this workplace. External union bodies chose it to establish initial concessions in wider campaigns, and domestic union organisation was both capable of playing its part in these wider schemes and of occupying the high ground in domestic industrial relations. The delegates did not see their role as taking the initiative upon workplace matters. Rather they held sufficient power that management normally found it wise to involve them in joint decision-making.

One outcome of the company's market power and the unions' strength was the standing of the plant as a good employer. Earnings levels were high, jobs secure and stable, and management generally considerate. Employment conditions within the plant made it attractive relative to other employers of semi-skilled and unskilled labour in the local labour market.

Within this general context there was scope for divergence in managerial styles. Prior to becoming a fully-owned operating group within the larger corporation, management possessed a degree of independence from head office which was employed to sustain a management style which appeared to be loose at times and punitive at other times. Little consistency and expertise was evident in this regime, although individual managers, especially in production, were considerably better at industrial relations than the general management system and style would suggest. Out of the old management were stamped the hallmarks of a particular type of industrial relations. It was largely devolved, often indulgent, informal and *ad hoc*. Interspersed within this general regime were bouts of managerial intransigence when attempts were made to redraw the frontier of control with the unions. It is difficult, in retrospect, to explain these convulsions. Those involved were inclined to attribute much to the personality of managers who tried to reinstate lost prerogatives or break down custom and practice. But equally, market or external corporate pressures could have played some role.

Into this haphazard management system has been introduced a corporate philosophy which, if implemented, may produce significant changes in both management style and industrial relations. It is too early to judge the impact of this corporate philosophy, with its emphasis upon devolution to profit centres, enterprise bargaining, and advanced human resource management strategies. Much of this has yet to be put in place.

What can be judged more positively are the effects of a changing external industrial relations environment. The second tier and award restructuring have set a climate in which more positive management–union relations have evolved. This may be contrasted with the years up to 1986 when external policies often induced plant confrontation in which the workplace's role as a 'cutting edge' site was most important. Two strategic approaches may be seen at work in this plant. The first, and older, strategy was for the plant to be linked into a network of external bargaining processes by which it could be used to establish beneficial precedents for union gain. This strategy depended on the ingredients we have outlined earlier, and worked successfully. The second, and more recent, strategy is a corporate one emphasising employee incorporation through human resource management techniques and an enterprise bargaining approach which could (although not necessarily will) detach the plant from the industry. It is possible to detect scope for conflict between these strategies.

John Benson and David Worland

4 Hotel International

Introduction

This chapter has as its subject the pattern of workplace industrial relations within Hotel International, a large five-star residential hotel in Melbourne. By focusing on a workplace of this kind we can examine the industrial relations setting of a workplace dealing with the provision of services rather than the manufacture of goods. We hope to identify some unique industrial relations structures, processes and outcomes associated with this setting.

The accommodation sector

The accommodation sector is an important part of the tourism and hospitality industry which has, within Australia, experienced rapid growth in recent years. This pattern of growth is attributed to a number of factors including a general expansion in demand for services which has accompanied increasing levels of personal income, the falling value of the Australian dollar, effective promotion of Australia as an attractive holiday destination, and significant tourism events such as the bicentennial celebrations and world expo. At the same time, some of these factors have discouraged Australians from holidaying abroad. Further, the government has introduced a more liberal air routes policy, which has led to an increase in the number of overseas airline flights to Australia and a resulting increase in the number of incoming tourists. In more recent times—from early 1989—tourism activity and business accommodation demand have slowed markedly due to the pull-back from the peak tourist demand of 1988 and the occurrence of the pilots' dispute.[1]

Business enterprises within the accommodation sector are categorised into two main groups—motels and guest houses, and licensed hotels.[2] Within each group the business units tend to distinguish themselves principally by size (measured in terms of number of rooms) location and perceived quality of service. Hotels are given a star rating category to identify quality of service. A five-star hotel is one which offers first class international standard service. The economic fortunes of the accommodation sector have generally mirrored those of other sectors within the tourism industry, although the demand for accommodation is not evenly spread across the various categories. For example, the pattern of demand for accommodation by the business traveller differs from that of the tourist. Notwithstanding, there is enough in common for an external factor such as a major airline dispute to have affected the demand for all types of accommodation.

The five-star hotel sector is a relatively small part of the Australian accommodation industry when number and capacity of those hotels is considered. In June 1989 there were only fifty-five five-star hotels in Australia. However, these hotels are large; they account for 12 per cent of guest rooms and 10 per cent of bed spaces and each had over 100 employees. In 1987 they accounted for 38 per cent of employment in the accommodation sector, 54 per cent of wages and salaries, 41 per cent of business and slightly less than 11 per cent of net operating surplus (ABS, *Tourist Accommodation Australia*, 1989, Table 1). So although few in number, they are a very significant part of the accommodation business in Australia.

In Victoria, where the hotel being studied is located, there were ten five-star hotels in June 1989 and they occupied a similar place in the industry to five-star hotels for the nation as a whole. For example, although they represented only 5 per cent of establishments in the Melbourne Statistical Division,[3] they accounted for 43 per cent of the accommodation business. The average length of stay in five-star hotels (1.9 days) was slightly lower than for other accommodation places (2 days) in the Melbourne Statistical Division (the location of all five-star hotels in Victoria). In Victoria the average stay in all kinds of accommodation was 1.8 days. Occupancy rates in June 1989 were slightly lower for five-star hotels (59 per cent) than for other establishments in the Melbourne Division (60 per cent), but higher than for elsewhere in Victoria (ABS, *Tourist Accommodation Victoria*, 1989, Table 2). It should be noted that the statistics for June 1989 did not reflect the effects of the pilots' dispute.

The most recent detailed statistics on employment in the

accommodation industry were provided in the 1986–87 services industries survey. It indicated that the industry's workforce has a high
casual proportion (approximately 43 per cent of the workforce are
casuals), a majority of employees are females (60 per cent) and a
smaller proportion of females than males were employed full-time.
Seventy-one per cent of male workers are full-time compared with 48
per cent of female (ABS, *Hotels & Bars and Accommodation Industries
Australia*, 1986–87, Table 5). Employment in the Melbourne five-star
hotels in June 1989 roughly mirrored the above patterns with respect
to full-time and casual status and there appeared to be a marginal increase in the proportion of casual workers over the last three years.
The Hotel International has a similar pattern of employment to other
hotels in Melbourne with approximately half the workforce being
casuals. However, the gender profile of the Hotel International's staff
differs markedly from the general industry pattern. There was a higher
proportion of males (56 per cent) employed at Hotel International in
June 1989 than for the industry as a whole (40 per cent). This mirrors
the gender profile of staff at large hotels, which in 1983 was estimated
at 56 per cent male (Charlesworth 1983, p. 101).

Hotel services

In the main, hotels provide a range of hospitality services, varying from
services associated with residence at the hotel—the provision of over-
night accommodation and meals during that period of residence—to
the provision of services of a short-term non-residential kind such as
conventions, banquets, entertainment, shopping and dining. There are
many characteristics of the 'product' of this industry that make the
workplace rather different from a manufacturing plant or office environment. Unlike the output of a typical manufacturing plant, the services
provided by hotels are highly perishable. For example, if there is an
event which interferes with the flow of guests to the hotel or prevents
the hotel from providing an advertised service, it is highly likely that
the business will be lost or at best be substantially reduced if re-
scheduled.

The quality of service provided is crucial to a hotel's capacity to
generate repeat business and thus is essential to its profitability. Further,
quality of service is inextricably linked to staff performance. Unlike
many other workplaces, staff in a hotel are exposed to the additional
pressure of having to deal directly with the guests. This makes the
quality of employee relations critical to the successful delivery of good

service. The unpredictable workload and non-conventional hours are additional factors providing obstacles to staff in their delivery of services.

The hotel industry universally experiences peaks and troughs in the demand for its services. In those areas involved in the provision of food and beverages, the peaks are associated with traditional meal times and normal entertainment hours. Such peaks often fall outside what are considered traditional working hours. There are also seasonal variations in the demand for accommodation and associated ancillary services. In the case of a major residential hotel, the surge in demand may occur with little notice.

The supply of hotel services is primarily determined by the cost of those services and whilst the cost structure varies between hotels and for individual services, there are some common themes to the model of employment and labour costs of a hotel. One theme has been the significance and growth in importance of casual employees in this sector with a bias towards the employment of females and young people. The attraction of casuals is in part the lower unit cost of a service when they are used in preference to full-timers. Not only are there savings in some of the on-costs associated with the employment of casuals but also the employer, by using casuals, is able to reduce the unit cost of a service by tailoring the labour input much more closely to the specific time requirement of that service. Another theme is the different cost regimes possible for large and small firms; it appears that small firms have some distinct advantages in labour costs over the large firms through lower payroll tax obligations and lower wage costs in those establishments where cash in hand type payments are used. Finally, non-wage labour costs as a component of the total unit costs has grown in importance over time and this may well have produced an employer response in terms of the kinds of decisions about labour inputs.

The industry therefore has relied mainly upon a non-permanent workforce with many casual employees. This has had a significant bearing on the labour market characteristics as well as on relationships within the workplace. Labour turnover is traditionally high and employers' perceptions of training and education may differ from those held within industries where the workforce is full-time and permanent. In addition, the industry tends to attract younger, more mobile workers who see employment in this industry as a second job or a source of income whilst they are engaged in study or on a working holiday. By attracting such people, the industry has benefited from a high quality labour source for the kind of work performed. It is possible that this source of labour will dry up due to demographic and other changes and the industry may not enjoy the benefits of this labour supply indefinitely. Finally, casual workers differ in other respects, for example, level of unionisation, attitudes to supervisors, and career aspirations.

Whilst casuals are suitable for some services provided by the hotel, there are other sections of the hotel which are staffed predominantly by full-timers. For example, the typical kitchen employee is a full-timer with trade qualifications. Another characteristic distinguishing various segments of the workforce is the degree to which staff seek promotion within the hotel group rather than participating in the external labour market. Many of the professional staff seek promotion within the group, whereas kitchen staff are more likely to see their long-term future elsewhere. The other distinction that is usually made (albeit rather blurred and contested) is that between 'award' and 'award-free' employees and this has important consequences for industrial relations at the workplace. This is discussed later in the chapter.

Hotel International

The major activity of Hotel International is the provision of accommodation in the form of fully-serviced guest rooms of an international standard. Complementary facilities provided include a cocktail lounge, a number of restaurants, a cabaret, a gymnasium and health club and a number of shops retailing a variety of services including international gifts, hair-dressing and wine and spirits. Included in the hotel are convention, banquet and meeting facilities for up to 1000 people. The hotel also caters for the business person with an executive floor within the hotel which offers a range of office support facilities.

The hotel was opened during the 1970s and is one of a number to be operated in Australia by International. International began life as the overseas subsidiary of International Hotels Corporation, and became an independent publicly owned company in 1964 with exclusive rights to the International name outside the United States and at one property in Hawaii. In October 1987 it was purchased by a British-based conglomerate already with sizeable holdings in accommodation as well as retailing. Head office exercises a major influence over the conduct of business at the Hotel International. In particular it sets profit objectives and promotes guidelines as to the preferred way of meeting those objectives. Furthermore, it puts a firm stamp upon the preferred direction of human resources management, for example, head office promotes an underlying theme of performance reward which has been taken up by the Melbourne hotel.

The primary financial objective of the International chain is to establish the most profitable cost-effective first-class hotel group. Local management sees both the expansion of revenue and a restraint on costs as necessary to achieve this financial objective. For this purpose the hotel is divided into two broad profit centres, namely rooms, and food and beverages. It is generally more difficult to earn a profit in some activities than others, so a degree of cross-subsidisation is required. For example, earning a given level of profit in food and beverage requires considerably more effort than in other segments of the business. Additionally, certain loss-making activities are retained solely to maintain the hotel's five-star rating. The provision of breakfast for guests is an example of this.

Profitability of the Hotel International has increased over the last four years when measured by the level of gross operating profit. In the previous financial year (1988–89) the hotel generated a gross profit margin of approximately 25 per cent. Further increases in profit depend on an increase in the room occupancy rate (which in June 1989 was 75 per cent) and the overall containment of costs. To achieve these objectives it is planned to fully refurbish the hotel and develop an associated marketing plan that builds upon an improved image by stressing the quality of the product.

In terms of the organisation structure, the general manager of the Hotel International is placed on the fourth level of the management hierarchy and reports to the vice-president of International's Australian operations. In practice, influence of head office is often transmitted directly to Melbourne, for example a video containing the chief executive's view is made available to all hotels within the chain simultaneously. The commercial relationship between the other hotels in Australia owned by the company and the Melbourne hotel extends to activities such as reservations, marketing and cross-selling. So there exists a level of cooperation between the various hotels in the group as well as a degree of subtle rivalry between them, not expressed in terms of market competition but in terms of market performance. That is, they are compared when performance is being assessed by the parent company and (presumably) by the decision-makers within the various hotels. The major residential accommodation market is highly competitive and is considered a price-sensitive business, especially within some market segments. Key indicators in determining the success of a hotel include such things as occupancy rates, turnover and productivity. Both the quality of service and price offered by a hotel will be significant factors in determining this although overt price competition is probably not as important as quality of service because the latter is critical in determining return business. The Hotel International typically has 60 per cent local business and 40 per cent international. It relies on air crew for a significant part of that international business. Approximately 19 per cent of business, at the time of the research, came from Japanese tourists.

The geographical layout of the hotel can be broadly divided into two main areas: 'the front of the house' and 'the back of the house'. This distinction reflects differing job functions undertaken by employees in the two locations, and the different level of exposure that each has to the guests. Back-of-house employees by and large are not required to communicate with the guests, yet they will often be seen by the guests and hence their appearance and efficiency will be as exposed to some guests as will employees in front-of-house locations. Within each profit centre there will be front- and back-of-house employees. The accommodation area will, therefore, have front office staff who process the accommodation needs of guests as well as back-of-house employees who maintain the guest rooms throughout the guests' stay and who undertake maintenance of the hotel facilities and guest rooms. Food and beverage staff also have differing levels of interaction with guests. Banquet staff will deal directly with guests in the restaurants and banquet rooms, however those involved in preparing food will not normally meet guests nor deal directly with them. Layout is critical in another respect. There are some jobs in hotels where the employees are quite isolated, whilst other jobs have a high degree of social interaction between the employee and the hotel guest, and between employees themselves. Each location can therefore be expected to produce a different social environment for the employees, and hence a different industrial relations environment.

Within Hotel International specific services are offered at varying times. Some of them are provided on a twenty-four-hour basis whilst others are offered only during more conventional business hours. The timing of services such as conference or conventions follow a different pattern again; when they are provided is determined by the specific arrangements made with the client, although the hours would follow a pattern normally established for the particular kind of event. In summary, this workplace has a very much wider spread of hours for most of its workforce than that experienced in a more traditional manufacturing workplace. Although some of the functions are operating around the clock, the normal shift-work model is probably not an appropriate way to describe the work arrangements in this workplace.

In June 1989 Hotel International had a total workforce of 630 people, eleven fewer than in 1987. Of these, 51 per cent were casuals—fairly typical for this type of establishment. Forty-four per cent of employees were female, and there was a higher percentage of females than males in casual jobs (56 per cent compared with 47 per cent). Within the last two years there has been a slight increase in the number of females within the management class, and the growth in casual employment amongst the non-managerial class was slightly more among men than women. As might be expected, there is considerable seasonal variation in the number of employees. This seasonal variation is absorbed mainly by the casuals; there is a sixty per cent growth in the number of casuals employed between the seasonal peak and trough in any year. This is consistent with the results of earlier studies (Worland and Wilson 1988).

More than one half of the workforce are considered as sales and personal service workers, with only a very small group of employees classified as management or professional. The occupational breakdown of the workforce employed at the hotel as at June 1989 is detailed in Table 4.1. It should be noted that some fifty-five casual employees, who were not employed at the time these figures were compiled, are not included in this table. These casuals are, however, considered by the hotel to be part of their regular workforce.

Table 4.1 Occupational Breakdown of the Employed Workforce at Hotel International, June 1989

Occupation	Number	Percentage
Managers	14	2.3
Professional	3	0.5
Para-professionals	1	0.2
Tradepersons	63	11.0
Clerks	17	3.0
Sales and personal service	323	56.2
Labourers and manual workers	154	26.8
TOTAL	575	100.0

(Source: Human Resources Department, Hotel International)

Terms and conditions of work for the majority of employees at the Hotel International are specified in the Hotels and Retail Liquor Award,

1983. The award applies to all '... persons employed in any capacity whether permanent or casual in hotels, taverns, wine saloons, wine and spirit merchants retailing to the general public and other retail licensed establishments, in or in connection with accommodation, with the selling of drinks, preparing and serving food and drinks, cleaning and attending to the premises and all other services associated therewith' (ACAC, *Hotels and Retail Liquor Industry Award*, 1983, Clause 4). The range of enterprises this award covers has led to the Hotel International claiming that the terms and conditions of employment contained in this award are not appropriate for the nature of the market they are operating in. For example, they argue that, unlike other respondents to the award, the major residential hotels provide full service twenty-four hours a day, seven days a week for the whole year. As a consequence inflexible working arrangements and penalty rates (including overtime and weekend rates) are major impediments to the efficiency and productivity of the hotel. The only exceptions to the applicability of this award are a small number of maintenance workers, such as carpenters and electricians, and the more senior management personnel.

The Hotels and Retail Liquor Industry Award has undergone some revision over the past two years, partly as a result of negotiations between the Australian Hotels Association (AHA) and the Federated Liquor and Allied Industries Employees' Union (FLAIEU) under the auspices of the second-tier principles.[4] The major changes include provision for 'regular casuals', traineeships, reduced working hours, redundancy provisions and new procedures to regulate the termination of employees. Despite these changes, which provide some protection to employees, the Award still protects the employers' traditional rights to 'hire and fire'. Thus whilst 'regular casuals' (defined as employees who have 'worked a roster of at least fifteen hours per week for a period of not less than six months' (ACAC, *Print No. H3480*, 8 July 1988)) now enjoy some of the guarantees afforded to monthly staff, the Award also stipulates that the mandatory period of notice for termination of employment

> shall not apply in the case of dismissal for conduct that justifies instant dismissal including inefficiency within the first seven days, neglect of duty or misconduct and in the case of casual employees, apprentices or persons engaged for a specified period of time or for a specific task or tasks (ACAC, *Print No. H6670*, 28 February 1989, Clause k).

Thus, in the case of the Hotel International, more than half the staff have little recourse in the case of unfair termination of employment.

The Award recognises, at least in part, the nature of the hospitality industry by permitting the standing-down of employees in the event of 'any cause for which the employer cannot reasonably be held responsible' (*Hotels and Retail Liquor Industry Award*, 1983, Clause 11), although 'slackness of trade' is specifically excluded. Presumably slackness of trade related to specific causes, such as an airline strike, would prove a justifiable reason for the stand-down of employees to occur.

In the main the Award provides the basis for employment at the Hotel International. The majority of employees receive award rates of pay, including penalty rates and allowances. Certain groups of employees, however, may receive higher rates of pay depending primarily on market conditions. For example, the kitchen brigade (chefs and related kitchen staff) as a group receives the highest over-award payments, which currently adds on average approximately 20 per cent to their gross wages. These arrangements operate with the agreement of the shop steward. With respect to conditions of work, Hotel International, in general, provides above-average working conditions. This has primarily arisen due to a desire by the Hotel International to be seen as a 'good employer', although over time they have emerged from agreements negotiated by the local shop steward. Further conditions of employment are laid down in the employee handbook. This document is presented to all new employees at the induction program and, in general, formalises management's expectations of workplace behaviour.

A hotel, in providing a range of services for its guests, is by nature a labour-intensive organisation. Most of the services provided by the International involve the direct interaction of hotel staff with guests. In some areas the labour input has been either augmented or replaced by technology although in this process new or supplementary jobs have been created. Some of the areas where the effects of new technology have been felt are the use of computerised reservations and accounts systems, an enhanced telephone network, the use of credit cards and electronic funds transfer as a means of payment, labour-saving devices used within the kitchen and restaurant areas, computerised bars in private rooms, and pre-prepared packaged food products. These developments have, to some degree, deskilled various jobs, although changes in technology related to food have been accompanied by an '. . . increased demand for variety and complexity of food services' (Charlesworth 1983, p. 21).

The role of management

The Hotel International is part of an international hotel group with headquarters in London. Management at the Hotel International reflects the corporate ethos of that group. A recent change in ownership of the parent company led to a revision of its management practices and this has flowed on to Hotel International's management strategy and its human resources management policy and practice. Head office directly intervenes in these areas and also intervenes indirectly as a result of decisions which it takes in areas such as marketing and finance. For example, a strategy directed towards projecting a specific marketing image for the hotel group can be expected to assist in shaping the corporate culture of Hotel International and this will impact upon the conduct of its management policy and practice.

Industrial relations policy

Turning specifically to industrial relations, we find that the degree of direct intervention by head office varies with the kind of issue under consideration. First, head office is responsible for the development of broad policy guidelines in human resources management. These are transmitted to the Hotel International through a Human Resources Development manual and reflected in a statement of Personnel Policies. The Human Resources Development manual (a document of 140 pages) is a comprehensive manifesto of personnel and training structures and practices. It outlines the organisational structure of the personnel and training areas and the job profiles of the associated positions. It presents a statement of human resources objectives and identifies critical success factors. The manual gives guidance on the personnel and training functions, the employment and training process, and employee facilities. Areas such as performance review and promotions, personnel transfers, and employee improvement programs are also addressed.

There are specific requirements as to labour relations policies and these extend to the type of human resources systems and reporting functions that are to be adopted by Hotel International. Further, head office is actively involved in some aspects of policy implementation. In the area of training, for example, head office is providing direct input into training the trainers. The success of the group's global corporate strategy 'to become the most profitable first-class hotel group in the world' and 'to enhance the overall quality of our customer service' will be highly dependent upon the quality of industrial relations achieved by the group. The quality revolution referred to by management is dependent upon a change in employee attitudes and this will occur only if the industrial relations climate has been appropriately set.

The role of head office in the determination of industrial relations policy and practice is supplemented by a prominent involvement by management at the Hotel International. This involvement is necessitated by local factors such as the vagaries of the employment scene, variants in the local industrial relations system together with the practice by head office of delivering autonomy to individual hotels. Although the extent of autonomy is difficult to gauge, from the evidence it appears to vary according to the issues and policies in question. For example, decisions taken within the constraint of local awards or agreements and decisions involving local issues are generally made locally.

Industrial relations practices

Local decisions are made within a fairly traditional hierarchical framework. The hotel has a general manager and there are thirteen department managers with functional responsibilities reporting to him. Within this structure, the general manager has established a management group consisting of these managers and the director of human resources. The director of human resources reports to the general manager as well as to the divisional or regional manager and (on certain matters) to head office. The management group meets regularly on policy matters. A wider group of twenty-five key personnel also occasionally meets, as does the group of sixty monthly-paid staff although this occurs rather less regularly. It may be called in response to a specific initiative such as the consideration and implementation of a new strategy from head office. Such a meeting occurred in April 1989, when Hotel International head office was considering the new corporate strategy and how it was to be interpreted and applied. The emphasis at that meeting was that:

(a)   change was the focal point. 'Success will come to those who can convince their employees to love change just as they have hated it in the past'. 'Targets must shock. Innovation must be faster' (managing director);

(b)   attempts must be made to introduce a new corporate culture which involves employees taking a different approach to the servicing of guests. The hotel seeks to be service-orientated; its total activities revolve around the guest.

    A number of changes to the structure and processes used by the organisation were also considered by the management group and some of these impinge upon industrial relations within the organisation. These include:

(a)   reduced number of levels in the management hierarchy,

(b)   more line management authority,

(c)   human resources management policy that promotes people who create excitement, zest and enthusiasm,

(d)   a number of innovations in the area of human resources management:
     — revised orientation program
     — performance review system
     — awards for excellence.

The focus on change is probably derived from both the change in ownership and the reorganisation of management structure at Hotel International which followed the recent appointment of a new general manager. A range of new managerial appointments (including the director of human resources) has contributed to the creation of a new workplace culture and introduced new ways of conducting industrial relations. Plans to remodel the hotel and a change to its marketing direction can also be expected to significantly influence the industrial relations climate within the hotel.

Within the workplace, responsibility for industrial relations is shared fairly evenly between line management and the director of human resources. The director of human resources is the only person within the hotel with specific responsibility for industrial relations. The job is seen as one in which approximately 35 per cent of the time is spent on industrial relations and employee relations matters, 30 per cent is spent on counselling, and 25 per cent is spent on administration. This person is playing a key role in implementing the new corporate culture and is also responsible for an intensive induction program conducted fortnightly and taken by all new employees. Line management and people responsible for the occupational health and safety function assist the training officer in the conduct of this half-day program. The human resources department maintains all records and the director of human resources is either an advisor or decision-maker in respect of interpreting corporate policy, making appointments, overseeing dismissals and applying industrial relations policy. The emphasis given to the various human resource functions reflects not only the direction of corporate human resources policies but also the background of the individual occupying the position of director of human resources and the philosophy and attitudes of the local management group.

Apart from the input of head office, line management, and the director of human resources, Hotel International may also rely on the major employer association for assistance in the resolution of industrial relations problems. The hotel is an active member of the Australian Hotels Association (AHA); it is represented at monthly meetings and is a participant at award negotiations conducted by the AHA and is, therefore, one of the high-profile industry members. In practice, however, Hotel International does not feel constrained by policies developed through this forum.[5] Assistance from the AHA is generally confined to matters such as information on award standards, advice and representation in negotiations, dismissals, and the provision of training. This degree of autonomy is seen as a necessary precondition to the development of industrial relations strategies consistent with the achievement of the overall group corporate goals. The major focus of these strategies is to develop flexible wage structures and improved skills within the workforce.

Management claims to practice a 'visible' management style; for example, they are required to conduct a policy of managing by walking around. There appear to be no issues in industrial relations where authority is sought beyond the workplace with the exception of matters going to tribunals. First line supervisors, whilst involved in industrial relations, spend less than 10 per cent of their time on grievance handling, discipline and recruitment.

After examining the way in which a range of industrial relations decisions are taken at the hotel, we conclude that there are several sources of inputs into the various decisions. For example, a decision about work rosters being local in character is made by the department head within the constraints imposed by the award and after seeking the advice of the director of human resources. On this matter no advice from head office would be sought. Details are provided in Table 4.2 on page 110.

The agreement with the union over compulsory union membership and the boundaries of exempt areas is also a local one. It was made in 1981, and since 1986 management has developed an understanding that the agreement should not be interpreted as a closed shop agreement, so that although management is prepared to hand out union membership cards, they are not prepared to force people to join. The making and modification of such an agreement rests with the general manager who is advised by the director of human resources. Interpretation and observance of this agreement has become a rather contentious issue between local management and the union and probably represents the most important issue to the union at the time of this study.

Table 4.2   Prime Responsibility for Tasks in Industrial Relations.

First line supervisor	Supervisor and P & T manager	P & T manager	P & T manager and senior management
• hours of work • staffing levels • speed of work • schedule of rests • work reorganisation • purchase of new equipment	• recruitment • employee transfer • training • promotion	• pay negotiations • negotiations of employment conditions	• dismissal

Decisions about employment at Hotel International are also taken at the local level. Those relating to the number of people employed are probably indirectly influenced by head office profit constraints but none the less are ultimately the responsibility of management at Hotel International. In turn, decisions about employment levels are devolved to departments which are required to keep within ceilings placed on numbers following quarterly staff reviews by management. Requests for additional staff are monitored by the director of human resources and department heads, whose task it is to administer such staffing goals.

The role and responsibility of management in the appointment of new staff varies according to the level of appointment and type of staff being employed. For example, the appointment of a new department manager will involve the area manager, whereas award employees are recruited through the human resources department. There are essentially three categories of award employees: full-time, regular casual, and casual employees. The regular casual employees are casuals who can expect to work a regular weekly workload. They are the preferred casuals who have made it to the regular list by their past conduct. This process is an important filtering device as it enables management to cull employees who do not meet the hotel's requirements, however that may be defined. It is possible that management may use this device to discourage a range of behaviours among casuals and the practice certainly removes the need for management to overtly dismiss employees whose performance is less than satisfactory.

The number of dismissals of full-time employees is very low. Although no firm data on the number of dismissals is available, the director of human resources estimated that (excluding those who might have involuntarily resigned) less than ten people have been dismissed within the last two years. The resignations during this time included two managers who were presented with the option of resigning or being dismissed. Their departure during a period of rapid change in the hotel was said to be related to performance.

The director of human resources stated that the dismissal of staff is to be avoided if possible. Counselling is used to prevent dismissals. Staff are said to be dismissed for neglect of duty and continued poor performance, theft of company property, and lack of reliability. Turnover of staff through voluntary separation differs across the various departments within the hotel. The relatively high turnover rate within the food and beverage department can be explained by the irregular hours, the stress component of the job (especially in the kitchen area and banquet supervision), the nature of the career path for a chef, and labour market competition (especially when major new hotels are established). The labour turnover experienced in the sales and administrative area was much lower than in the kitchen and functions area and this is attributed to the more regular work pattern of this section.

Reward systems

Employees at the hotel are classified by management as either salaried staff or wage employees. For wage employees there are differences in the hourly wage paid to permanent and casual employees, with casuals earning $10.68 per hour and permanent wage employees earning $9.80 per hour (as at June 1989). Differences occur in the wage rates paid according to when the work is performed. For example, a much higher hourly rate is paid to workers engaged on public holidays ($18.67 per hour for casual employees and $19.71 per hour for permanents working overtime on a public holiday). Wages paid to employees as overtime are quite a small proportion of wages overall (less than 1 per cent) and this reflects the desire by management to use casual employees rather than permanents to reduce the incidence of penalties associated with overtime rates paid to permanents.

Most wage employees are paid according the hotel industry award and approximately one third of these ninety-six receive over-award payments. There appear to be three possible reasons for over-award payments. For some employees, particularly those working in the kitchen area, the over-award payment has been negotiated between the union and management. For others, the over-award payment reflects management's perception of the responsibility attached to the job. This means that employees in supervisory positions can receive substantial over-award payments. The third source of over-award payments is related to the prevailing labour market. Some employees receive additional payments as a result of individual bargaining with management using labour market conditions as a source of power.

Although over-award payments are mainly confined to permanent staff, six casual employees are listed as receiving over-award payments because of their specific supervisory responsibility. Apart from people employed in the kitchen, most over-award payments appear to attach to the job rather than to the individual. Overall, the level of over-award payment varies between job classifications but is approximately 10–20 per cent of the award wage. People in supervisory positions receive between $20 and $55 per week in over-award payments and kitchen staff receive between $25 and $110 per week.

Over-award payments for salaried staff in the middle management area are rather more difficult to ascertain as salary packages are often negotiated on an individual basis without any reference to award rates. Salaries are reviewed annually and the general increase is likely to approximate community standards although individual bargaining may provide outcomes which differ from this. Recommendations arising from the annual salary review are ultimately approved by the area manager for the South Pacific region. In addition to the salary, staff receive perquisites such as laundry, car parking and some meals.

The wages and salaries bill was analysed to determine the relative importance of each category of labour and to enable an understanding of the contribution of wage costs associated with the various classes of labour to the overall labour cost. Salaried staff excluding executives accounted for approximately 20 per cent of the weekly wages bill in June 1989. Based on a working week of 42.6 paid hours, the average hourly cost of salaried staff was $12.24 in June 1989. If unpaid overtime is included the hourly cost of labour is reduced and it becomes clear that there are some labour cost advantages from promoting people to salaried staff positions, particularly when they can be expected to work unpaid overtime at times when the alternative labour costs are high.

Employee participation

Within this establishment, the application of formal employee participation appears to have been quite limited. There is evidence of information sharing by management but the type of information made available to employees is restricted to that which is required by legislation (for example, communication of pay and conditions) or that which is directly related to improving market performance (for example, marketing information or revisions to the corporate plan). Employees are not informed about changes to staffing or provided with information of a financial kind. Participation in decision-making by employees is also rather limited. For example, the only direct involvement by employees is through the suggestion scheme and other meetings with supervisors where (presumably) some two-way communication takes place. Occasionally management briefing meetings are held and are attended by monthly-paid personnel (eighty staff) where senior managers form a panel and address questions from the floor. Much of the interaction in these forums was information flowing from the top down rather than participation by middle management in the decision-making within the organisation.

The company publishes a quarterly staff magazine primarily to convey information to staff. The contents of a 1988 edition (eight pages) contained a message from the general manager together with a range of professional and social news about staff at the hotel including photographs of specific events and achievements. As well, the general manager, from time to time, produces a staff newsletter before a significant event where the support of staff is required.

Formal schemes of financial participation are restricted to a select few members of the senior management group who are involved in a profit sharing arrangement—rewards being related to profit levels. However, there is no share ownership scheme. In terms of formally structured participation schemes, quality circles represented the only form attempted at the workplace and these were discontinued because of their inadequacy: they were found to be 'unworkable'.

Many of the management practices described above have been directed towards the incorporation of the workforce. By identifying employees, above all else, as members of the company, management is creating a culture that insulates employees from the effects of outside influences. This approach has been most obvious in recent times by Hotel International's approach to trade union membership.

The role of unions

All non-managerial employees at the hotel, with the exception of tradepersons, are 'technically' required to be members of the Federated Liquor and Allied Industries Employees' Union. This policy, the outcome of an agreement between the major residential hotels and the union, has resulted in an overall unionisation rate at Hotel International of over 80 per cent. This figure varies substantially for the various occupational groups within the hotel. Clerical workers, for example, have a unionisation rate of 70 per cent which compares to 90 per cent for sales and personal service workers and close to 100 per cent for the unskilled hotel employee classification. The only other group of union members within the hotel are the tradepersons who belong to a variety of unions such as the Amalgamated Metal Workers' Union and the Electrical Trades Union. Of the sixty-three employees in this group over 95 per cent were members of their respective union. Few conflicts occur between the unions on site and when potentially damaging issues arise they are usually settled quickly.

Union fees are deducted from most employees' wages. The union has a notice board for the display of union material and the local union representative has access to a telephone and is given time off work as required to carry out his functions. Management will, if the need arises, distribute notices on behalf of the union and provides union members with the necessary rooms in which to conduct union meetings, including stop-work meetings of members.

Workplace trade union organisation

Within the workplace the Federated Liquor and Allied Industries Employees' Union has only one endorsed shop steward. This is normally the case for major residential hotels, although it would appear to be considerably lower than for most unions that encourage workplace representation. The problems associated with such a large membership to service have been partially overcome at the hotel by the formation of a shops committee. This committee does not have any delegated responsibilities from the union and is primarily used by the designated steward to gauge members' attitudes, to provide a more immediate union presence in the various sections of the hotel and to coordinate union activity within the workplace. The committee consists of four FLAIEU union members, one of whom is the shop steward. The remaining members, all of whom are women, come from the major areas of the hotel such as laundry, front office and food preparation. Full-time union officials have expressed some concern over the effective functioning of this committee due in part to the absence of one member resulting from injury, and the strong personality of the shop steward. The shop steward is certainly the dominant personality in terms of the union's presence at the Hotel International and has significant power, much of which has derived from his long employment at the hotel and his involvement in employee affairs.

The shop steward is normally elected from all FLAIEU union members at the hotel, although in the present case he was nominated by the union and elected unopposed by the membership. He has occupied the position of steward for the past six years; prior to his election he was acting as an assistant to the shop steward and had gained most of his knowledge of industrial relations from this experience. The steward had not undergone any formal training for this position either with his union or through the Trade Union Training Authority. The steward estimates that, on average, he would spend about six hours a week acting as a steward, about half of which would be in his own time. These hours, in the main, are spent in negotiations with management, discussions with full-time union officials, and consulting with members. The major issues negotiated with management tend to be individual grievances or working conditions. Rarely, if ever, would wage increases be the subject of these negotiations.

Membership meetings are conducted infrequently, usually averaging two to three each year. These tend to be held during working hours and for at least one of these meetings the members will receive full pay. These meetings are usually called only when particular issues need to be considered by the full membership. The last such meeting was arranged to discuss issues associated with award restructuring and for full-time union officials to report the progress of such developments. A full-time union organiser would visit the hotel about once every three months, usually to keep contact with the steward and shops committee, provide members with the latest copy of the journal (*On Tap*) and to ensure all eligible staff are members of the union. Eligible staff who have not joined the union have, in the main, gained exemption from the shops committee. The full-time union official would only be involved in local negotiations in those circumstances where the grievances had not been able to be resolved by the steward.

Employees belonging to other unions on site do not have any local workplace organisation. In general these union members would consult with their own union and tend to be relatively self-contained in terms of industrial relations. Rarely would meetings between these unionists or the full-time representative and the local steward take place. When these meetings have occurred they have almost solely been concerned with industrial action.

Current union issues

Union membership has declined over the past two years at the hotel, although this decline has not exceeded 10 per cent of the membership. This decline is indicative of the mode of employment that exists in large residential hotels as well as local management's unwillingness to enforce the membership agreement. The large number of casual staff employed (whose members have increased by 6 per cent in the past two years) and the seasonal and cyclical nature of their employment makes it difficult for the union to recruit and retain such employees. Whilst this is a problem that exists in most of the larger hotels, one other factor peculiar to Hotel International has contributed to this decline. A major reorganisation of managerial positions and the accompanying increase in responsibilities over the past two years have led to a number of the relatively more senior staff resigning from the union. This has included employees occupying managerial positions and a number of more senior kitchen staff such as chefs. Full-time union officials claim that this has been a deliberate strategy of senior management at the hotel, and that, accompanied by a failure to administer the agreement, this represents a concerted attempt to reduce the effectiveness of the union and to break down award conditions.

It is difficult for the union to enforce local agreements as their presence at the workplace is weak, notwithstanding their numerical strength. The high proportion of casual staff, the profile of employees (young, ethnic, students), the seemingly endless supply of workers, and the restrictions on industrial tactics such as secondary boycotts mean that any bargaining strength will depend to a large degree on the negotiating ability of the organiser and the strength of the local representatives.

Clearly, union organisation at Hotel International is centred upon the local shop steward. In some respects the steward's role is akin to that of a personnel officer in that considerable time is spent on resolving individual grievances. Considerably less time is spent by the steward in developing an awareness of potential issues and developing a collective consciousness amongst the hotel's employees. This finding, coupled with the presence of little overt industrial conflict, would suggest a degree of incorporation of the steward into the management hierarchy. This view is rejected by the steward, who claims that the good working relationships of the past have given way to a 'them and us' mentality.

Full-time union officials have in the past visited the hotel infrequently and have not provided adequate support for the steward. This has led to a feeling amongst members that for all intents and purposes the shop steward is the union. The union recently recognised these problems and has increased the frequency of visits to the hotel by full-time officials. It has also attempted to recruit more stewards and thus expand the shops committee. The recruitment of more stewards is a problem, however, due to the high number of casual staff and the isolated nature of parts of the workforce.

Consultation, negotiations and dispute settlement

A high level of consultation and bargaining occurs within the hotel over a range of issues. In part this represents the new style of management which has as a prime objective the involvement of all staff in improving the quality of the service provided. The outcome of such a policy is the settling of disputes, where possible, within the workplace. Only in this way, management argues, can they be assured of a commitment by employees to a final decision or agreement. Equally, this approach may represent a realisation by management that not to do so runs the risk of having the issue resolved externally to the satisfaction of neither party.

Consultation within the hotel is achieved through the direct involvement of the shop steward as well as by workforce briefings by senior management and supervisors. From time to time other forms of consultation and participation have been used, for example quality circles, but as discussed earlier these have proved to be of little use and, in the main, unworkable. The shop steward has direct access to the general manager of the hotel, although for most matters the normal course of action would involve working through the director of human resources. On matters relating to the introduction of new products and services, the introduction of new technology, and changes in work practices and staffing levels, the steward is normally kept fully informed.

The same philosophy is apparent with respect to negotiations. The prime objective is to resolve disputes within the hotel with the minimum involvement of 'outsiders'. If the issue is of an individual nature (for example, individual grievances) then the negotiations normally occur between the shop steward and the appropriate line manager. Only if the issue cannot be resolved at this level, or if the matter involves alleged unfair disciplinary action or dismissal would the steward take the matter directly to the director of human resources. The procedure for handling such issues was introduced by management and to date it has been successful in containing the issue to within the workplace and preventing industrial action. It should be noted that this process closely resembles the grievance procedure contained in the Award. This procedure was introduced in 1985 and provides for disputes to be settled, wherever possible, by discussions between the shop steward and management. Only when this cannot be achieved will external people (full-time union officials, representatives of the AHA) become involved. Failure at this level will result in the issue being referred to the Australian Industrial Relations Commission. Both the procedure and the apparent effectiveness of the procedure consolidates the pivotal role of the steward in industrial relations matters.

Issues of a more general nature that affect a group or groups of employees are usually settled via negotiations between the shop steward and the director of human resources, who may in turn involve other senior management. Rarely does the steward involve the shop committee or full-time union officers in such negotiations. Thus, staffing levels, general working conditions, health and safety concerns, new technology, and work organisation will, at least initially, be subject to negotiations at the local level. Only if the issue involves award wages or standard conditions (for example, hours of work or leave entitlements) would the negotiations extend beyond the workplace and involve full-time officials of the FLAIEU and representatives of the Australian Hotels Association.

Certain issues may, by necessity, involve other personnel within the hotel in negotiations. This is particularly the case (excluding individual grievances) with discussions concerning working conditions, changes to work organisation, and health and safety issues. In these cases more-senior management will become involved, and in the case of health and safety matters the full-time nursing officer will play a key role. The final outcome of such negotiations would normally be an unregistered written agreement or simply a verbal agreement. Rarely would either party seek to register such an agreement with an industrial tribunal, which illustrates the willingness, in the past, of both the union and management to honour such agreements.

This approach to union–management negotiations can be readily observed in the negotiations emanating from the March 1987 decision of the Australian Industrial Relations Commission, better known as the second-tier or 4 per cent negotiations. Whilst the wage outcome of 4 per cent was settled outside of the workplace, many of the 'trade-offs' were negotiated within the hotel. These included wages to be paid fortnightly by electronic funds transfer, management to be afforded greater flexibility in determining staffing levels and rostered days off, agreement on dress standards, prior warning of industrial action, and an increase in the number of hours a part-time employee can be engaged for. With the exception of the part-time employment provisions these issues were resolved locally without the need for the involvement of a full-time FLAIEU official. At this stage, all aspects of the agreement have been implemented and, in the main, accepted by the employees. Ironically, whilst management perceives this exercise to have strengthened union–management relations within the hotel, local union representatives believe this form of negotiations, which involves trading-off certain conditions, has diminished the level of trust between employees and management. Other issues of significance to management and unions recently have included the question of positions to be exempted from union membership, occupational health and safety, training, and employee dismissals.

Industrial action

Overt industrial action is not a feature of industrial relations at this hotel. In part this is a product of the attempts by management, particularly over the past two years, to resolve issues via consultation and workplace negotiations. Equally it may reflect the nature of the hotel's workforce and the organisation of work, in particular the number of casual employees, the existence of shift work, and the physical separation of groups of employees.

In the past two years no industrial dispute has resulted in strike action. Just prior to this period a 24-hour stoppage was held over negotiations related to the second-tier 4 per cent wage increase. In that instance over 95 per cent of FLAIEU members at the hotel took part in the stoppage which was part of a wider industry campaign. The final settlement was negotiated between full-time union and industry officials, although at the local level the hotel's Chief Executive became involved in the negotiations. The matter was ultimately referred to the Australian Industrial Relations Commission for final resolution.

More recently the union has organised a number of stop work meetings (four over the past two years, usually averaging one to one-

and-a-half hours in duration), although in each case the issue under consideration was not specific to the hotel. The last stop work meeting occurred in April 1989 over the issue of award restructuring. Only FLAIEU members were involved and the meeting was primarily organised to allow full-time union officials to report the progress of award restructuring within the industry and to allow the hotel's shops committee to put a number of recommendations to the membership. The key recommendations, which were subsequently accepted, related to training, salary grades and penalty rates. As this had important implications for management, management encouraged all employees to attend, and also provided the facilities for the meeting and guaranteed all employees that they would not suffer any loss in pay. During the period of the meeting managerial staff carried out the duties of those attending the meeting. From discussion with union officials it appears that employees are reluctant to participate in work stoppages and this factor has been an important determinant of the pattern of industrial action.

Other forms of industrial action may be more covert in nature. These forms of conflict are more difficult to measure but can include absenteeism, labour turnover and a range of occupational health problems. Absenteeism at Hotel International is less than 2 per cent of staff in any one day—a relatively low figure. Absenteeism is greatest amongst permanent staff; these employees account for 97 per cent of all recorded absenteeism. More than half of all absenteeism is concentrated in four sections: engineering, front office, housekeeping and the kitchen. Whilst these are areas that employ large numbers of staff (over 150), they do account for a disproportionate amount of absenteeism.

Labour turnover at this workplace is also low by industry standards. Notwithstanding, it is a significant factor affecting the hotel with about one-third of employees expected to leave in any given year. Only 12 per cent of all employees have currently worked for the International for over five years. Turnover rates appear reasonably standard across all work areas, with the largest turnover of staff occurring immediately after the winter period. Occupational health problems appear to be few, with only six employees being eligible for Workcare benefits during the past twelve months. Of these only three remained off work as at May 1990. Taken collectively these findings would indicate that the level of conflict in terms of covert forms is little different from the more observable forms of work stoppages.

Conclusion

Our discussions with key participants in industrial relations at Hotel International have yielded a rich supply of information from which we can draw a number of conclusions about the texture of industrial relations at this workplace. Industrial relations policy and practice appears to have been shaped by many factors, including the formal role of tribunals and related award arrangements. These influences have been complemented by a range of other factors related more specifically to the enterprise and the workplace. In particular we can identify the nature of the workplace, the kind of labour force employed, management ideology and rules both at the workplace and in Head Office and trade union attitudes and behaviour.

The business strategy adopted by Hotel International of ensuring profits through quality of service is central to the determination of industrial relations policy and practice in the workplace. This strategy emanates from head office (located overseas) and is transmitted to Hotel International through a number of key management people in head office, and the regional office in Australia. It provides for a degree of financial control over the individual business units by head office, leaving the decisions about how to meet corporate objectives up to the management of those business units. The devolving of authority is also practised by management within Hotel International which passes on significant degrees of authority to department managers. However, this devolution of authority is contained, in that head office has retained a degree of control in a number of areas. The global corporate strategy is for International to become the most profitable first-class hotel group in the world, and a major plank in this strategy is enhancing the overall quality of customer service. So, whilst management at individual hotels has been encouraged to act autonomously, there is a significant degree of intervention by the corporate head office to ensure standardisation of the quality of service. Moreover, head office has taken a deliberate stance on the kind of industrial relations and human resource management practice that is consistent with the corporate business goals and these are reflected in the human resources guidelines and procedures. Further, there are checks and balances to ensure that corporate human resources policy and practice is followed. For example, responsibility for the appointment of the human resources specialist goes beyond the manager of Hotel International. Procedures for many other decisions are also monitored by head office. Therefore, whilst management at

Hotel International has been given a degree of autonomy within broad profit objectives and other business objectives, there is a significant level of intervention by head office in human resource decisions through corporate involvement in this area.

There is direct evidence of management at Hotel International having developed a style which incorporates the workforce. It sees this style as being consistent with improved performance and profitability. This process of incorporation, promoted by head office, can be identified from a number of recent decisions taken by local management:

- It has changed course on its interpretation of the union membership agreement in so far as being prepared to collect dues on behalf of the union but no longer requires employees to fill in the 'blue card' as a condition of employment;
- it has expanded the number of employees promoted to staff positions;
- it has introduced an elaborate induction program which has as part of its focus the corporate image and objective the kinds of expectations that management has of its employees to achieve those objectives;
- it provides incentives to employees for performance, ranging from over-award payments for people in supervisory posts to the promise of security and better work for the casuals who perform well.

Promotion of the corporate image (currently through promoting the excellence of service) is also an important part of this process.

Individuals in the management level are also important contributors to the climate of workplace industrial relations at Hotel International. The high profiles of both the director of human resources and the general manager in articulating a style of incorporation have been most important in setting the direction of industrial relations policy, and local management also has significant areas of autonomy about workplace matters. This is most visibly (but not exhaustively) displayed in areas such as decisions about recruitment and termination of wages employees, and negotiations with staff and unions regarding employment conditions and union security.

The level of unionisation at the workplace is over 80 per cent although it varies between the different occupational groups. Whilst this degree of unionisation could provide the basis for a strong shop-floor organisation, this is not the case. There is only one endorsed shop steward and a small non-elected shops committee which is primarily of use by the steward to assist feedback and for some limited organisational activities. The shop steward, in becoming actively involved in local disputes, provides a significant restriction on management decision-making. However, this restriction does not appear to have constrained management in a number of critical areas such as the level of casual employment, management style, retrenchment and dismissal policies, and moving staff into non-award classifications. The major union, in recognising the trend to incorporation, has responded by attempting to raise the union profile, planning to increase the number of delegates, more frequent visits by full-time officials, and proposing to strengthen the shop committee structure in the hotel. The structure of the workforce, the service orientation of the business, and non-conventional working time arrangements all contribute to the texture of industrial relations and help to differentiate the characteristics of this workplace from those found in a typical manufacturing environment. Part of the difference can be attributed to the geography of the workplace: many employees are in much closer contact with the customers than might be expected in a traditional manufacturing plant. This relationship may enhance the quality of working life and therefore improve industrial relations and, as well, it will be essential for the hotel to project an environment where staff are competent and satisfied in their jobs.

The major workplace rules are derived from two principal sources: tribunal decisions and company rules. Tribunal decisions, primarily in the form of awards, provide the baseline with respect to wages and conditions of employment. The award is very prescriptive about pay rates and terms and conditions of employment. The management of the Hotel International would argue that this award represents a significant constraint on their ability to develop a flexible workforce that can meet the pecularities of the hotel industry, and the five-star sector in particular. Penalty rates are cited as an obvious example of this, but other constraints would also include tightly-defined job classifications and inflexible working arrangements.

These perceptions partly explain the hotel's recent moves to upgrade a number of jobs to non-award staff positions. These perceptions also, at least in part, explain the key role played by Hotel International's director of human resources in the industry-level negotiations on award restructuring. That is, for five-star hotels, award restructuring is seen as a possible means of reducing the constraints imposed by the award system.

Nevertheless, whilst the hotel operates within these constraints, the system of conciliation and arbitration has little impact on the day-to-day pattern of industrial relations. From time to time a number of employment conditions are negotiated directly with either individual employees or trade unions. Supplementing these arrangements are company rules which specify requirements about the delivery of service by and conduct of staff. In addition, these rules specify a number of staff benefits such as provision of meals, parking benefits or additional pay. Often these benefits are tied to salaried status, and the practice of rewarding these employees in this way is related to the management's strategy of increasing the number of salaried staff as well as reducing the significance of unions in the company.

In many workplaces the formal industrial relations rules are complemented by a series of informal work rules that have grown out of custom and practice. This kind of work regulation does not appear to be important to Hotel International. Rather, the complaints by Hotel International's management about workplace inefficiency appear to be about the restraint imposed on work organisation by tribunal decisions. Much of management's current thrust in industrial relations is to attempt to make changes to the award via the structural efficiency principles. It appears that the union's perception of the agenda is similar. It sees the key issues as being those arising from management's attempts to reform some of the formal workplace rules such as the removal of penalty rates and the repeal of the agreement about compulsory union membership. This is not to say that there is a total absence of informal work practices; rather they are not seen to be an important determinant of workplace industrial relations.

Hotel International has very few industrial disputes and most of the problems that do emerge are handled internally. Matters of substance which involve questions of award revision are generally handled through the employer association with which the hotel has a close and active involvement. However, the association does not play a significant part in the day-to-day industrial relations of Hotel International.

In the case of the Hotel International it appears that the developments arising from recent tribunal decisions have been co-incidental to the drive for greater efficiency, although these decisions have allowed the process to proceed more smoothly than would normally have been the case.[6] The major impetus for greater efficiency at the Hotel International, and indeed within the whole chain, was the purchase of the International chain by a British-based conglomerate. Following this purchase the Hotel International, under new management, embarked upon a process of reform that would create a more profitable organisation and improve the quality of the product. This approach occurred in some 50 per cent of all hotels in the chain immediately following the takeover. Management attempts to increase efficiency have therefore been independent of, although not unrelated to, the decisions by industrial tribunals.

In conclusion, Hotel International is characterised by high employee morale with corresponding low levels of disputation, absenteeism and labour turnover. Employees appear to have accepted the new corporate culture of the hotel and are prepared to place a significant level of importance in achieving its operational goals. This new culture, developed by the International chain and adopted enthusiastically by local management, has significantly influenced the industrial relations processes and outcomes at this workplace. Clearly, industrial relations at Hotel International differ substantially from that which may exist in the traditional manufacturing establishment and it is therefore not possible to use established models to analyse industrial relations in this hotel nor, we would suspect, the hospitality industry in general.

5 Comel

Background

The plant which is the subject of this case study is located in the eastern suburbs of Melbourne and is one of a number of similar regional establishments of a division of a large firm in the electronic communications industry known as Comel. The others are located in Sydney, Brisbane, Adelaide and Perth. These regional arms overlap somewhat in their range of output, however, they do not compete with each other and tend to specialise in different activities in accordance with the division's national business plan.

The Melbourne plant of Comel emerged in 1987 from the rationalisation and consolidation of three main workshops and a few small stores in the inner metropolitan area of Melbourne following a major reorganisation of the parent company (to be referred to henceforth as the 'corporate body'). Some hundred workers chose to move to other divisions of the corporate body for geographical reasons. No retrenchments occurred. In the year before the move, workforce numbers were allowed to run down with the object of building up staff drawn as much as possible from the new locality.

The activities of the division are wide-ranging—reconditioning, servicing, designing, and manufacturing of equipment and parts for the electronic communications industry. Its main customers are the various divisions of the corporate body, which take as much as 98 per cent of its output. The activities at the Melbourne plant are roughly split evenly between servicing or reconditioning and manufacturing of new products, mostly on a jobbing basis involving a large number of small runs of output. Although the establishment operates in a competitive environment and must submit tenders to the corporate body without any preferential treatment from its parent, in practice it has a competitive advantage in that its potential competitors are not interested in the myriad of small jobs based on old technology which characterises most of the corporate body's demands. By the same token, this activity does not allow economies of scale and high profitability. The opportunity for specialisation on a limited range of products and supplying the communications market generally is limited by the extent to which the plant is required to meet its primary role to service the needs of the corporate body. In that sense, the division is more accurately an 'in-house' establishment of the corporate body rather than a completely independent enterprise. This is despite the reorganisation of the corporate body in 1988 and the development of a new corporate strategy which included decentralisation of management and competition. It is relevant to note in this connection that the division forms a comparatively small and ancillary part of the corporate body's total operations in the communications industry.

Following the reorganisation of the corporate body and greater emphasis being given to service to the customer, competition and productivity, the financial performance of the plant has improved. These commercial pressures, together with award restructuring, have added tension to industrial relations. However, as discussed later, the incidence of industrial disputes has actually fallen since the move to the new plant location.

The physical work environment at the Melbourne plant is good— spacious and attractive and generally considered to be a great improvement on the earlier workshops. There were initial problems with lighting and heating but these appear to have been overcome. The layout of the workplace is appropriate to the various functional areas— production, maintenance, design, storage, administrative offices, and cafeteria.

The organisational chart shown in Figure 5.1 outlines the present formal structure of the workplace and the lines of authority. There are seven managers of functional areas who report to the plant manager. The devolution of operational responsibility down the line is reflected in the chart.

The overall size of the workforce is about 560. Some 350 are in the production area and are made up of the electronics and mechanical/artisan groups. The rest perform administrative, clerical, cleaning, commercial, and engineering functions. The total workforce, broken down into designations as at the middle of 1989, is outlined in Table 5.1.

Figure 5.1 Plant Managerial Structure

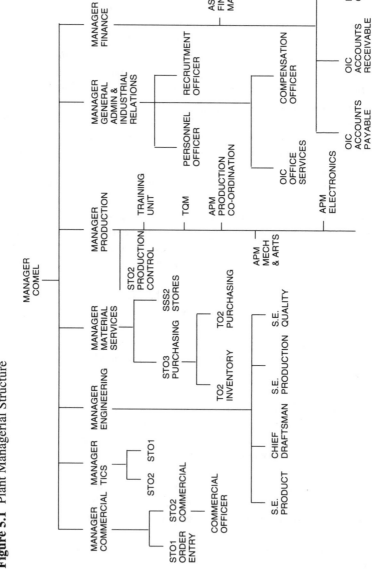

Table 5.1 Plant Workforce

Artisan	163
Building services	19
District management	1
Drafting	14
Engineer	9
Production and other	129
Storeman	31
Technical	108
Trainee	36
Transport	2
Administrative	49
Total	561

The majority of the production workers are female. The ethnic composition of the workforce includes Greeks, various Arabic speakers, Mauritians, and Maltese. A single shift operates for all except for a handful of the workforce. Recently, two shifts were introduced in the metal fabrication section, affecting some eight tradespersons and second-class tradespersons, to overcome the excessive overtime which was both unpopular with employees and costly for the establishment. The production staff work a nine-day fortnight from 7.30 a.m. to 4.15 p.m. Every second Monday is a rostered-day-off for all except administrative, clerical, and management staff, who are on flexi-time.

The plant is covered by fifteen Federal awards, most workers being affected by more than one award. As a matter of employer policy, no over-award payments or standards are granted. This has caused difficulty from time to time in retaining and recruiting skilled workers in competition with other employers. However, it is expected that award restructuring currently being negotiated will provide greater flexibility, and be more attractive to employees.

For the period from May 1989 to April 1990, 100 work care claims were made, on which liability was admitted in ninety-four cases. The accident frequency rate was slightly above target for most months of this period. No figures were kept of (unauthorised) absentee rates but it was estimated at about 8 per cent per month. Total staff wastage varied between four and sixteen people per month; the total for the 12-month period being 100, or about 18 per cent.

Data on the number of employees and their average pay at April 1990 for the different groups is contained in Table 5.2.

Table 5.2   Employees' Average Pay

Number of Employees		Group	Average Pay $
8		Engineers	39,733
115		Technical	31,327
16		Drafting	31,117
57		Administrative	29,255
173		Artisan	22,900
27		Stores	21,776
114		Production	21,616
32		Trainee	20,314
17		Building services	18,724
559	Total	Average	25,167

Trade apprentices follow the normal procedure of on-the-job and formal class training at TAFE. Training and retraining arrangements of the non-trade skills are conducted on the job as and when necessary. In some instances, training packages are contracted with companies or TAFE to facilitate the introduction of new equipment.

Considerable emphasis has been given to 'quality' training under the direction of specialist instructors. At first Quality Circles, and later Total Quality Management techniques, were used in training lower and middle management. Under the latter, first line supervisors and above from various areas of the establishment are brought together to engage in problem-solving exercises and to discuss issues relevant to improved performance over a period of seven days. Also, short residential team-building courses involving this level of management have been conducted for groups of fifteen to twenty. Underlying these 'quality' training exercises is the objective of promoting a culture for change and improving workplace morale in line with a program commenced by the corporate body in 1984. Unions have generally not been enthusiastic about this program and regard it as a waste of money and a threat to the loyalty of workers to their unions.

The importance of training at various levels to promote efficiency and harmony at the workplace is recognised by management, which freely admits that there is not enough training for developing supervisory skills, in particular interpersonal skills. Training of middle management in industrial relations conducted by the corporate body is infrequent, and often staff cannot be spared to attend such courses. The low incidence of industrial disputes may be related to what is described as a 'common sense' approach to industrial relations.

The technology in use ranges from basic 1950s-type technology applied by the mechanical/artisan group, to most recent technological advances used by the electronic group. The standard of technology used is driven by the needs of the customer—other divisions of the corporate body—and the nature and volume of the products demanded. Because of the small-scale jobbing nature of most orders (there were some 800 orders extant at the time the study was undertaken), it is in most cases not economically efficient to use ultra-modern technology which calls for large-scale production. However, in some smaller 'hi-tech' projects, the establishment has a competitive edge against other firms.

The technological innovations that have been introduced have not resulted in retrenchments or redundancies. Those displaced from particular areas have been absorbed elsewhere in the establishment, usually with a little retraining. No demarcation problems or serious resistance from unions and employees have occurred in introducing new technology. Nor has there been a significant change in the employment profile as a result of new technology despite the displacement of lesser-skilled process workers by a smaller number of more skilled workers operating sophisticated electronic equipment. On the other hand, some resistance was encountered to the organisational changes arising from the rationalisation and consolidation of the three Melbourne workshops into a single establishment.

Management

Relationship with the corporate body

The management structure was outlined earlier. Every functional manager is responsible for the performance of each area but there is a policy of devolving operational responsibility as far as possible down the line. The costs of each area are analysed and incorporated in monthly and annual reports to the corporate body, forming the basis of an internal feed-back mechanism.

In considering managerial operations, it is useful to distinguish between policy formulation including the setting down of guidelines, the implementation of such policy, and an accountability system which facilitates a regular evaluation of the performance of the enterprise.

For some years, a devolution of operational responsibility and decision-making has taken place progressively to the various divisions within the corporate body. This included the devolution of responsibility for operating industrial relations and human resources management. However, as noted earlier, the devolution on the production side is restricted by the requirement to service the needs of certain other divisions. Productive efficiency is reflected in financial returns and cost performance which are regularly reported to the corporate body as part of the accountability process.

In respect of industrial relations and human resource management, the autonomy of the establishment is circumscribed by centrally determined policy laid down in guidelines and by awards. These awards reflect the input of the corporate body in proceedings before the Industrial Relations Commission. The implementation of the guidelines and awards in the day-to-day operations of the workplace is the responsibility of the plant manager and those entrusted by him lower down the line at the establishment; and their performance is monitored both by the division head office and by the corporate body through regular reporting by the plant manager.

The operational authority and responsibility of plant management is therefore constrained by policy and rules, and accountability requirements imposed by the corporate body. Further, while the establishment is free to obtain independent legal advice and run its own cases in civil law and compensation matters, any case which is likely to affect other divisions must be referred to the corporate body. The views of local management in industrial relations may influence the policy of the corporate body. But decisions on policy are made centrally.

Thus, in essence, the change from earlier days is that there is less need to refer matters for decision by either the division or the corporate body: greater responsibility and accountability for the *operation* of the enterprise has been devolved to the establishment subject to policy, rules, and accountability requirements prescribed by the corporate body.

The managerial personnel

Managerial personnel are appointed on a continuing basis rather than on a contract for a specified term. Pay is based on a particular level of appointment and not on a specific position; this allows flexibility between different positions. There are corporate plans afoot for executive-level management to be appointed on a contract basis at market-related salaries.

The plant manager is a professional engineer with long service with the corporate body. Some of the functional managers have moved up the line with experience in their particular areas. Others have been brought in from outside. The industrial relations manager has been with the parent company for twelve years and in his present position for eight years. Middle management is drawn from the lower supervisory levels and the latter mostly from the shop floor. More recently, in order to widen the choice of lower supervisory staff, recruitment has been extended outside the establishment. This move was opposed by some of the unions who declined management's offer to participate on selection panels.

Although the day-to-day responsibility for the operation of human resource management and industrial relations rests on the industrial relations manager, the philosophy of the plant manager sets the tone generally on industrial relations matters. He is known as a 'no-nonsense' man who departed from the more indulgent approach of earlier managers. Although not regarded with affection by the unions who view him as a hard-liner on industrial relations matters, he is respected as a person. Since he took over as plant manager in 1985, the number of disputes has fallen markedly. While it would be difficult to attribute this mainly to him, because other factors such as the move to new premises were operating, his influence cannot be excluded from any explanation about the reduced incidence of disputes. He keeps a keen eye on industrial matters, spending an average of between half and one hour a day on them, mostly being briefed on the subject by the industrial relations manager rather than being directly involved in them. While having an open-door policy for employees and union delegates, he is a strong believer in devolution, intervening directly only when potentially serious disputes are not resolved lower down the line. The functional managers see him individually as and when necessary; and *ad hoc* meetings of managers are called when issues arise for discussion. This may occur two or three times a week.

At managerial level, the only person with specialist training in industrial relations is the manager, general administration and industrial relations, who is assisted by specialists in personnel, worker's compensation and office services. The implementation of guidelines prescribed by the corporate body and awards are under his direction. He is effectively the day-to-day source of advice for those who make decisions on routine industrial relations matters down the line. Apart from being accountable to the plant manager for industrial relations generally, the industrial relations manager is responsible for:

- maintaining employee records,
- maintaining and communicating award information,
- administration of earnings,
- worker's compensation claims,
- chairing the Health and Safety Committee, a standing body consisting of equal union and management representatives, which advises the plant manager on the resolution of particular problems as they arise,
- framing policy on induction of new employees in accordance with corporate guidelines for implementation by the training officer.

There is a great deal of informal communication and interaction on a daily basis between the industrial relations manager and other functional managers. This is facilitated by the comparatively small size of the plant and by the personalities involved.

Although some of the union officials regard the industrial relations manager as essentially the mouthpiece of the plant manager, we have an impression of soundness and competence in the industrial relations manager's approach to industrial relations. The low level of disputes may partly reflect the way industrial relations matters are handled.

The other functional managers are more immediately responsible for, among other things:

- the daily allocation of tasks,
- dealing with shop stewards in their particular areas,
- dealing with grievances not resolved lower down the line,
- discipline and termination,
- day-to-day training requirements,
- promotions and upgrading of those two or more levels below them.

Management operations

Much of the direct day-to-day dealings with employees fall on first- and second-line supervisors who make decisions which have industrial relations implications and who act as the first stage in the (at present) informal grievance procedure. The more difficult decisions are referred up to middle management.

It appears that, apart from the industrial relations manager, other management personnel, and especially those at middle and lower levels, have not attended the training courses in industrial relations designed and conducted by the corporate body. Work pressures and the timing of such courses have prevented their attendance. Nevertheless, there is a belief expressed by management that a 'common sense' approach is the essential feature of successful industrial relations management. This belief is probably sustained by the absence of any major disputes for some years, possibly the result of improved working conditions and good management, but also because of the absence of union militancy. Day-to-day industrial harmony depends more significantly on the selection of lower level management personnel with good inter-personal skills rather than on industrial relations courses. Grievances have arisen in a number of cases because such personnel, while having technical skills, may not have shown adequate human relations skills. Selection and training processes may need to give more attention to these skills.

A point worthy of special mention is that management, even those in middle and higher levels, are members of unions to which those they manage may belong. There is no corporate attempt to discourage such membership. However, in a number of cases supervisors and middle managers are also shop stewards. This results from shop stewards who are promoted to the management line not relinquishing shop stewardship. On its face, such a dual role presents risks of conflict of loyalties. Indeed, in one case which occurred in 1989, the supervisor concerned appeared to give primacy to his shop steward role, resulting in his dismissal. (He was later reinstated on appeal.) On the other hand, some of the managers interviewed claim that on worker grievances, supervisors can act as speedy mediators and assist in resolving issues before they become heated. The unions regard many of their supervisor members as staunch and helpful unionists.

The Melbourne plant is a member of the Metal Trades Industry Association (MTIA). But because it is not a respondent to the Metal Industries Award, advice on award matters, representation in proceedings before tribunals and advice generally on industrial relations are not sought from MTIA. Contact with MTIA is minimal and is virtually confined to participation in certain training courses organised by MTIA.

Overall, management at various levels appears to be satisfied with the policy and guidelines on industrial relations and the way they are being administered. There was some dissatisfaction with the corporate body in the early stages of reorganisation when various responsibilities were devolved from that body at some speed and with little help in training for adjustment. But the establishment has now adjusted to its new responsibilities and has a good working relationship both with the division head office and with the corporate body. The prevailing view is that there is about the right amount of importance given to industrial relations matters; that the processing of grievances should be more structured; and that more training in industrial relations and human resource management should be given to managerial personnel.

Trade unions

The workforce of about 560 is represented by seven unions, all of which are occupational in form. The largest union, with a membership of 350, covers production workers (185), technical staff (100) and some trade staff (sixty-five); other unions with significant membership cover draughting and technical employees (fifty members), stores (sixty members) and clerical employees (thirty members); the remaining three unions cover specialised craftsmen and have only a handful of members in the plant. Although the coverage of some of the unions overlaps, this has not been a source of tension or open disputation. Union membership is generally encouraged and information about unions forms part of the induction briefing. There is, however, no closed shop or preference. Overall union density is estimated at about 90 per cent. Check-off is applied for a charge of 2.5 per cent of union dues.

The various unions are represented in the establishment by shop stewards elected by their members. Their numbers are recorded in Table 5.3.

Table 5.3   Number of Shop Stewards

Production/Technical	8	(2 women, 1 non-Anglo-Saxon immigrant)
Draughting	4	
Stores	1	(non-Anglo-Saxon immigrant)
Clerical	1	

Shop steward elections are rarely contested. Despite the large proportion of immigrants and women eligible for election, very few are willing to nominate for shop stewardship. Since the move to the new plant, the turnover of shop stewards has been high partly because of the loss of long-standing stewards in the move and because of the high turnover of the more skilled workers. In most cases, the present shop stewards have held office for from one to three years, but an exceptional case is one who has been a shop steward for eight years.

Shop stewards generally handle the complaints of their members, mostly about pay discrepancies, health and safety issues, and worker's compensation. They are given adequate opportunity to contact members during work time. Except when special and contentious issues arise (e.g. RSI, reorganisation), shop stewards spend between one and three hours a week attending to members' needs.

A majority of stewards had attended a training course, such as those organised by the Trade Union Training Authority. A number, however, had not participated in such courses and, overall, stewards appeared to have little interest in training.

The Combined Union Shop Committee, which was active in earlier times, has gone into decline, coming to life spasmodically to promote issues of common interest (e.g. car parking, ID-cards). Inter-personal difficulties and apathy militate against an active committee. Management is divided on the usefulness of the committee. Some regard it as a valuable means of co-ordinated discussion; others see it as a potential source of militancy.

The lack of interest by shop stewards in the Combined Union Shop Committee is parallelled by a general lack of interest in establishing a joint management–union consultative standing committee holding regular meetings. One *ad hoc* joint meeting was held in 1989 involving only the production–technical union. A joint working party on the implementation of award restructuring has been formed consisting of management representatives and shop stewards from the production–technical and draughting unions; but at the time of writing the working party had not met.

The overall impression is that the union presence, as reflected in the activities of shop stewards, is not one of enthusiasm and energy. It may be that pay, working conditions, and management performance are generally satisfactory, and there is no real wish among the rank and file for shop steward militancy. It may also be that the dual role of supervisor–shop steward has been a moderating force.

The participation of members in union business appears to be minimal. The production/technical union, by virtue of its numbers, is exceptional in having a plant-based sub-branch. The periodic sub-branch meetings held at lunch-time attract between thirty and a hundred out of a membership of 350. Apart from general union business and the election of office-bearers of the sub-branch, the agenda has also included local issues related to the plant. As for the other unions, when issues arise for resolution by the members a lunch-time meeting may be called, usually attended by union organisers. In the case of stop-work meetings authorised by management (e.g. to deal with award restructuring), an extension of thirty-five minutes beyond the lunch break is allowed on company time. Four such meetings occurred in 1989. There were two unauthorised stop-work meetings in 1989—one in connection with the dismissal of a supervisor–shop steward, and another called by one union, in connection with award restructuring.

The involvement of branch officials in plant-level affairs is mostly by shop stewards seeking advice by telephone. Normally, organisers are expected to visit the plant once a year, but when issues crop up which cannot be resolved locally or need official explanations (e.g. award restructuring), union officials are drawn into local negotiations or attendance at stop-work meetings. The impending visit of branch officials is communicated to the management, usually the industrial relations manager, as a matter of courtesy.

Bargaining processes and issues

Both the range of issues over which bargaining has taken place and the processes through which bargaining has been conducted have been, in the post-1987 era, quite limited. In one sense this is not surprising given that the division is part of a larger organisation which has traditionally conducted negotiations with trade unions at a centralised level. This central control of key industrial relations areas, such as wages, has continued despite the general devolution of managerial authority (noted earlier) within the corporate body to the divisional level. For example, the corporate body's *Personnel and Industrial Relations Guidelines and Procedures*—all three volumes—constrain divisional activities. In addition, plant managers are also subject to divisional policies and guidelines. Despite this top-heavy control, a number of issues over which bargaining might have occurred has arisen in the normal day-to-day worklife of the plant. In this section, we focus on these issues and on the processes through which they were resolved. We commence with a brief outline of formal bargaining processes.

Although many stewards were unaware of its existence, a formal procedural agreement, the Employee Complaint Settlement Process, has been negotiated between the corporate body and all unions (see Appendix to this chapter). This document is a fairly standard settlement process outlining the various stages through which an employee complaint may be pursued. The procedure ranges from the initial step of discussions between the employee(s) and the immediate supervisor, to the fourth and final step which provides for negotiations between 'the representative of the employer and the federal body of the staff organisation'. Neither conciliation nor arbitration is part of the agreement although, presumably, the awards allow matters to be taken to the Commission for resolution. Issues related to discipline and health and safety could also be regarded as subject to procedural agreements. A corporation-wide procedure covers the areas of discipline and dismissal. At the peak of this procedure is the Disciplinary Appeals Board, a three-person board chaired by an individual from outside the corporation, which possesses the authority to vary and indeed rescind any disciplinary penalties including dismissal. In 1987, an Occupational Health and Safety Committee was established in the plant. The terms of reference of this committee are fairly wide although, as discussed below in relation to a dispute over poor lighting in the production area, its effectiveness must be queried.

Management has attempted to introduce a formal, all-encompassing grievance procedure at the plant level but, in the words of the production/technical union sub-branch president, his union 'won't have a bar of it'. This absence of an accepted formal mechanism has, as is discussed later, allowed management to unilaterally determine a number of issues, such as changing job technology.

Inevitably, given the non-existence of a formal mechanism, an informal substitute has evolved. Both unions and management are clear as to their preferred first step in this informal procedure: direct discussions between the employee and the supervisor. Occasionally however, for reasons such as language difficulties or employee preferences, the steward may take part in these initial discussions. The second and later stages can differ substantially from issue to issue, largely depending on the particular issue and the preferences of the steward. As a general rule, and where the issue is relatively minor, the steward will go directly to the source most likely to resolve the issue. For example, disputes over incorrect salary payments would be taken directly to the pay office. In at least one dispute over heating in the factory, a steward bypassed management and liaised directly with maintenance employees. This informal system extends up to the plant manager who claims to maintain an open-door policy. However, he does insist that issues are discussed with lower-level management prior to his involvement. In practice most issues seem to be resolved at the lower to middle levels of management. This range of choices available to stewards is enhanced by the fact that, traditionally, a number of senior stewards were, and some still are, also supervisors. For example, the production/technical union sub-branch president is a senior supervisor. Such stewards possessed a keen sense of how best to resolve a problem and also, in many cases, the ability to leave their work station without permission in an attempt to resolve an issue. In general, management supports this strategy and is not averse to stewards spending 'an hour or so a week' on union duties. In at least one case, however, management took disciplinary action against a steward who, it was claimed, spent too much time on her union functions. This action culminated in her dismissal, a decision which on appeal to the Disciplinary Appeals Board was amended to a job transfer to another division of the corporate body.

In cases where the stewards cannot resolve issues themselves, two further avenues are open to them. In the last few years this is increasingly the case due to turnover of experienced stewards, or where the issues are of some importance. The first option, the internal option, is to raise the issue within the sub-branch, or alternatively within the Combined Union Stewards Committee. As noted earlier, however, this Committee has become virtually defunct and use of the sub-branch structure is not conducive to a quick resolution of the issue. Accordingly, the practice which has developed is a degree of informal consultation between stewards, and in particular between individual stewards and the president of the sub-branch. This has resulted in the President being involved in most industrial relations issues, including those involving unions other than the production/technical union. The relatively high turnover of stewards has also increased the importance of this advice-giving role of the President. The second option, the external option, is to seek advice and, if necessary, call in a full-time union organiser. Full-time officials indicated that this is an option which they are not keen to encourage, preferring the stewards to settle local matters.

Prior to 1985 it could be argued that such an informal, flexible system of resolving problems kept open a range of options for both stewards and management. And this is still quite a valid view given the traditionally cordial management–union relationship. In the post-1985 period, however, and under a new management with a brief to 'fix up' the Melbourne plant, the lack of a formal, local negotiation structure has allowed management to exercise a substantial degree of unilateral decision-making on a variety of industrial relations issues. This decision-making is, of course, subject to corporate guidelines and within the framework of awards. In effect, where the issues are substantial, negotiations take place between management and full-time officials; however, where issues are not important enough to warrant full-time official involvement, management attempts to impose change unilaterally. Frequently, because of both the lack of local negotiating forums and a strong, shop-floor union organisation, management is successful in these attempts. In the words of one senior management figure, 'they let us get away with a lot'.

Perhaps the best way to illustrate the respective roles of the parties is to briefly outline how some substantial issues were resolved. The main issue in the post-1985 period was the relocation of the various workplaces in the inner Melbourne suburbs to one location in the eastern suburbs. Not unexpectedly, the implications of this move were the subject of quite lengthy negotiations between management and full-time union officials, resulting in a twelve-month relocation allowance. Subsequently, and following the appointment of a new production manager, full-time officials were again involved in negotiating a major organisational change, although their interests focused fairly narrowly on threatened job declassifications or staff cuts. Unions and stewards were not, however, consulted on 'local' issues such as the introduction of new technology in 1988 or the issue of quality circles or total quality management. Similarly the introduction of a second shift in late 1989 was not negotiated with unions although, as indicated earlier, this affected only a small number of employees. Other items of traditional managerial prerogative which come under union challenge in some factories, such as the allocation of overtime, are also solely the domain of management at Comel.

Overall, therefore, the range and number of issues over which bargaining takes place are fairly limited and are usually issues of substance which draw in full-time union officials. An informal system of resolving individual grievances also exists. Issues which fall between these two levels are largely determined by management. Only a very few such managerial decisions draw an industrial response from the workforce.

Industrial action

There has been relatively little overt industrial conflict at the plant over the last two years. One manager regarded the plant as being 'pretty tame industrially'. The disputes which have occurred have been fairly minor and, in most instances, have not led to any loss of production. No strikes have taken place at the plant. Over the twelve months to February 1990, however, 1535 hours were lost through industrial disputes, mainly stop-work meetings—an average of about 2.75 hours per employee per annum. Working conditions, dismissals and an attempt to introduce identity cards were the main causes of these minor disputes.

The new plant was not a 'greenfields' site; rather, the corporation purchased the plant and attempted to modify the factory to suit its production needs. Some teething problems were probably inevitable. However, problems with lighting and heating continued beyond what the employees considered a reasonable time. Ultimately, the issue of lighting on the production floor led to a walkout by employees. Management responded by hiring consultants and experimenting with different systems but, as late as 1989, still 'hadn't quite got it right'. Along similar lines, levels of heating in the office block were a frequent source of complaint by clerical staff. Finally, the staff staged a walkout on a day when no heating at all was available and, because of a rostered day off for the production workers, no maintenance staff were available to resolve the problem. These two issues were frequently discussed at the meetings of the joint Occupational Health and Safety Committee. The inability of discussions in this forum to resolve these issues has lowered the status of the Committee in the estimation of shop stewards. Two managerial edicts on working conditions caused some degree of employee dissatisfaction which did not, however, result in any overt conflict: no smoking in the plant and no eating in the workplace outside the canteen. The edicts do not appear to have been totally accepted by the workforce and policing varies from section to section.

A number of dismissals of employees had the potential to cause industrial conflict. The dismissal of a locksmith in 1985 led to a stop-work meeting and a 'walk-off' for the rest of the day by all members of the main union. This action contributed to the employee being given another job within the corporate body—a job arranged by the plant assistant manager, according to one shop steward.

Two further dismissals also caused industrial action. In April 1987 a shop steward was charged by management with unauthorised absence from the workplace. Her defence was that she was absent on union duties; ultimately, she was fined $20. Management believed that the steward was spending too much time on union duties and certainly far more than they regarded as a reasonable time. In May, her union applied to the corporate body for the steward to be released to perform work in the branch office connected with a specific campaign. Management refused the union's request, claiming that the steward could not be released due to a backlog of work in her section. On June 2, the union sub-branch met and requested the Victorian branch to call a stop-work meeting of all sub-branch members. It recommended that the State executive direct the steward off the job. This recommendation was put to a stop-work meeting at the plant on 5 June and was overwhelmingly carried. The meeting also voted to undertake a campaign of industrial action commencing the following Monday. This action was suspended when management indicated they were willing to meet with the union to discuss the issue of industrial relations at the plant. However, that meeting never took place. Subsequently, after being directed off the job, the steward was charged on a further two occasions, the first time being fined $40, the second time being dismissed. On appeal, the steward was reinstated by the Disciplinary Appeals Board to a similar-level job within the corporate body but outside the division. Subsequently, this steward became a full-time industrial officer with the Victorian Branch of the union and, among other duties, assumed responsibility for industrial relations at the division plant. Consequently, she was the full-time union representative involved in discussions over the dismissal of another union activist.

The individual dismissed in June 1989 was the president of the production/technical union sub-branch. For a variety of reasons, including his experience and outspokenness, this individual was quite clearly the public face of unionism in the plant. The dismissal arose from his actions, in his supervisory capacity, of sending employees home early on an extremely hot summer day. Ultimately management decided that his action, when viewed in conjunction with previous problems, warranted dismissal. The union responded with a stop-work meeting which was also supported by most of the other unions. Between 250 and 300 employees participated in the meeting but, after voting to condemn management's action, voted against a recommendation to not return to work. Possibly they were swayed by the argument advanced from the floor of the meeting that this was a matter for the Disciplinary Appeals Board. Ultimately, the Board ordered that the employee be reinstated in his old job.

In many ways, the ID-card dispute is illustrative of the industrial relations processes at the Melbourne plant. Management unilaterally decided that all staff should wear a personal identity card which included a photograph. Security reasons were advanced as the main rationale. These cards could also be used to record the start and finish of work times. The suspicion or rumour quickly spread that these cards would also be used to record the length of time each employee spent doing a particular job. This threat of personal performance monitoring led to informal meetings of members of the clerical union who decided not to wear the cards but also not to tell management of their decision. They also supported the concept of a 'go-slow and general non-cooperation' should management introduce such monitoring. Stewards from the production/technical union supported this action. It also appears that a substantial number of employees conveniently 'lost' their ID-card. Finally, management assured the unions that it would not seek to use these cards for monitoring purposes prior to discussions with the unions. Subsequently, management has not sought such an outcome and, indeed, does not police the wearing of cards.

In addition to these three areas which caused some low levels of conflict, a sectional claim for a particular allowance by painters led to some minor action.

Conclusions

Several points emerge from this study which call for special emphasis.

The importance of the Federal industrial tribunal in shaping the processes and outcomes of industrial relations at the establishment is evident from the comprehensive award coverage of all employees. As a matter of corporate policy, the pay and conditions prescribed by these awards are strictly adhered to and no over-award payments are made. This sometimes puts the establishment at a disadvantage, particularly in the recruitment and retention of more skilled personnel in a labour market in which over-award standards are common. However, at the time this study was being conducted, the recruitment problem had eased greatly. The viability of award pay and conditions is reflected in the lower overall turnover rate compared to manufacturing industry generally, and in the low level of industrial action on pay and conditions. The rate of absenteeism was also not a matter of serious concern.

Based on the material available to us, it is not possible to say what effect adherence to award conditions has had on the establishment's efficiency. More positively, the implementation of the Commission's Restructuring and Efficiency Principle of March 1987 and the Structural Efficiency Principle of August 1988 has provided both management and unions with the need to negotiate for more efficient work and management practices as a basis for pay increases. The overall outcome of these developments cannot be measured at this stage and a longer period will be needed for the developments to work through the enterprise. However, independently of the Commission, the recent corporate restructuring has produced pressure for greater efficiency at the workplace, and has resulted in greater decentralisation of operational responsibility, and the drive for greater competitiveness.

Despite substantial devolution of operational responsibility from the corporate body to the divisional level, the autonomy of management is heavily qualified. The range of products which are produced is largely determined by the requirements of other divisions of the corporate body which take up the bulk of the establishment's output. On industrial relations matters, all the awards covering the establishment are the result of the corporate body's direct involvement in negotiations and arbitration before an industrial tribunal. It is important to note that the awards covering the various regional establishments of the division also cover other divisions of the corporate body. In the interest of consistency and avoidance of comparability flow-ons, centralisation in the making of agreements and awards is necessary if only because the same unions are covered in the different divisions of the corporate body. The corporate body's guidelines on human resource management, reflecting corporate policy, form the basis of day-to-day operations at the workplace. The discipline imposed by the accountability process of regular reports to the corporate body ensures that corporate policy on industrial relations and human resource management is adhered to. Thus operational flexibility provided by the devolution of responsibility operates in the context of corporate policy and accountability requirements: it is a case of 'flexibility within a centralised system'.

The appointment of a new plant manager in 1985 resulted in a different managerial approach to industrial relations within the plant. Previous plant managers had accorded a significant role to trade unions, and particularly to the production union, within the workplace. The new manager preferred to emphasise employee relations at the expense of industrial relations; he has encouraged the view that day-to-day issues and problems relating to the workplace should be discussed and resolved directly between employees and appropriate managers, rather than by involving an 'external' third party (a trade union). However, despite an attempt by the corporate body to develop a corporate culture, no concerted attempt has been made to imbue the plant workforce with this unitarist philosophy. Given such factors as the high union density rate and the corporate policy of encouraging union membership, such a strategy would have been too ambitious. Rather the local management's thrust has focused on convincing lower and middle managers—most of whom are union members and, indeed, some of whom are shop stewards—that their allegiance should lie with the corporation rather than with their trade union. This development has created some degree of ongoing tension within these managerial ranks.

Although the workforce is heavily unionised the plant-level union organisation is relatively inactive. The Combined Union Shop Committee is virtually moribund, turnover of stewards is high and elections for these positions are very rare, and sub-branch meetings of the dominant union are poorly attended. Overall, interest and participation in their union of rank and file membership appears minimal. There are, of course, occasional spurts of activism centred around a particular issue but such involvement is both unusual and infrequent. Accordingly, what union activism does exist is restricted to a small minority and, in particular, to a few senior stewards. Given this context, management, by and large, operates the workplace relatively free from trade union constraints. This is not to claim that managerial prerogative goes unchallenged. Rather it is to claim that with few exceptions and within limits, rights, duties and obligations imposed by national agreements and awards, management is the dominant influence in the plant workplace industrial relations.

Appendix

Employee Complaint Settlement Process
If an employee has a complaint arising out of an official instruction or from any other cause the following procedures shall apply:
(a) A complaint shall first be discussed by the concerned employee(s) with the immediate supervisor.
(b) Any complaint not settled under (a) above shall be discussed between the employee(s) and the supervisor or more senior line management. The employee(s) may wish to be accompanied by an accredited staff organisation representative or have the union represent the case to management.
(c) If the matter is not resolved, it shall be further discussed between the Branch Secretary of the staff organisation (or representative) and the appropriate Regional/Branch Manager or nominee.
(d) If the matter cannot be resolved at that level, it shall then be discussed between the representative of the employer and the federal body of the staff organisation.
(e) Sensible time limits shall be allowed for the completion of various stages of the discussions. Unless otherwise agreed by the parties, at least 7 days should be allowed for all stages of discussion to be finalised.
(f) Throughout all stages of the procedures, all relevant facts shall

be clearly identified and recorded and provided to the individual.

(g)   Until the matter is settled, the employee shall, so far as possible, carry out any instruction given him/her until it is countermanded by proper authority. No individual shall be prejudiced as to the final settlement by the continuance of work.

6 Automakers

Background to the case

Automakers, which began operations in Australia in 1925, is part of a multinational enterprise that is divided into three main operating groups worldwide: vehicle manufacturing, diversified products (including aerospace and glass) and financial services (being the second largest credit provider in its home country). Within the vehicle manufacturing group there are two main geographical divisions: the home country and overseas. The overseas division is further divided into three parts: Europe, Latin America and Asia-Pacific. The Australian company is part of the Asia-Pacific group. Other separate entities within that group are New Zealand, Taiwan, Korea, and Japan, although there are no manufacturing facilities in either Korea or Japan. Within Asia-Pacific, all companies are self-contained profit centres. Each company submits an annual business plan and budget to the President of the Asia-Pacific group, who then refers it to the head of the Overseas Division. Product development for the Asia-Pacific region is located in Australia. The Asia-Pacific regional office is currently located in Melbourne but is in the process of moving to Tokyo. The organisation of the world-wide operations is represented in Figure 6.1 (page 149).

The first assembly plant in Australia was established in Victoria, and the Sydney operations began eleven years later in 1936. A company publication on the 50th anniversary of the NSW assembly plant in Sydney gives a flavour of the early years:

> Assembly operations began ... on 17th March 1936, without any fanfare, as Australia was still in the grip of a depression. Employees numbered 386, only 6 of whom were female. The plant was run by a superintendent and one foreman in charge of production ... Employees were hired (or

fired) by the hour, the rate being 1s/10d per hour. For a 44 hour week you were paid £4. There were two models built at that time, a V8 De Luxe Sedan (£389) and a 10 Horsepower sedan (£289) . . . Production in the early days was approximately 15 cars per day.

Figure 6.1 Organisation of Automakers World-wide

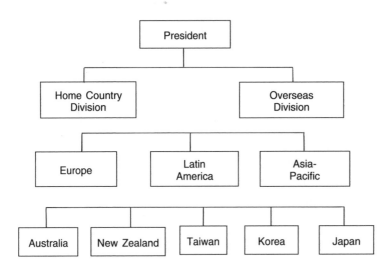

The organisational structure of the Australian company has remained fairly stable for the past twenty years. Initially, the company was organised around state branches, each with its own assembly plant. This changed when the Victorian plant was built in 1959 and plants in Adelaide and Perth were phased out. The state branches then became regional sales offices and plant managers reported to the director of manufacturing. The organisational structure of the company is set out in Figure 6.2 (page 150).

The number of employees in the company has varied in recent years but is currently approximately 12 000. The majority is based in Victoria at two locations. At one site there are some 5000 employees engaged in manufacturing and product engineering. At the main Victorian plant, however, where the head office is located, there are approximately 5500 employees working in the major assembly plant, truck plant, plastics plant, and national parts depot. The company also has smaller assembly plants in Sydney (900 employees) and in Brisbane (400 employees).

Figure 6.2   Organisation of Automakers in Australia

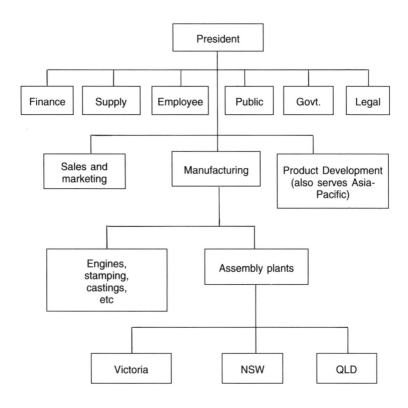

A large proportion of the workforce was born overseas and many do not speak English as their first language. In all, over fifty nationalities are represented and this is an important feature of the workforce at all the assembly plants including that in Sydney. Courses in English, some of which are available in work time, are an important component of the company's employee training and development program. According to the 1988 annual report almost three times the amount of money recommended by the federal government was spent on training during that year. Some 1280 structured courses were conducted and their content ranged from engineering and technological skills to basic report and letter writing. Induction and initial training are highly intensive and can take up to seven weeks.

The company is also the largest private employer of apprentices in Victoria.

For a significant proportion of the workforce who were born not only outside Australia, but in countries where industrialisation is relatively recent, unionism and collective resistance to management often takes a different form. This is particularly the case for workers of Asian origin, who comprise an increasingly large segment of the workforce. Thus, especially at the Sydney plant, high levels of union activity at the shop-floor would appear difficult to sustain and the ethnic composition of the workforce is rather more conducive to the formation of direct links between workers and the company. However, it should be acknowledged that the Sydney plant has had stable industrial relations over a long period of time, supported by close links between the company and the main union. Evidence of these links is provided by the number of plant-specific agreements covering matters such as rehabilitation, shift work, and drug and alcohol abuse.

The workforce is highly unionised. The Vehicle Builders Employees Federation (VBEF) has a closed shop agreement covering production activities and covers 85 per cent of the blue-collar workforce. The other major unions for blue-collar workers are the Metal and Engineering Workers' Union (MEWU), the Federation of Industrial, Manufacturing and Engineering Employees (FIMEE) and the Electrical Trades Union of Australia (ETU). Approximately 50 per cent of the white-collar employees are unionised and are members of two unions: the Federated Clerks' Union of Australia (FCU) and the Association of Draughting, Supervisory and Technical Employees (ADSTE). The company has had two major disputes in recent decades but otherwise the industrial relations climate has been relatively stable.

The nature of the product market has been highly influential in shaping the company's strategies. It is one of five vehicle manufacturers in Australia, but competition for the domestic market extends well beyond these companies to include manufacturers from all over the world. Furthermore, under the Federal government's plans for the industry, the levels of protection for the domestic industry will continue to be lowered so that competition from overseas will become more intense. Thus, decreased costs of production and increased vehicle quality are essential to the company's profitability with increasing emphasis being placed upon the latter in recent years. Indeed, it is planned that the new model sports car currently being assembled in Victoria will be of sufficient quality to compete successfully in its price range on at least one major overseas market.

The company has held a very strong market position for some years now and profitability has continued to improve accordingly. This period of dominance has paralleled the tenure of one particular president who emphasised the need to improve industrial relations (through the introduction of the Employee Involvement program) as well as the necessity to raise quality and the image of the company in Australia.

Employee relations (ER) in Automakers

The company, worldwide, had long had a reputation for poor industrial relations and highly autocratic management. In Australia, the Victorian plant of the company achieved notoriety from a strike in the early seventies when photos of police confronting massed workers were prominent in the media. From the beginning of the eighties, however, head office overseas initiated a dramatic change in industrial relations policy centred around the building of trust and commitment through the implementation of an Employee Involvement (EI) scheme (see below). The newly-appointed president of the company immediately embraced EI and the new industrial relations policy in a most enthusiastic fashion. Thus, at least in its home country and in Australia, the company has transformed its industrial relations image and is now known as one of the more progressive employers in the industrial relations field.

In Australia, employee relations (or ER as it is currently known in the company) first became a separate function at head office in 1951, having previously been part of the state manager's responsibilities. Initially there were tensions between the central industrial relations function (as it was then known) and the state managers, who felt that their authority had been eroded. ER was centralised from the outset because of the interdependence between plants; i.e., if one plant sought to change wages and conditions, these would quickly flow to other plants, hence the need for a common policy. But ER policy is less uniformly administered than was previously the case; for example, at one time even the colour of work clothes had to be the same in all plants. Now there is more discretion given to the plant manager. Foremen or supervisors used to refer all ER problems to the plant ER manager. Now there is more emphasis on foremen resolving problems at the workplace level.

The degree to which the ER department becomes involved in decision-making depends on the issue. Where changes in wages are concerned, the vice president, employee relations, will decide strategy together with the president and then inform line management. If dismissal of an employee is involved, line management will be heavily involved. The two most recent major disputes (in the early seventies and early eighties) both concerned wages and were primarily handled by the ER department and the president, with occasional input from manufacturing management.

There are approximately twenty employees in ER at head office, who are divided into four functional groups: labour relations, salaried personnel, research and training, and personnel services (including occupational health and safety). There are ER managers with professional and support staff in each assembly plant. They report directly to the plant manager but also have a 'dotted line' relationship with the vice president, employee relations, in head office. The ER department receives monthly reports from all plants on absenteeism, labour turnover, lost time, occupational health and safety, workcare statistics, and training. Each plant submits its own ER budget.

The plant ER managers have a difficult balancing act to perform in terms of maintaining loyalty to both the plant manager and the vice president, employee relations, especially if the plant manager is seeking to take a course of action different from that of the company (i.e. head office).

The relationship between the ER department and line management is illustrated by recent award restructuring activities. Plant managers were asked to submit ideas for productivity improvement, and manufacturing management was involved in discussions about the implementation of the new agreement. Details of the new award and negotiations with the unions, however, were the responsibility of the ER department. There was some criticism of plant managers by the ER department regarding their failure to 'follow through' on the second-tier agreements (which preceded award restructuring) in order to achieve optimum gains (for example in areas such as prevention maintenance and demarcation problems).

Industrial relations tends to be centralised throughout the vehicle building industry in Australia. Eighty per cent of negotiations over award restructuring, for example, were conducted at an industry level, although there were some company-level negotiations. The Metal Trades Industry Association (MTIA) provides a venue for meetings between the companies but there is constant contact between them. The Vehicle Manufacturers' Association collapsed in the early 1970s and there is no formal body which represents all employers in the industry on industrial relations matters. But since the early 1980s informal relationships between the firms, especially in regard to industrial relations, have greatly improved. There are separate company awards, but these are fairly standardised, especially in regard to wages.

With respect to the relationship between the company and its head-quarters overseas, it seems the Australian industrial relations system has provided the company with somewhat greater independence in the area of employee relations than may otherwise have been the case. ER managers at the overseas headquarters have conceded that unique features of the Australian system, including the high degree of centralisation, necessitate the relevant Australian managers operating with a certain degree of autonomy.

The case studies

The main case study was conducted at the Sydney plant. However, a less detailed case study was also conducted at the main Victorian assembly plant.

The Sydney assembly plant was established in 1937 and is the smallest of all of the assembly plants in Australia. It does not supply products or parts to any other plant and was operating at full capacity at the time of our research. Although expenditure on capital equipment has increased substantially during the past two years, labour costs are still approximately 65 per cent of total costs.[1] The plant manager felt that costs at the Sydney plant were a little lower than comparable plants (of equivalent size and sophistication) due to more effective work practices and better utilisation of people.

The plant has 927 employees of whom 882 are male and forty-five are female. Some 95 per cent of employees are covered by a total of four awards. The main award is a company award which covers 87 per cent of all employees. Absenteeism in 1989 was approximately 4 per cent and employees averaged two days off work on worker's compensation during 1989. The total number of employees increased by 197 during 1989.

The production process in Sydney is totally concerned with the assembly of the company's most popular small car. Apart from plastic mouldings, no components or parts are produced at the plant; they all come from either Victoria or overseas. Beginning with the basic frame of the car's chassis, an assembly line takes the car through the various phases of assembly. These include the building of the body, application of paint, installation of the engine, transmission and electrical components, and finally the fitting of the trim. While work organisation revolves around traditional assembly line procedures, it is subject to ongoing modification and innovation. The introduction of the new model, scheduled for early 1990, provided some impetus for change. However, many changes have also come out of the strongly-supported EI program, which has yielded a steady stream of suggestions. There is considerable multi-skilling and job rotation and some development of team-work although this has not gone as far as the recent innovations in Victoria associated with the assembly of the new sports model. Thus supervision is generally structured in the traditional mode although there has been an increasing emphasis on employee responsibility for quality. The EI scheme provides wide-ranging opportunities for employees to influence their work lives, and the unions, and particular groups of workers, are consulted at times of change. However it seems the pace of work, manning levels, and allocation to work tasks remain within the province of managerial prerogative.

The Victorian assembly plant was built in 1959 and currently employs 4200 (i.e. more than four times the number employed in Sydney). Labour costs were estimated by the plant manager to be approximately 59 per cent of total costs. The plant was operating at full capacity in 1989. There has been substantial investment in new capital equipment associated with the manufacture of the new sports car at the plant. Also work organisation has been altered considerably in this area with an emphasis on team-work. The first-line supervisor has taken on the role of team leadership, and quality control is a collective responsibility. Even here, however, traditional assembly line technology predominates with each team being limited to a reasonably small part of the total assembly process.

The plant manager estimated that unit costs at the Victorian plant were lower than at comparable plants because of higher volume production. However, individual worker productivity was regarded as being a little lower than at comparable plants. The Victorian plant produces more than 70 per cent of the company's total output.

The role of management

There are approximately three levels of management between the plant manager and the president or managing director of the company. A plant manager reports to the general operations manager, who reports to the vice president, manufacturing, who reports to the president. There is currently an executive vice president but this post will probably be deleted when the present incumbent returns overseas.

At the plant level there are typically seven or eight levels in the hierarchy between plant manager and the lowest level operator (Grade 1). All positions in the company are graded. Any position at Grade 11 or above is automatically called manager, although some positions at Grade 9 and above may be classified as managerial. There are approximately 300 employees who are at Grade 9 and above. About two-thirds are in Engineering and Production.

There are three main avenues into management: promotion from within, those who originally came through the graduate recruitment program (usually about fifty people a year), and recruitment from the external labour market directly into management (of whom there are few). The vice president, employee relations estimated that about one-third of management would have come originally from the graduate recruitment program (which has been in operation for twenty years or more). About one-third to half of the graduate intake each year have engineering degrees and it has been found that a number of senior people in other automobile companies have come through this company's graduate recruitment program. Quite a few managers from the company go to the Asia-Pacific group, within the overseas division, as part of their career development.

Most managerial training (about 90 per cent) is conducted within the company. Only about 2 per cent would be conducted externally although this is gradually increasing. About 8 per cent of training is conducted overseas within the corporation.

Performance appraisal is used extensively within the company, especially at the managerial level, mainly for the purposes of counselling and developing employees. There is a trend towards more frequent performance appraisals (once every six months). Approximately one third of the management—i.e. the top management group—are included in the company's world-wide performance appraisal system. The company does not have many non-salary fringe benefits for management—mainly cars and superannuation. Management salaries are reviewed every twelve months and increases are based mainly on job performance in the previous year.

Plant managers' perspectives

In Sydney, the plant manager saw decision-making within the company as highly centralised. For example, head office would make all major decisions in regard to appointments of senior managers in the plant, any reductions in employment, and the introduction of new bonus or incentive schemes. Plant costs are monitored daily, and weekly reports are sent to head office. When seeking to introduce major new equipment in the plant, the overseas headquarters are informed because they have to agree to the decision. However, both head office in Australia and the senior plant managers have a significant input. All major industrial relations decisions are made by head office (Australia) and the plant manager felt that the circumstances of the Sydney plant were often not taken into consideration. He would like that plant to have greater independence in these matters.

In Sydney, the plant manager estimated that he spent about 30 per cent of his time on employee relations matters. His stated philosophy was 'to achieve goals through the development of trust between employees and management'. He felt that he achieved this by walking around and talking to people. He rated employee relations at the plant level as very good, based on

- the low number of grievances and disputes,
- the fact that approximately 52 per cent of employees voluntarily participated in the EI programs (the highest rate of participation in any plant in Australia),
- the positive attitude of the shop stewards towards management, and
- the high level of personal recognition which he received from employees during his frequent plant visits.

The plant manager claimed that his philosophy was unchanged from five years ago but that he now placed greater emphasis on building trust than he did previously.

The most significant change which the Sydney plant manager would like to make would be to upgrade the paint facility. However, the larger plant in Victoria also needs a new similar facility and this has higher priority. He would also like to be able to take greater initiatives in regard to award restructuring but is unable to do so until the new car model has been launched.

In Victoria, the plant manager indicated that, with respect to his relationship with head office, he could recommend the appointment of a senior manager and could decide on a reduction in full-time employees up to 10 per cent. However, head office would have the final say on any redundancies. The introduction of any incentive scheme would have to be referred overseas for approval. The plant manager estimated that he spent about 10 per cent of his time on employee relations issues (narrowly defined) but up to 30 per cent of his time on broader ER issues (such as career development and training). He felt that the ER department at head office was less intrusive now than it was five years ago and that it usually gave the plant manager a favourable hearing on issues which concerned him. While the broader industrial relations system remained centralised, he acknowledged that there would need to be control by head office.

The guiding philosophy of the Victorian plant manager was 'trying to get people to accept common objectives and to work as a team'. He felt that during the 1980s there had been a move away from the previously autocratic style of management, but that it was very difficult to communicate this to people: 'we are still in a transition stage . . . the issues are very complex . . .' He felt that management had not been able to exercise significant influence at the shop-floor to bring about the major changes which were needed: 'it is difficult to put these ideas into shop-floor language'.

The main change which the Victorian plant manager would have liked to make, but felt constrained from doing, was to gain employees' acceptance of the need for increased work loads, i.e. greater productivity per person. He felt that there was commitment to greater efficiency at the top levels of the union movement, but not among the rank and file. 'We can't (as management) push too hard because we don't want to risk a dispute' (especially when there is a high demand for vehicles and the plant is running at full production).'

Employee relations managers' perspectives

In Sydney, the employee relations manager estimated that 75 per cent of his time was spent on industrial relations matters. He had seven years experience in employee relations with the company, having graduated with an economics degree (with a major in industrial relations). He had worked briefly as a secondary school teacher before joining the company. He had twenty-four staff directly reporting to him, of whom thirteen worked on ER matters. The employee relations manager listed a large number of issues for which he was responsible but it appeared that most significant industrial relations decisions were taken by head office, particularly in award matters. This is understandable given the fact that all employees work under federal awards, and the highly centralised nature of decision-making within the company. For example, all negotiations over award restructuring were conducted by head office, as were appearances before the Australian Industrial Relations Commission.

The employee relations manager noted that most decisions about changes in work organisation or working conditions were made by the plant manager. The main responsibility of the ER manager was to ensure that such changes were not contrary to the award. He saw the most satisfying aspects of the job as 'those issues which I can do something about ... investigate what has happened, involve line managers, get advice and arrive at a decision ... such as improving occupational health and rehabilitation, reducing absenteeism, developing grievance procedures and handling disciplinary matters'.

In Victoria, the employee relations manager was directly involved in industrial relations negotiations. 'There tend to be lot of plant-level negotiations here because the VBEF drives issues through the larger plants.' Hence, although major award negotiations were handled by head office ER personnel, the plant-level ER manager and his staff were involved in implementation of their decisions and setting the pace for other plants. The ER manager had responsibility for sixty-six staff of whom twenty-eight were involved in ER matters. He had been in his current post for one year but had been with the company for seven years, including a period in the UK.

The issues most frequently negotiated at plant level included local staffing and working conditions. There were a number of local agreements on issues such as productivity and quality improvement. The most recent issue to be negotiated concerned manning levels. The plant ER manager discussed issues with the union delegates at least once a week on average. The main concerns raised by union delegates tended to be health and safety matters, working conditions, and manning levels.

The role of unions and unionism

Unionism has been present in the Sydney plant almost since its establishment. In 1939 the company was a respondent to the Motor Body and Coach Building Award and union records reveal the active involvement of VBEF organisers at the Sydney plant in the early forties.[2] The unions with members currently at the Sydney plant are the Vehicle Builders Employees Federation of Australia (VBEF) (New South Wales Branch), the Federated Clerks' Union (FCU), the Association of Draughting, Supervisory and Technical Employees (ADSTE) and the Transport Workers' Union (TWU).

The most important union, by far, is the VBEF which covers virtually all payroll employees and is the only union with such coverage.

This situation is consistent with the industrial unionism policy of the VBEF which it has pursued consistently, especially in New South Wales. It seems that at the Sydney plant tradespersons became disenchanted with the services offered by their previous unions and were very happy to join the VBEF. The FCU covers clerical staff of which there are relatively few, while ADSTE has some members among the technicians and supervisors. The TWU covers only two employees in the plant.

In Victoria, while the VBEF is again the most important union, the MEWU, the ETU, the FCU and ADSTE have a presence as well as the FIMEE, the Association of Professional Engineers (APEA) and the Federated Engine Drivers and Firemen's Association (FEDFA). The last three unions, however have very few members and have no delegates on site. The main area of overlapping coverage and potential disputation concerns the maintenance tradespersons, who can belong to either the VBEF or the MEWU. More will be said on this below.

At both the Sydney and the Victorian plants there is a closed-shop agreement for both the VBEF and the FCU with a cheek-off system in operation for the collection of fees. Thus all employees eligible to be members of these unions are unionised. The closed-shop arrangement is in the form of agreements between the union and management that are not, however, ratified by the Commission. Such agreements apply in all the company's plants and are consistent with the national industrial relations policies. Apparently the advantages of the closed-shop agreements, for management, are that they eliminate the potential for disharmony over non-membership and, especially in Sydney, help to strengthen the relationship with the unions involved. The check-off system means that delegates do not have to leave their work stations to collect fees and it was claimed to have made the relationship between delegates and the membership more harmonious and more effective. It means that delegates are not perceived as debt collectors, and provides them with more time to pursue members' grievances and assist with personal problems.

The occupational groups belonging to the VBEF are para-professionals, tradespeople, plant and machine operators, drivers, labourers and process workers. The largest single group is plant and machine operators and drivers. The membership as a whole has been growing in the Sydney plant as a result of an increase in the size of the workforce; at the present time it numbers approximately 800. In the Victorian plant the membership has started to grow during 1989 after a period of gradual decline, and currently numbers approximately 2800 in the car assembly section. There is a greater percentage of women there than in Sydney and this should rise, especially in the section devoted to the assembly of the sports model.

There is a VBEF delegate for each section of the plant in Sydney and for each of the two shifts, giving a total of nine. At present there are no female delegates but this has not always been the case in the plant. There is one FCU delegate and one ADSTE delegate, both of whom usually meet separately with management. On occasion, however, there are combined union meetings with management, usually concerning particular issues such as occupational health and safety or superannuation. There is nothing resembling a shop committee but all VBEF delegates meet together as a committee with the union organiser at least once a month.

At the Victorian plant there are fifty-six delegates: thirty-six from the VBEF, eleven from ADSTE, five from the MEWU and two each from the FCU and the ETU. Although there were no female VBEF delegates at the time of the relevant interviews, three delegates' positions had been held by women previously. One impediment to the involvement of women was the attitude of certain ethnic groups. Despite the multiplicity of unions among payroll employees at the plant, there is no shop committee—a situation which is apparently supported by both management and the leadership of the VBEF. As mentioned above, maintenance tradespersons can belong to either the VBEF or the MEWU. Their final choice of union can depend on a variety of factors, some as relatively incidental as the conscientiousness of the respective delegates. Despite the potential for conflict in this situation it seems to have been avoided so far. This is especially remarkable given the VBEF's ambition to be the sole union in the industry, even covering clerical and supervisory positions.

The main facility provided by management for delegates is time off for the conduct of union business. The company's policy on this does not extend to full-time delegates or convenors, but in Victoria the senior delegate spends all his work time (and more) on union business and this is accepted, at least unofficially, by management. In Sydney it seems there is no limit placed on the time the senior delegate spends pursuing union matters, and delegates have access to the phone for union business. Meeting rooms are available on request, and while secretarial and printing facilities are available, the union rarely utilises these, preferring to remain as autonomous from management as possible. A delicate balance is attempted, it seems, between a cooperative relationship involving the use of certain company facilities and overdependence on management which may compromise the union.

When a delegate's position becomes vacant in Sydney, nominations are called and, if necessary, an election is held by secret ballot. However, it seems that elections are rarely conducted. This does not necessarily indicate low level of interest in union affairs, at least according to the union. It was claimed that there is often more than one nomination but in most cases informal agreement is reached among the nominees and thus elections are avoided. While there are ethnically-based factions within the workforce, there are no divisions, it seems, on political grounds.

In Victoria, political factions are more evident and vacancies for delegates are frequently contested. The manner of the election is decided by the members involved, and while secret ballot is most common there have been instances where the matter was decided by a show of hands. To assist in overcoming language problems generated by the extensive ethnic mix, photos of candidates are sometimes displayed on voting papers.

In Sydney, there was no evidence of tension or conflict between delegates and full-time union officials, with the delegates apparently happy to abide by union policy and to accept the advice of the officials. Award and safety matters, worker's compensation, and dismissals appear to be the main issues on which the senior delegate would normally seek the advice of a full-time official. Should members be contemplating industrial action, the matters in dispute would first be referred to the union branch. However this is a rather hypothetical question in Sydney as such action has not been taken on plant-specific matters recently.[3]

In the main, general meetings of the membership are held at lunchtimes or, more frequently, at the change of shift. For example, in the only two stoppages at the Sydney plant in recent years (see below) the full-time officials addressed a general meeting of the membership the day before. Indeed management claimed that the union organisers were instrumental in generating sufficient support, especially for the latter stoppage. However, having voted to strike, there was 100 per cent participation by the membership. Any union meetings held in work time result in loss of pay. The last general meeting called by management was about immigration, especially the status of certain Chinese employees following the June 1989 uprising in their homeland, but there was no union involvement.

Senior delegates' perspectives

The senior Sydney delegate at the time of our research was employed as a quality control inspector, and had worked at the plant for twenty years. However he had only been a delegate for the last five years and required more assistance from the full-time officials than had his two immediate, more-experienced predecessors.

Approximately half the paid work time of the senior delegate in Sydney is spent on union matters, which include dismissals, safety, rehabilitation, and working conditions. His most time-consuming task, however, is handling grievances on behalf of individual members. In the months preceding the interview he had been spending more time than usual in his senior delegate role as a result of negotiations concerning the introduction of the new model. In Sydney, the senior delegate did not find it necessary to spend much of his own time on union matters. However, as a member of the state council of the union, he was obliged to attend meetings twice a year and he also attended meetings in his own time.

This contrasts with the situation in Victoria where, as would be expected with the much larger, more industrially active membership, the senior delegate spent all his work time and between ten and twenty additional hours on union business. As in Sydney the most time-consuming task appears to be the handling of individual grievances, but at least a couple of hours a week are spent in negotiations with management. In Victoria, the senior delegate is very experienced both industrially and politically. He has served as a delegate for eighteen years, has been a member of the state executive of the union, and has a long record of active involvement in the political wing of the labour movement.

The Victorian delegate stressed the need to ensure that the union was not compromised over the provision of facilities for delegates by the company. Additional facilities, especially assistance with secretarial tasks, were not sought by him because of the dangers they could pose for the autonomy, or perceived autonomy, of the union. He pointed out that certain of his members refused to have their fees deducted from their pay, insisting that he collect them personally, for much the same reasons. Both senior delegates have had training in union matters and, in accordance with the relevant award provision, spent at least five days during the past year at training courses, all of which were run by TUTA.

The main point of contact between delegates and management in Sydney is at the supervisor level and the relationships at this level were perceived as good. Matters are generally raised by the senior delegate on behalf of the delegates and the membership, and if the issue cannot be resolved at the supervisor level the next point of contact in the management hierarchy is the labour relations coordinator. On some occasions, however, the matter may be taken directly to the employee relations manager. The relationship between management generally and the delegates was described as 'good' to 'very good'.[4]

While accepting that management had changed its approach to employee relations during the last decade, the Victorian senior delegate indicated his belief that this change in attitude had to be demonstrated more dramatically. He felt more effort and resources had to be put into the training of managerial staff, especially as there were certain older managers who were reluctant to change. In addition, he claimed that a more radical form of worker participation should be introduced; he personally preferred a form of profit-sharing. In the senior delegate's view certain elements of distrust and suspicion remained in the workforce, and management would have to signal its new intentions more clearly to overcome the rather prevalent scepticism. This viewpoint is consistent with a statement by the plant manager in Victoria on the need for management to pursue its revised employee relations policy very consistently as any deviation may create the impression that it was regressing to the previous, highly authoritarian approach.

Union officials' perspectives (NSW Branch of the VBEF)

A full-time official, usually the assistant secretary, visits the Sydney plant at least three times a fortnight. Such officials enjoy right of access to the plant, and the relationship between senior union personnel and management was perceived as positive and cooperative. The union officials appeared to hold the plant manager in particularly high regard but felt that the employee relations staff lacked some experience, especially with industrial action. The incumbent senior delegate in Sydney had succeeded two people regarded as highly experienced and capable, and his lack of experience necessitated a greater involvement of full-time officials at the workplace. Although much of their time in the plant is spent in meeting with delegates and management, full-time officials also spend some time in discussing grievances with individual members. Indeed the assistant secretary was insistent that an important part of his role was to take up matters of concern on behalf of individual members even though such action contravened the provisions of the grievance procedure. Apparently union policy dictates that officials, once approached by members, have a responsibility to pursue matters to their conclusion.

Some of the immediate matters of concern to union officials related to award restructuring and the recent operation of the national wage system in general. Uncertainty over the future of paid rates awards[5] (such as the company's main award) has been generated by comments in recent wage decisions, and more generally the officials were somewhat sceptical about the adoption and implementation of both the second tier (4 per cent) and the structural efficiency principle. They claimed there was still considerable membership antagonism about the trade-offs under the 4 per cent and were adamant that attempts to secure further concessions would be strongly resisted.

Negotiations, consultation and dispute settlement

Some of the main issues over which bargaining occurs at the Sydney plant are working conditions, dismissals and disciplinary action, and changes to work practices. It seems the main issues raised by delegates during the past year related to the work environment (for example, a request for fans) and the personal grievances of individual members. Generally health and safety issues are dealt with separately by the relevant committee or safety representative.

It seems there is no formal schedule or timetable for bargaining; rather it occurs as required, that is, when either management or union representatives feel a need to hold discussions with the other party. At a time of significant change, such as that associated with the introduction of the new model, bargaining occurs more frequently and even in normal times it can be said that bargaining takes place almost on a daily basis.

Most bargaining initiated by the delegates takes place, at least initially, at the level of the supervisor, while management-initiated discussions generally take place at the level of the plant manager and often involve full-time officials from the outset. In any cases involving dismissal the senior delegate is immediately involved. At least once a month delegates meet as a committee with the relevant full-time union official, but this committee has no role in negotiations with management.

One of the most important representative bodies at the plant level is the Health and Safety Committee. This committee is comprised of an equal number of employee and management representatives and meets at least once every month. For the appointment of employee representatives, nominations are called and elections are held if necessary.

A formal written agreement also applies to worker's compensation. An associated rehabilitation agreement was recently finalised at the Sydney plant after lengthy negotiations between the company, local delegates, and union organisers. The employee relations manager was the principal negotiator on behalf of management but all proposals were approved by both senior plant management and senior ER management in Melbourne. There are various agreements covering issues such as new technology, equal employment opportunity, training, or redundancy (some of which are incorporated within awards).

The union clearly resented the lack of autonomy enjoyed by the management negotiators in Sydney, claiming that they were unable to make virtually any decisions without first obtaining approval from Melbourne. This, according to the union, greatly hampered the negotiation of initiatives such as the rehabilitation agreement.

The officials talked of the Sydney plant as the 'jewel in the crown' as far as the company was concerned. In terms of industrial harmony, cooperative relationships, employee satisfaction, and productivity, it had a record which was clearly superior to that of plants elsewhere, especially those in Victoria. While this was a source of pride for union officials as well as management, it was perceived as a form of constraint on management. The officials claimed that managers had to be very careful to preserve the record and special status of the Sydney plant, and their decision-making and strategy formulation was influenced by this consideration. Any manager found to be jeopardising the special reputation of the plant would be quickly transferred and his future prospects with the company would suffer accordingly.

There is a grievance procedure written into the main award and it seems that a large proportion of grievances are handled by the procedure. In the main, industrial action is not contemplated until the procedure has been exhausted. Certain grievances, however, are dealt with by the senior delegate outside of the procedure, and others are taken up directly by the union organiser after approaches by individual members. In addition, occupational health and safety matters such as pollution, fumes, and noise are usually taken straight to the relevant committee and/or safety representative. The most frequent source of grievance appears to have been conflict of personality between employees and supervision.

The steps in the procedure are firstly an approach to the foreman, followed, if necessary, by the matter going to the industrial relations staff. If unresolved there, the senior delegate becomes involved; the final step is the involvement of the union organiser. The grievance procedure was seen by both parties as being generally effective, but some scepticism was expressed by the senior delegate in Victoria, who felt that management would be better served by removing common sources of grievance such as poor working conditions rather than wasting time talking about them.

Approaches to employee consultation and participation include joint consultative committees (particularly dealing with health and safety matters), various *ad hoc* joint working parties, and workplace meetings at which management provides briefings to the workforce. The company makes extensive use of internal newsletters and bulletins to inform employees about the performance of the company and other activities.[6]

The EI program

The most enduring and far-reaching approach to employee consultation and participation has been the Employee Involvement (EI) scheme which was first introduced in 1983 in Sydney and has gradually been extended to all plants. The scheme originated overseas in the late 1970s following several years of adverse conditions for the automobile industry. An economic downturn had led to severe reductions in annual vehicle sales and, within a shrinking market, domestic producers were suffering a decline in market share due to the rising popularity of imported Japanese vehicles. Out of this adversity came recognition by both the management and the union that greater labour–management cooperation was needed in order to improve the company's chances of survival. Thus, the union and the company jointly sponsored the introduction of the EI program within all the company plants and offices.

Although the Australian company was not facing the same traumatic conditions as those which prevailed overseas, a serious industrial dispute did halt the main assembly plant in Victoria for six weeks in the early eighties. Consequently, management decided to reassess its approach to employee relations and to introduce an EI program which was based largely on the overseas model, albeit with some important local modifications. The stated objectives of EI are

> to unlock the creative potential of employees by involving them in decisions affecting their work. At the same time, the aim of the (EI) process is also to provide employees with a self-fulfilling and self-enhancing sense of achievement (EI: Sydney Assembly Plant Booklet, p. 3).

The EI program began in Australia in late 1982 when an orientation session was conducted for managers and union representatives at the assembly plant in Sydney. Agreement was achieved for the introduction of a pilot program at the Sydney plant in early 1983 to test the EI approach. After several months of successful operation, formal endorsement of the EI program was obtained from the federal officers of the main unions and in due course, from the ACTU secretary. Thereafter EI was presented as a joint ACTU/company initiative and was progressively introduced throughout all the company's plants and offices during the next three years. A national steering committee was established which was chaired jointly by the federal secretary of the VBEF and the director of employee relations at the company. Local steering committees of a similar kind, with union and management representations, were subsequently formed in each plant.

The central feature of the EI process is the establishment of EI groups comprising volunteers who meet for approximately one hour per week in company time in order to resolve issues which they see as important to improve the work environment, productivity, or product quality. Problems are chosen by the groups, subject to approval by the local steering committee, which must lie outside those issues normally the matter of negotiations and resolution between the company and the unions. Each steering group has one or two EI facilitators who carry out their EI responsibilities on a full-time basis and ensure that the process operates in an effective manner within the agreed guidelines. The EI facilitators are also responsible for providing both group members and group leaders with training.

Perceptions of the EI program

The EI program has been judged by management to be a success and it currently has a participation rate of approximately 30 per cent of employees throughout the company. The highest rate of participation, approximately 52 per cent, is at the Sydney plant, where it has been longest established. The main advantages of EI cited by management include the achievement of a more collaborative and trusting relationship within the plants, and the associated improvement in employee relations. EI was also seen as having assisted in the implementation of change. Productivity and quality were also regarded as having improved with EI, but it was difficult to determine the precise contribution made by EI in these areas. Indeed, the company has deliberately avoided any attempt at undertaking a cost–benefit assessment of EI, on the grounds that the process of introducing EI has been intrinsically worthwhile.

Some minor criticisms of EI were nevertheless voiced by various parties. While most of the unions gave EI their tacit support, the MEWU has never been officially part of the process. The VBEF representations were generally positive about EI but maintained that the limitations on issues discussed (i.e. non-industrial) were overly restrictive. They saw that the overtime rates paid for attendance at EI sessions acted as a strong incentive for a number of employees to become involved. Some of the managers mentioned negative reactions among supervisors who felt 'left out' and even 'undermined' by the EI process. It was also felt that some of the initial expectations raised by advocates of EI were set too high and led to a degree of disappointment. There also remained a good deal of scepticism among those who had chosen not to become involved. Some managers are disappointed that absenteeism and labour turnover has remained relatively high despite EI.

The future of EI

It remains to be seen whether EI will continue to expand throughout the company, especially in the larger plants where its penetration remains relatively low. It is also evident that an important factor in the widespread application of EI in the company has been the strong support given by the former president of the company. Although formal commitment to the EI policy remains, it is not clear whether the new president will give it the same degree of emphasis. The success and continuity of EI depends strongly upon the enthusiasm of local plant managers and support from the head office employee relations group which provides training for the facilitators. It is also uncertain whether EI will be sustained if enthusiasm wanes at world headquarters and an alternative employee relations strategy emerges. For the time being, however, the EI program remains a high priority in the company.

Industrial action

In terms of collective/organised action versus individual/unorganised forms, virtually all industrial action in Sydney belongs to the individual/unorganised category. Turnover is high, absenteeism, although now reduced to a relatively low level, has traditionally been a problem, and pilfering is a serious problem. In addition fighting between employees and physical threats to supervisors are common causes of disciplinary action, and various incidents of sabotage and vandalism occur from time to time. It is appreciated that forms of employee behaviour such as turnover, absenteeism, and sabotage should not necessarily be conceived of in terms of conflict or industrial action (see Edwards and Scullion 1982). Notwithstanding, for the purposes of this analysis these forms of behaviour will be treated under the heading of 'industrial action'.

With respect to the collective/organised category of industrial action the only strike to be held in recent times was the 24-hour stoppage in support of the state-wide 'day of outrage' against the Greiner government in NSW with the particular concerns of the union membership in this plant being the changes to the worker's compensation legislation. Such incidents, when action has been taken in support of national or state-wide campaigns, constitute the only instances of strike action at the Sydney plant in the last twenty years.

Collective action is much more common in Victoria, with two days having been lost in the second half of 1989, for example, as part of the campaign of protest against delays in the national wage case. This stoppage translated into a loss of 10 000 working days and there was an increase in overtime in the attempt to make up for the substantial loss in production. Recent changes to the leadership of the Victorian branch of the VBEF were seen as instrumental in the staging of this strike. A 'reform group' has gained power in the branch, and management was apprehensive about the approach this new leadership may take in the future.

Turnover is relatively high at 11 per cent and is costly for the company. It appears to be concentrated in particular categories only and in a relatively small proportion of the workforce. In other words a significant majority of the workforce has been at the Sydney plant for a long time (over twenty years employment is quite common) but beyond this stable core there is a rather transient group. Some of the factors associated with this turnover rate appear to be relatively low rates of pay, unpleasant working conditions, lack of career opportunities and the particular ethnic composition of the workforce. Also, at the time of the research in 1989, there was a serious labour shortage experienced by enterprises such this. This meant that workers were recruited from far afield (such as Wollongong), or from those who were traditionally employed in other industries. They are more likely to leave when opportunities arise either closer to home or in their traditional fields of employment.

It is interesting to note that turnover is markedly lower in the section of the Victorian plant devoted to the assembly of the sports model than it is elsewhere in that plant. This appears to be related to the more careful recruitment procedures and the improved working conditions that apply in that section.

Absenteeism was once a serious problem for Sydney management at 10 to 12 per cent, but this has been significantly reduced in recent years and at present is running at between 4 and 5 per cent. The reduced absenteeism indicates higher morale and the more positive atmosphere now prevalent in the Sydney plant. Absenteeism is a more serious problem for management in Victoria than it is in Sydney, despite a marked improvement in recent times. Considerable effort by management has seen the rate fall from between 12 and 13 per cent to approximately 9 per cent.

While pilfering is common to many industries it appears to be particularly endemic to car assembly plants where many of the component parts are highly marketable (e.g. car radios) and often urgently required to complete repairs to workers' cars. It seems pilfering falls into two main categories: large scale operations perhaps associated with organised crime, and minor incidents where parts and materials are taken for immediate use rather than for sale. It was claimed by union sources that the latter category could be considerably reduced if parts were made available to employees at lower prices. Once detected, pilferers are handed over to the police, and culprits are dismissed automatically without any opportunity for representation by the union.

Physical violence among workers, and attempts to physically intimidate supervisors, occurs from time to time in Sydney but is apparently less of a problem than it is in Victoria. Its occurrence may be seen as an indicator of dissatisfaction and frustration, especially among non-English-speaking workers who have communication problems both with management and with each other. It was felt, at least in Victoria, that the extent of physical violence would diminish as the proportion of female workers increased and the work culture became less 'macho'.

Conclusions

Automakers provides an interesting example of an enterprise in which the conciliation and arbitration system has a major influence in shaping the processes of industrial relations at the workplace level. As noted above, the company deliberately chose to follow a centralised approach in order to minimise the variations in conditions of work and payment systems between plants and to prevent the unions from playing one plant off against the other.

Part of this centralised approach was strict adherence to the awards of the federal tribunal—a strategy encouraged also by the structure of industrial relations in the vehicle building industry which emphasises a uniform approach through the paid rates award. Automakers and the other manufacturers have supported this approach because it ensured that wages and conditions did not vary between employers in the industry. However, there were indications that some of the other vehicle companies were considering options such as the adoption of minimum rates awards and certified agreements which would enable them to offer different employment conditions. This approach may, indeed, become more prevalent if the Australian Industrial Relations Commission encourages the extension of certified agreements to permit greater enterprise-level bargaining. At the time of the study, however, the vehicle building industry represented one of the clearest examples of the tribunals exercising strong influence over the parties, albeit with the tacit support of both management and unions.

With respect to the question of the relationship between plants and head office, the corporate management of Automakers sought to exercise strict control over all important strategic industrial relations decisions at the plant level. Nevertheless, the comparison between the two assembly plants, which were of contrasting size and in different locations, demonstrated that even within a centralised approach, diversity could still be found. The larger plant, in Victoria, was more central to the Australian operation which meant that employee relations policies were more likely to be initiated there. It was also closer to the scrutiny of head office. The smaller and more remote plant in Sydney appeared to have greater autonomy in some aspects, yet employee relations within this plant were more constrained by head office control than was the case in its Victorian counterpart.

Numerous factors influenced the relationships between each of the plants and corporate level management. First, the Victorian plant was of great significance to both the unions and the company so that it tended to lead the other plants in regard to any changes in pay or conditions. Although the corporate ER management had greater formal authority over ER policy, plant management (including the local ER manager) played a major role in the decision-making process since they had to implement any agreements which were negotiated. By contrast, the Sydney plant was small and remote from the decision-making process, both in terms of management and union activities, and was thus obliged to follow the lead set in Victoria.[7] In certain issues, however, such as employee rehabilitation and programs to help overcome problems of drug and alcohol abuse, Sydney has been the leader. Agreements reached on these matters, through the more cooperative union–management relationship, have been seen as providing models for the rest of the company.

Second, the location in Melbourne of the Australian Industrial Relations Commission, the federal office of the VBEF, and corporate ER management, meant that all of the key participants in the industrial relations process were near each other. ER management in Victoria was inevitably swept up into discussions and negotiations within and around the Commission. There was greater possibility for both formal and informal exchange of information, so that the management and union representatives in Victoria could intervene in matters more quickly and easily. By the time the Sydney plant became aware of matters, they had often been already decided.

Third, the size and complexity of the Victorian plant meant that there was more scope and necessity for local agreements between plant management and unions. Hence, although the main industrial relations matters were still regulated by the federal award, many other issues affecting employees' working lives were covered by local plant-level agreements. This provided both ER management and unions at the local level with scope for negotiation. In Sydney, where there was only one major union and fewer employees, there was less need for formal agreements. Issues were settled more informally and activities proceeded under custom and practice.

A fourth factor which affected the degree of autonomy experienced by the management in Sydney was the more junior status of management at that plant. As would be expected in the case of one of the smaller plants, managers appeared to lack some of the authority and confidence in decision-making enjoyed by their counterparts in Victoria. This was most noticeable in the case of the ER management.

Some of the characteristics outlined above have also been significant in the development of employee relations and labour productivity at the Sydney plant, which has been labelled as the 'jewel in the crown' for Automakers. Thus workers, their representatives, and management point with pride to their record in a variety of areas and to the 'flagship' role played by the Sydney plant in schemes such as Employee Involvement and, more recently, employee rehabilitation. However, the 'jewel in the crown' syndrome also constitutes a constraint on management because it must be careful to ensure that the status of the Sydney plant is maintained. Thus, the issue of autonomy from corporate head office in a multi-site organisation is more complex than it might initially appear.

Another distinctive feature of Automakers was the clear strategy adopted by corporate management to 'changing the culture of industrial relations' from one which had been strongly adversarial to one which emphasised mutual interests and collaboration. It should be noted that this company was not the only one to adopt this type of strategy in recent decades. Quality of Worklife (QWL) and related programs were initiated by various automobile manufacturers in the mid 1970s, but these were often not sustained, and various other employee participation approaches were pursued during the 1980s. Automakers was more thorough-going in its determination to introduce the EI process in all of its plants. Even though only 30 per cent of all employees are currently engaged in the process, it is still expanding and the company has won wide recognition and acclaim from business, government, and unions for its initiatives in this field.

Broadly speaking, the company can be described as having a dual or two-strand strategy in regard to employee relations. One strand involves strong support of unionism, particularly the VBEF, with an important role for both full-time union officials and workplace representatives. This is generally consistent with a pluralist ideology. The second strand is grounded more in a unitarist approach and involves attempts to forge more direct links and stronger loyalties between individual employees and the company. In other words, this involves 'incorporating' the workforce into a management-initiated program of change. While EI is an important part of this second strand in the overall strategy it is only one part of the total picture. In Sydney, the plant manager considers it very important to be known personally to as many employees as possible. Thus he attaches considerable significance to his frequent walks around the shop-floor when he talks individually with employees.

In Victoria, where plant size means that such an activity is hardly feasible, and the involvement rates in the EI program are significantly lower, much of the 'human relations' activity is centred on the section of the plant devoted to the new sports model. Here recruitment is more selective and the induction program more intensive. Also much more effort is devoted to training which is necessitated, in turn, by the group-work approach that is in operation. Employees enjoy greater discretion and greater variety with respect to their work tasks but in turn bear greater responsibilities for work quality. While all these initiatives have the full support of the unions, it seems they are likely to encourage greater individual worker commitment to the company rather than strengthening links between the unions and their members.

The nature of unionism at the workplace level, and the extent to which the unions constrain management decision-making, also varied considerably between the two plants. The NSW and Victorian branches of the VBEF appear to differ markedly in the policies and strategies used in their respective relationships with the company. In New South Wales the emphasis has been on the improvement of members' conditions through a generally cooperative relationship with management, while in Victoria a more confrontationist stance has been adopted. The number of union–management agreements in place in Sydney attest to the level of union activity but they have been reached without the industrial action that has occurred in Victorian. In Sydney the VBEF's sole coverage of the blue-collar workforce has meant that inter-union competition, important in Victoria, is absent. This, along with a much smaller workforce lacking apparently in political factions, has resulted in relatively little militant shop-floor activity.

Another factor conditioning union attitudes in New South Wales is the perceived danger of the Sydney plant being closed. Such a possibility in Victoria is far more remote. Stability in union leadership has also been a differentiating factor. In NSW the branch has been dominated by long-serving officials subscribing to moderate industrial and political philosophies, while in Victoria a recent election saw a left-wing 'reform' group take over the leadership. This leadership change was seen as instrumental in the promotion of unrest at the Victorian plant. Thus in NSW a situation of industrial stability and harmony, at least in comparison with that prevailing in the company's Victorian operations, has resulted, at least in part, from a long-serving, moderate union leadership in combination with a smaller, less union-conscious workforce.

The nature and influence of unions is greatly influenced by the strategies pursued by management. It has been noted that Automakers, unlike some employers who followed the BCA policy on enterprise-based bargaining, sought to develop its industrial relations strategies within the broad context of a centralised system. Automakers also strengthened the pre-eminence of the VBEF as the main union within the industry and tends to promote the Sydney plant (where the VBEF has its widest coverage) as setting an example for others to follow. At the same time, however, it recognised that the Sydney plant was too small to provide a model for the typical car assembly plant. Thus, in Victoria, the company sought to develop an effective industrial relations strategy within the current framework of multi-union bargaining, while simultaneously developing other supporting policies such as employee involvement.

At the plant level, neither management nor the unions felt that they had achieved significant gains from negotiations over the second-tier wage increases or award restructuring. Management felt that while there was commitment to achieving greater efficiency within the industry at the senior levels of the trade union movement, this was not shared by the rank and file. To some degree, this view was shared by the union officials who noted that there was considerable antagonism among their members to the concept of 'trade-offs' between working conditions and wage increases. These findings tend to confirm the view that, in a highly centralised approach to industrial relations, as represented by the vehicle building industry, neither management nor union representatives at the local level are likely to feel strong identification with decisions made elsewhere. Indeed, increased efficiency was more likely to be the result of negotiations between the parties at the workplace level than of decisions at the industry level.

As demonstrated, the character of industrial relations in the two plants of Automakers examined here contrast markedly. In terms of the categories suggested by Callus *et al.* (1991), the Victorian plant was an 'active bargainer' while the Sydney plant exhibited elements of both the 'structured inactive' and the 'reactive bargainer' workplaces. Both plants are highly structured with respect to the union workplace presence and the management of industrial relations. Furthermore, in the Victorian plant the level of multi-unionism and disputation, and the extent to which bargaining occurs on the initiative of the union representatives, all qualify it for the 'active bargainer' category. At the Sydney plant, however, bargaining occurs on a regular basis but generally in response to management initiatives rather than as a result of union leaders or the membership seeking concessions from management. Moreover, strike action was almost non-existent, being confined to support of state-wide and national campaigns. Thus the Sydney plant tended to straddle the 'structured inactive' and 'reactive bargainer' categories.

By the end of the 1980s, Automakers had been largely successful in reducing the level of overt industrial conflict and disputes at both plants, despite their contrasting characteristics, through a range of consultative activities with the workforce, such as the EI program. Yet recent changes in the leadership of the Victorian branch of the VBEF may pose a greater challenge to the company management, especially in the large Victorian plant. Similarly, new appointments to the senior management ranks, following the retirement of the company's former president and the vice president of employee relations, both of whom championed the shift in industrial relations strategy from an adversarial to a consultative approach, may result in changes to workplace industrial relations during the coming decade. The future course of events may also be strongly influenced by the company's ability to maintain the market dominance which it achieved during the 1980s, and which underpinned many of the industrial relations initiatives.

7 FoodCo

Until the Australian Workplace Industrial Relations Survey (Callus *et al.* 1991), there was relatively little research on workplace industrial relations in Australia. The neglect is particularly apparent in relation to retail distribution and most other elements of the service sector, which have received much less attention than manufacturing and mining. This study focuses on the back-end of retailing—warehousing—which is neglected in comparison with the front-end—shops. We explore managerial and union strategies and behaviour in two large modern warehouses that were commissioned in the 1980s. Although they are almost identical in technology and are owned by the same firm, these warehouses exhibit quite different patterns of management and industrial relations.

Background

During the 1970s, a large Australian retailer, FoodCo, increased its number of shops, turnover and volume of sales. As it aimed for further increases, it proposed to modernise its distribution facilities to cope with the receipt of goods, inventory control, storage and despatch of the 5000 different items of stock carried at any one time. The company decided to invest in two large dry-food warehouses, which it called distribution centres (DCs) that would utilise the latest technology.

The planning and installation of the two DCs took about three years and was guided by an American management consulting firm. Each of the new DCs would be among the largest (32 000 m²) and most sophisticated retail DCs in Australia. They were designed to have a total capacity of 21 000 pallets, about two-thirds of which were in conventional low-bay storage, with the other one-third in high-bay automated storage and retrieval. These DCs introduced several applications of information technology which were novel in the context of food warehousing. The main features of each DC included:

- automated pallet storage and retrieval system for holding reserve stocks;
- slow-moving full-case lines to be assembled using automated high-rise order selectors (order pickers);
- store orders to be assembled using radio controlled, double-pallet jacks (rather than manually operated single-pallet jacks);
- carton live storage to be used for 'broken lines', small or low-demand items;
- air and noise pollution levels to be reduced by good ventilation and the use of battery-powered mobile warehouse equipment;
- comprehensive fire protection, tunnels and other safety arrangements;
- pleasant lighting, restaurant, and relaxation facilities for employees.

Computer systems were used to locate stocks and provide picking lists for truck loads. Fork-lift drivers were given scheduled instructions from the computer; these advised of let-downs and pick-ups. All pallets received into the DC were addressed to a specific location. Although not completely automated, each DC was highly computerised.

The first stage of distribution centre A (DCA) was opened in Sydney, NSW, late in 1981, while distribution centre B (DCB) was opened in Brisbane, Queensland, in 1983. These new DCs aroused a great deal of interest. DCA was described in a contemporary trade journal as 'a milestone ... the most sophisticated computerized handling system available ... an example of ''total concept'' materials handling on the grandest scale ... a very impressive facility and worthy of the awe with which its opening has been greeted in the materials handling industry'.

DCA is essential to the smooth operation of FoodCo retail outlets in NSW. While the company has two other dry goods grocery DCs in NSW, these others carry only the 2000 fastest-moving lines. DCA carries the full range of goods (8000 lines) and it services the other warehouses. The DCs were built to carry 5000 lines and early in 1990 an extension added a further 50 per cent in storage space to enable DCA to house the expanded number of lines more conveniently. DCB stocks 7000 lines—nearly as many as DCA. It is also extending its space so that it too can carry the full range.

More than half of all the goods sold in FoodCo stores in the area of Queensland and Northern NSW come via DCB. DCB stocks groceries of all types, but because of space restrictions it is supplemented by a fresh food warehouse, a frozen food warehouse and another warehouse which stocks slow-moving items. These warehouses, in conjunction with one in Townsville, service FoodCo stores in the area.

As warehouses owned by a large retail chain, the DCs are not in direct competition with other similar operations; it is difficult to measure their efficiency in comparison with those of rival companies. However, we can compare them with each other: DCB costs about half what DCA costs to provide a comparable service. DCA's extra cost is largely because of its low productivity. The differences in productivity at the DCs first became apparent as DCB was commissioned. Using the measure of average rates of 'pick per person hour' (ppph), DCB was achieving 145 ppph in 1984, compared to 98 ppph at DCA. This contrast in productivity levels was still apparent in 1990, when managers at both DCs agreed that productivity was still about 50 per cent higher at DCB than at DCA, though the number of shops serviced and volume of turnover was higher at DCA.

What could explain the difference in productivity? The technology used in the two DCs is virtually identical. In both cases the initial workload and the original employees were transferred from FoodCo's manually-operated warehouses in the same city, which were much less capital-intensive. But their subsequent histories showed marked divergence. While DCB has been characterised by low levels of disputation, and managerial continuity, DCA has had high levels of disputation, and managerial discontinuity. The DCA management says that the difference in productivity is almost entirely due to differences in union behaviour. But the union blames the management.

Management and the workforce

FoodCo's corporate structure is illustrated in Figure 7.1 (page 181). DCA was situated in Sydney, as were the company's regional and national head offices. Its management was subjected to close scrutiny from various superiors who arbitrarily intervened in increasingly desperate attempts to try to 'heal this gaping wound' of low productivity. But such interventions were counter-productive; they undermined the authority and independence of the site management.

By contrast, DCB was in Brisbane, a thousand kilometres from the

Figure 7.1 FoodCo Corporate Structure

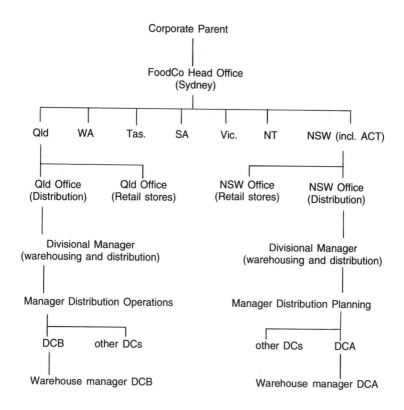

Source: adapted from a FoodCo in-house diagram

national head office, and it experienced less intervention from its regional head office. The DCB management had a strong sense of independence; they exercised their authority confidently in the workplace without fear of unwanted intervention.

At DCA, however, the company initially transferred a manager from a small old warehouse to become the DCA manager. He had worked his way up into management and was neither specifically trained nor experienced in using the new technology. DCA suffered a discontinuity of management as FoodCo became impatient to find a remedy for the escalating problems of this DC. Managers were moved in to improve DCA and sometimes were moved on before they had time to tackle the problems thoroughly. Other managers left voluntarily. DCA acquired a reputation as a 'career destroyer'. Its managers were caught in the cross-fire of industrial disruption against the background of a power struggle between the regional and national head offices. There was also considerable inter-functional conflict, especially between the supermarkets, distribution, and electronic data processing functions. The DCA managers became demoralised as their superiors interfered in local decision-making and quarrelled among themselves. Sensing the weak position of DCA managers, the delegates demanded that their grievances be resolved by higher-level managers either from the regional or national head offices. This further undermined the authority of managers at the site.

In its formative period, no one individual associated with DCA was sufficiently competent and strong to be the 'champion' of change. There was confusion about who was in charge: the DC manager, the regional office, or the national head office. As one company executive put it: DCA was 'a ship without a skipper'. Especially in its early days, there appeared to be no *strategy* there; the various managers connected with it adopted short-term *tactics*, which were not always consistent. More recently, however, there has been a more consistent management at DCA.

By contrast, for DCB, the company initially recruited a professional DC manager already experienced in logistics and in computerised warehousing. As the best-qualified person in this field in the company, he was able to take charge as a strong leader from the start. He formulated a series of strategies to commission and subsequently to operate DCB. Not only did he become the champion of innovation, but he developed other managers with complementary skills who stayed with the project through its formative years.

The senior managers at each site decide employment levels for the warehouse, purchase major capital equipment, allocate resources for in-house training, and when appropriate they refer matters to the industrial relations commission. Managers at DCB say that they are generally consulted about decisions made higher up in FoodCo regarding, for example, the use of financial surplus, the introduction of bonus or incentive schemes, or the appointment of new managers. They claim to have significant autonomy in the operation of DCB, and that head office supports them when required. This is also the case under the current DCA management, in contrast to the pattern in the earlier periods, when there was more head office intervention at DCA.

Figure 7.2 Distribution Centres' Management Structure

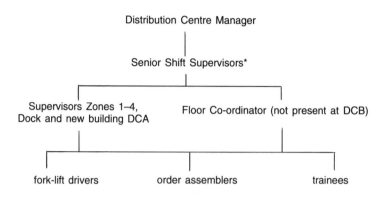

* Structure from senior shift supervisor down is repeated for each shift.
Source: adapted from a DCA in-house diagram

The DCs' organisational structure is illustrated in Figure 7.2. Senior shift supervisors (middle managers) have always had the authority to make important decisions about the operation of DCB. They recruit, deploy, dismiss, and promote non-managerial staff; they determine levels of overtime, and attempt to change work practices. In the early period of its operation, middle managers at DCA were constrained in these decisions by the feeling of being watched by head office. They were constrained throughout by the militance of the workforce which, they say, determines levels of overtime and constrains decisions on deployment, promotion, and dismissal of staff, as well as levels of overtime.

At each DC, most industrial relations matters are handled by the senior line managers. At DCA, in particular, such matters are a major preoccupation for the senior managers. Neither DC has the exclusive use of a specialist industrial relations manager, however, each can call on the services of such a specialist who has broad responsibilities and is based at the state head office, rather than inside the DC.

The workforce

In 1985, there were 285 people employed at DCA and 225 at DCB. As shown in Table 7.1, by 1990 the workforce had grown significantly at DCA, but was still almost at the same level at DCB.

Table 7.1   Occupational Groups in DCA and DCB

| | DCA | | DCB | |
Occupations	number	%	number	%
Managers	19	4	12	5
Professionals and				
para-professionals	3	1	2	1
Tradespersons	7	2	7	3
Clerks	8	2	7	3
Sales and personal				
service workers	0	0	0	0
Warehouse workers	388	91	203	88
Total	425	100	231	100

Source: data provided in mid-1990 by DC managers; percentages are rounded.

DCA was located in Sydney's old western suburbs—a large and competitive labour market in which the available supply of workers was 'industrially sophisticated'. Many of the supervisors and workers were transferred from an old warehouse nearby, despite the union having warned FoodCo about a few known trouble-makers, some of whom had become workgroup leaders. By contrast, fewer of DCB's workers had a manufacturing background. (There is less manufacturing in Brisbane than in Sydney.) DCB's management was more selective about who was transferred from its old warehouse, especially into the supervisory team. In both cities, FoodCo had outgrown its old warehouses. It continued to use them, however, but only for the slower-moving non-food stocks.

The largest occupational groups in the DCs are order assemblers and fork-lift drivers. The occupational profiles of DCA and DCB are summarised in Table 7.1. The bulk of the warehouse workers assemble orders, check orders in and out, and re-deploy goods in the warehouse. In addition, FoodCo employs managers, nurses, tradespeople and clerks in its DCs. The tradespeople are electricians and mechanics employed to maintain the machinery. One trainee is employed at DCB, but there are none at DCA. Computer operators, accounts staff, and stock control personnel are also employed in each DC. These staff are not included in Table 7.1 since they have other responsibilities apart from servicing the DCs where they are located. Jobs are polarised into full-time per-manent and part-time casual, as shown in Table 7.2. Also each DC engages contractors for specialist maintenance work and to provide catering.

Table 7.2 Gender and Employment Status of the Workforce

| | DCA | | DCB | |
	number	%	number	%
Full-time permanent: Male	372	88	190	82
Female	13	3	16	7
Part-time permanent: Male	0	0	0	0
Female	0	0	0	0
Full-time casual: Male	0	0	0	0
Female	0	0	0	0
Part-time casual: Male	40	9	7	3
	0	0	18	8
Total	425	100	231	100

Source: data provided by DCA and DCB managers in mid-1990

There are some significant differences between the workforces at DCA and DCB. Many of the casual workers at DCA have second jobs, so are not dependent on a single employer. This is especially the case on the afternoon shift, which has more stoppages than the morning shift. DCA employs some people who already have a second job at another warehouse. Senior managers at DCA are ambivalent about their employees working two jobs. On the one hand such workers are less productive on the job, and are less dependent on the income from their work at DCA; on the other hand, they are less likely to want to work overtime, which reduces the overtime bills substantially (for reasons discussed later). The employment of people who have another full-time job is less common at DCB. In Brisbane, because of the current shift times, workers cannot work two shifts in two different warehouses. Those workers who do paid work outside of DCB generally do irregular work from home.

About a quarter of the workers at DCB and one of the union delegates are female. Initially there were no female storeworkers at DCA. Apparently the workers at DCA did not want women employed there. However, union officials and managers at DCA say that they favour the employment of women at DCA. By 1990, 3 per cent of its workforce were women. Some male workers at DCA opposed the recruitment of women on the grounds that, if they were hired, the men would be required to do more of the heavier jobs, which hitherto were shared among all the workers. (In NSW a restriction on the maximum weight which women can lift restricts women to jobs where loads less than 16 kg are lifted.)

Until 1988 the same restriction existed in Queensland. Although only a quarter of all storeworkers at DCB are women, about one-third of storeworkers on the day shift at DCB are female. No women are employed on other shifts, because all jobs on the night shift and many on the afternoon shift are fork-lift jobs, involving the lifting of heavier weights. Since the weight restrictions have been removed, no women have applied for jobs on these shifts.

Wages in the DCs, as shown in Table 7.3, are comparable with wages in similar occupations under other awards. While pay can be favourably compared with pay at the front-end of retailing, which is the alternative for most of the women employed in DCs, it is low in comparison with pay in other typically 'male jobs'. The base wage rate at DCB in 1990 was $372.70. This rate is boosted by shift allowances of $58.35 for the afternoon shift, and $69.35 for the night shift. At DCA the wages are higher for the order assemblers and fork-lift operators, with a 'Storeman Grade One' earning a weekly wage of $441.60 with 17.5 per cent afternoon-shift allowance, and 27.5 per cent night-shift allowance. In comparison, under the federal metals award an assembly line worker is paid less than the DC workers: $318.00 plus a 15 per cent shift allowance raising the wage to $366.00. A trades assistant under the federal metals award is paid about the same as the DC workers in Brisbane: a basic wage of $314.00 with an average over-award payment of $70 and a shift allowance of 15 per cent raising the wage to $441.60. Under the federal metals award storemen are paid a basic rate of $323.70, with typical over-award payments of $75.00

Table 7.3   Gross Weekly Earnings

		DCA $	DCB $
Clerks: despatch, freight charging		396.40	385.00
Storeworkers:			
Day shift	Storeman grade 1	441.60	372.70
	Fork-lift driver	451.90	385.70
	Checker	468.10	387.70
Afternoon shift	Storeman grade 1	518.88	431.05
	Fork-lift driver	531.00	444.05
	Checker	550.00	446.05
Night shift	Storeman grade 1	563.04	442.05
	Fork-lift driver	576.17	455.05
	Checker	596.82	457.05

Source: Managers at DCA and DCB: mid-July 1990

and shift allowances of 15 per cent raising the wage to \$458.50 for shift workers.[1] This is more than a DCB storeworker and less than a DCA storeworker.

Additional employee benefits at both DCs include: a canteen, a social club, clothing, a rostered day off, discount on FoodCo's products, security of employment for most workers, and recreational facilities. All employees qualify for the superannuation scheme if they have been employed for more than six months, and for more than an average of twelve hours per week.

Employment costs at DCB are about 40 per cent of total costs. At DCA employment costs are about 70 per cent. This difference is because DCA's productivity is much lower, so there are more employees at DCA, which is working at closer to full capacity. The cost of each labour hour is also greater at DCA (Table 7.3), and is increased by the large amount of overtime worked. At DCA there is a one-in-all-in principle of overtime, resulting in 35 per cent of workers in any one week working overtime. There is an expectation of overtime among workers at DCA to boost their wages on a regular basis. At DCB, in contrast, there is no such expectation, and there is no one-in-all-in custom. Weeks pass without many workers being involved in overtime. Nevertheless, overtime is worked by a substantial number of workers at DCB in weeks which include a public holiday, since five days work has to be completed in four days.

At DCA approximately 9 per cent of employees are casual, whereas at DCB 11 per cent are casual. The casual employees at DCB are used to provide the extra labour required for normal weekly fluctuations in demand. This is cheaper than using overtime, since casuals are paid a 25 per cent loading, rather than a 50 per cent or 100 per cent loading for overtime. At DCA such use of casuals is not practicable since almost the maximum proportion of casuals allowed in the industrial agreement is used in the daily running of the warehouse.

Contrasting industrial relations experiences

When these warehouses first opened, managers claimed that the jobs in the new DCs required new skills, since people had to learn to operate the new equipment. However, the new tasks were not very difficult and workers were supposed to follow instructions from the computer, rather than rely on their own knowledge and experience. At DCA, the 'pick routes' seemed disorganised; workers complained that the computerised 'pick list' would sometimes instruct them to pick heavy goods to stack on top of breakables. Therefore they did not always follow the recommended pick route, nor unload goods exactly where the computer instructed. But once goods were put in a different place, chaos could soon follow: the pick list might say 'pick baked beans at a particular location', but actually dog food was there!

People seemed to work inefficiently and slowly at DCA. The work organisation seemed to be more efficient at DCB, though one shop steward there assured us that the people did a 'fair day's work'. DCB workers were told to pick orders so that the stack of cartons remained as level as possible; they picked 'level layers'. At DCA, some workers picked around a pyramid of cartons, which was more likely to cause breakages as the pyramid collapsed.

A 'them and us' division was apparent at DCA. It was like a barricade between the workers and supervisors who adopted an autocratic style. As one manager put it, 'the supervisors used a piece of "four by two" [wood] when a feather was needed', resulting in confrontation with workers. Also, there were entrenched demarcation customs among the workers, for example, between fork-lift truck drivers, order-assemblers, checkers, packers, and cleaners. Furthermore, there were allegations that recruitment and the allocation of jobs were determined by favouritism (or on the basis of religious or other links).

Rather than a division between 'them and us', DCB supervisors had a more consultative style and there was some flexibility among the workforce. Everyone did their own cleaning. If a worker broke a carton at DCB he or she would clean it up, but at DCA it might simply be left for the cleaners. Each of DCB's zones was managed by a supervisor, but with a quasi-autonomous workgroup approach. By contrast, at DCA, there was no such clear association between zones and supervisors. Some said that, as they had to confront an intransigent union, the supervisors there had 'lost the ability to motivate' and had 'given up their managerial responsibilities; there was no discipline'.

The DCB management designed an induction and training program for all employees, who quickly became confident about operating the new technology. At DCA, by contrast, training had a lower priority, so neither the managers nor the workers became competent or confident about operating the technology.

As DCA was being established, the workgroup leaders took the opportunity to win extra pay and generally to maximise the workers' advantage by further restricting the working practices which had prevailed at the old warehouse. There was the opposite process at DCB, where managers sought to maximise their advantage by increasing their control over the labour process and, where possible, changing the prevailing working practices which they saw as restrictive. Although the workers claimed extra pay for working with the new technology at DCB, managers made no concessions.

Unions

Most employees at DCA belong to the National Union of Workers (NUW) (formerly the Storemen and Packers' Union), one of the most powerful and reputedly militant Australian unions. At both DCs, the managers said that they preferred to deal directly with the delegates, rather than with the full-time union officials. Perhaps the industrial disruption at DCA was exacerbated by the managerial tactics, which sought to separate the employees from their union officials. This approach was based upon managements' view that the workers were being 'misled' by the union. The result of these tactics, however, was to strengthen the power of unofficial workgroup leaders at DCA, who frequently called for industrial action independently of their delegates and the full-time union officials. As one manager put it, the NUW state leadership had its own 'political agenda'. Another said: 'there was industrial anarchy'. And perhaps the stoppages at DCA were not solely to pursue serious industrial grievances. As many workers on the afternoon shift had second jobs, it was suggested that one reason for them instigating stoppages was to gain a much-needed break from work.

Retail warehouse employees in Brisbane usually belong to the Shop, Distributive and Allied Employees' Association (SDA). In the late 1980s, the SDA claimed more members than any other Australian union, but many of them are part-time and it is generally seen as a moderate right-wing union and much less powerful than the NUW. Industrial disruption was negligible at DCB. There was some criticism by delegates that pay levels were lower there than at DCA and about the high productivity levels (i.e. pick rates) which the DCB management demanded. In 1984, the DCB manager dismissed a worker who was seen as a poor performer. The SDA contested this case successfully at an arbitration hearing. Even so, some workers at DCB complained that the SDA was too weak, but others claimed that this reflected the workers' fear that the DCB management would dismiss people whom they saw as trouble-makers.

In spite of such claims, managing industrial relations at DCB was more akin to 'fire prevention', in comparison with the 'fire fighting' approach at DCA. DCB management aimed to be 'firm but fair'. They made positive attempts to establish and maintain a high level of trust between all levels of their organisation, as a foundation on which to build industrial peace and employee commitment to corporate goals. Key differences between DCA and DCB are summarised in Table 7.4 (page 191). None of these factors should be considered in isolation. They are all interrelated. Perhaps it was part of FoodCo's problem that managers at DCA sought to resolve the problems by treating individual symptoms rather than seeing their interconnections. However, DCA managers were demoralised by their many industrial battles with the union, which precipitated frequent hearings in the industrial commission.

Retail distribution is within the jurisdiction of the state industrial commissions. The storeworkers at DCA are covered by an industrial agreement between FoodCo and the NUW: *The Storemen and Packers Grocery and Variety Chain Warehousing Agreement of 1986*, that is registered in the Industrial Commission of NSW. The storeworkers at DCB are covered by an industrial agreement between FoodCo and the SDA. The agreement is based on the *Shop Assistants' (Retail Stores) Award—Southern Division*, and is registered in the Queensland Industrial Relations Commission.

Although the NUW and SDA are the dominant unions at DCA and DCB, at each DC clerical employees belong to the Federated Clerks' Union (FCU), and a few workers at each DC belong to the Federated Miscellaneous Workers' Union (FMWU). Some maintenance workers at DCB belong to the Amalgamated Metal Workers' Union (AMWU), while some of those at DCA belong to the Australasian Society of Engineers.

The SDA has seven delegates on site at DCB: three in the (largest) morning shift and two in each of the afternoon and night shifts. In each shift the delegates are elected as 'number one', 'number two', or 'number three', with 'number one' being the most senior. In each shift the number one delegate has several years experience as a delegate. The number one delegate of the largest shift is female; all other delegates are male. The FCU, which has the second-largest membership (thirty-seven people) on site, has no delegate at either of the DCs.

Foodco managers have entered into national agreements with the SDA, FCU, and NUW which ensure 100 per cent membership of the appropriate unions, and automatic payroll deductions. No managers or professional employees at either site are covered by industrial awards.

Table 7.4 Factors Influencing the Success of Technological Change

DCA in Sydney	DCB in Brisbane
Management	
No 'champion'	A specialist 'champion'
Short-term tactics	Long-term strategy
Discontinuity	Continuity
Demoralised by failure	Motivated by success
Intervention from superiors	Relative autonomy
Poor supervision	Good supervision
Work organisation	
Disorganised	Organised more effectively
No performance appraisal	Performance appraisal
'Them and us'	'One big family'
Demarcation	Flexibility
Autocratic supervision	Consultative supervision
Little training	Training
Inefficient work practices	More efficient work practices
Industrial relations	
Workgroup leaders are not necessarily stewards	Workgroup leaders are stewards
Power struggles between workgroup leaders, stewards, NUW, and managers	More collaboration between stewards, SDA, and managers
NUW 'militant'	SDA 'moderate'
'Fire-fighting' management style	'Fire-preventing' management style
Labour force	
Industrially sophisticated	Less industrially sophisticated
Some with second job	Mainly only one job
Location	
Sydney's industrial western suburbs	Brisbane's light industrial outskirts
Near national headquarters	Distant from national headquarters
Under scrutiny of superiors	Relative autonomy for local managers
Product market	
Includes a large city and a large rural area	Smaller urban area with larger rural component
Shorter delivery cycles	Longer delivery cycles
Technology	
Management initially preoccupied with commissioning difficulties	Similar technology but fewer difficulties

Source: the authors' interpretation

Negotiations, consultation and dispute settlement

In 1985, largely because of the increasingly apparent failings of DCA, FoodCo was losing market share in its most important market, Sydney.

FoodCo shares were becoming the focus of take-over speculation. Managers were getting more and more nervous about the company's survival (and their own job security). In these circumstances, the managing director made a radical move. He decided to retain DCA as the main warehouse for the Sydney area, but in view of his satisfaction with FoodCo's sub-contracted transport arrangements, he proposed to sub-contract the management of DCA to the same contractor, TruckCo. FoodCo continued to own the premises and the stock, but TruckCo took over the mobile equipment and became the employer of nearly all staff at DCA. TruckCo was a rapidly growing road haulage business which already held several transport contracts with FoodCo.

There has been an international trend in retail distribution towards sub-contracting transport and, to a lesser extent, warehousing. An argument often used to justify this type of development is that it releases retailers from the 'distractions' of transport and warehousing, and leaves them to concentrate on their 'core missions' and do what they know best: buying and selling. However, as one competitor of FoodCo warned: 'It's a frightening thing to have a large part of your business in the hands of someone else'.

Immediately after TruckCo took over, DCA's fortunes appeared to be transformed. There was a significant reduction in stoppages and an increase in productivity. DCA appeared to be almost 'a new place'. The transformation can be explained in terms of three factors in particular: the management, work organisation and industrial relations.

TruckCo's style, strategy, and tactics appeared to be different from those of the previous bureaucratic style of managers. Although already a millionaire, TruckCo's founder and owner, Mr Truck, saw DCA as a great personal challenge. He began by spending a month of intensive work at DCA. He gave pep talks to the workers and was able to infect them with enthusiasm. He asked them directly what was wrong with DCA and offered cash payments for useful suggestions. Mr Truck demanded major improvements in productivity at DCA before he would offer job security there. He negotiated a redundancy scheme with the union which initially applied to fourteen long-service workers on a voluntary basis, but the 'volunteers' included two of those whom the managers (and the union) had seen as trouble-makers.

Although the big retailers had been hesitant about confronting the 'restrictive practices' endemic in warehouses in Sydney (and Melbourne), TruckCo insisted on measuring productivity. He did deals with the union to win its agreement to changes in several work practices at DCA: greater flexibility in the deployment of labour, the abolition of one-in-all-in overtime, the abolition of casual employees, and an arrangement whereby workers would do their own cleaning (this had previously been undertaken by sub-contract cleaners).

TruckCo did not engage in 'union busting'. When meeting union negotiators, however, its managers had a tough approach. They did not simply listen to their claims, but countered them with their own claims. While taking over the running of DCA, its owner, Mr Truck, personally negotiated with the union at three levels: with the federal officials on national issues, with the state secretary on state agreements and awards, and with the DC delegates on workplace issues.

He offered continuity of union coverage and job security for the union's members in return for its cooperation. Significantly, he also offered to restore the union's authority at DCA by insisting that the managers and the employees abide by the agreed disputes procedures. Thus he strengthened the authority of the delegates and full-time organisers, so that they too would be responsible for the conduct of any industrial disputes, thereby establishing a more orderly approach to grievance handling at DCA, and getting the union 'on side' with the managers. Delegates at DCA indicated that initially they respected the new TruckCo manager. 'We know where we stand with him; he can hire and fire. Under the old managers we didn't know where we stood. We couldn't negotiate with them. Decisions were made at about six levels above them.'

TruckCo initially appeared successful at changing the productivity and patterns of industrial relations at DCA. The sub-contracting of DCA was potentially traumatic for all concerned: FoodCo, the workers, the delegates, the NUW, and even for TruckCo. Mr Truck personally became 'a champion' at DCA. To help him learn the business, he borrowed a manager from DCB for two months. Together, they investigated urgently the industrial, organisational, and technical systems at DCA and proposed changes. Then, to take over the day-to-day management, TruckCo recruited a warehouse manager from another firm.

His new DCA managers followed examples from DCB. For instance, TruckCo reorganised the DCA layout to emphasise the importance of workgroups and to give more responsibility to the first-line supervisors for the performance of their teams. This was in an attempt to change the balance of power between the supervisors and delegates, so that each would have a complementary role in managing and in dealing with discontent. The abolition of casual employees was designed not only to cut labour costs, but also to ensure that the workers were fully committed and could be held accountable for achieving specific performance levels. The new DCA layout included four clearly separated zones with a computer installed in each. Employees were trained to use the computers to monitor the movement of stock and respond to the information provided. TruckCo arranged a booking-in system for deliveries to eliminate congestion at the delivery bays, and it encouraged FoodCo data processing staff to be more responsive to the needs of supervisors and workers. The work organisation was thus adapted to be more conducive to the efficient handling of materials.

Mr Truck had a novel approach to negotiations, consultation, and dispute settlement. None the less, he personally continued to be 'a champion' for only a few months. After he moved on to other issues, productivity dropped, the deals were not fully honoured and industrial disruption increased again. The extra cost of the sub-contracted DCA could be justified only if it maintained a much higher performance than under the old regime. Once it became obvious that TruckCo was not maintaining its early success, FoodCo grew anxious about this sub-contract. After less than three years of the new regime, FoodCo terminated TruckCo's contract and DCA reverted to FoodCo's direct management. Again, there were initial improvements, but these were not maintained. Evidently, such short-lived improvements were a 'Hawthorne effect'.

Management at the DCs in the 1990s

Two FoodCo managers were moved to DCA to replace TruckCo managers: the NSW divisional manager of warehousing, and the manager (distribution planning) were re-located to DCA to manage the warehouse, as well as to coordinate the operations of other NSW warehouses. The DCA managers were then all located at DCA and its directorate was all on site. Workplace managers were obliged to inform head office of any industrial or other problems.

The current NSW divisional manager of warehousing has had a long involvement with DCA. He was the manager who had been responsible for monitoring the performance of DCA when it was under TruckCo management. After TruckCo's contract was terminated, he resumed control of DCA, but with little expectation of raising productivity in the short term. Rather, his brief was to provide a reliable and consistent service to the stores. This involved also cutting costs and restoring some control of the timing and nature of disputes to FoodCo. He comments:

The same issues generate disputes at (DCA) as they do in other warehouses. But the industrial climate here is different ... People have different expectations regarding how matters will be resolved. There is a history at DCA that management can't criticise or reprimand ... My job is mainly to size up whether we can afford a particular stoppage. While TruckCo was in charge a lot of (restrictive) work practices were introduced which we are trying to remove. This is a slow process. Even a half day stoppage is very expensive. So we can't do very much very quickly except for preventing new work practices from being introduced.

In the past, the number of first-line supervisory positions was cut in an attempt to make workers more responsible for their own productivity. According to managers, this has not worked, so more supervisors are currently being recruited to manage discrete groups of workers and to boost their productivity. Supervisors are being sent to Australian Institute of Management training courses in an attempt to provide them with management skills. DCA has difficulty attracting good supervisors from the external labour market, but it is even more difficult to promote people via the internal labour market. This is partly due to the potential for personality conflicts generated when a worker is promoted to a position of authority above his workmates. When supervisors are promoted internally, they used to be chosen according to seniority. Latterly, however, the DCA management has been aiming to promote on the basis of merit.

At DCB, the management has always aimed to identify employees with promotion potential using aptitude tests. First-line supervisors are made responsible for managing their own workgroups. In an attempt to build a spirit of cooperation, DCB's managers have emphasised the importance of direct communications between managers, delegates, supervisors and individual employees. Periodically, the DCB manager talks to meetings of all employees on each shift. The current DCA manager is now also adopting such an approach. However, this style has emerged more recently at DCA after a period of comparative industrial militancy.

Consultation

In both DCs, managers claim to consult the employees extensively on matters which directly affect them, for example, changes in the work process or the introduction of new technologies. Shift managers hold regular meetings to obtain suggestions from workers regarding the operation of the warehouse. In one instance at DCB, some workers who were sceptical about the benefits of a proposed technological change were taken to another warehouse to observe the operation of the new technology.

In contrast to the earlier periods, the current DCA managers are striving to improve productivity through consultation and training. Their management style aims to be visible and approachable. To this end they have regular meetings with about twenty representatives of the storemen, including some delegates, at which they discuss ways of improving the efficiency of the centre. In 1990, it was higher-level managers, concerned primarily with FoodCo's shops, who decided to change the DC layout to facilitate stock handling at the front-end. Nevertheless the DCs' managers recognised that the operators them-selves would be best informed about precisely how to organise the new layout to be most effective. Therefore the managers went to some lengths to consult the operators.

In order that members from all shifts can attend, there are two health and safety committees at DCB, each of which consists of three workers and one manager. These committees meet monthly. While health and safety matters are frequently raised by the delegates, they do not generate much conflict. The SDA delegate says that she receives a fair hearing when she raises these matters and she characterises managers' attitudes as 'sensible'. A health and safety committee also operates at DCA, with representatives from each shift. As at DCB, it meets monthly and appears to generate little conflict. A nurse is employed at DCA.

In comparison with their predecessors, the current managers at DCA are more positive about the role of the union. Some say that the NUW has a reasonable approach and generally abides by the agreements which it makes with the employers. They claim, however, that the workers do not always abide by the agreements. As one manager puts it: 'the union has created a tiger over which it has no control'. This is supported to some extent by one union official: 'Some of our members are not angels'. But this is denied by another: 'our membership is well disciplined and active at [FoodCo] . . . Members will rarely take action without consulting us. I am grateful that I have such a well disciplined membership, therefore, the employers have to take us seriously . . .'

Industrial conflict

DCA services more shops, and has a higher turnover of stock. As it is a busier warehouse, DCA managers argue that even with good industrial relations it could probably not achieve as high a level of productivity as DCB can. However, the apparently endemic industrial conflict at DCA has contributed to its low productivity, as it loses many working days through industrial stoppages. These reflect an attitude that industrial differences will not be settled until workers walk off the job. Moreover the management is committed to improving work practices as much as possible. In one year, which was a relatively peaceful one for Australia as a whole, there were thirty-eight recorded industrial stoppages at DCA, and more that were not recorded. Between January and August 1990, DCA lost 1250 worker-days through industrial action.

At DCB there has been comparative industrial peace. Management and union delegates perceive industrial relations there as 'good'. An indication of this is that between 1988 and 1990 there were no strikes and only one half-hour stop work meeting at DCB. Its management encourages any employee with a complaint to settle it directly with the shift manager. The dispute is considered at a higher level of management at DCB only if shift supervisors fail to settle it. All the parties agree that most problems are solved on site in an informal manner. A union delegate noted that managers are polite to workers, treating them 'as people, not as tools'. SDA officials and DCB managers have a productive and informal relationship. Indeed the major complaint of SDA officials about site managers is their failure to notify the union formally about relevant matters. SDA officials say that information is generally passed to them informally by managers or by union delegates, rather than in written form.

DCB managers characterise their approach to industrial relations as one of decentralisation and delegation. There have been few sackings of permanent employees. When workers have been sacked, the SDA has seldom been able to mount a case for reinstatement at the Queensland Industrial Relations Commission. The SDA officials admit that usually they have been consulted from the early stages of any disciplinary action, and that dismissals are avoided where possible by the company. In contrast the DCA managers say that the union there will back any sacked worker, even if the state secretary of the union is aware that the worker in question is not doing 'a fair day's work'.

While collective industrial conflict has been minimal at DCB, there have been pockets of explicit conflict. In particular, the afternoon shift has a higher rate of disputation. It is staffed by men, some of whom have second jobs. There is not complete harmony at DCB, for labour turnover is relatively high (22 per cent per annum in 1989). The union officials and managers explain this as a consequence of the nature of the work (which is repetitive), the low wages, and the poor career opportunities. They note that despite the high turnover rate, there is a core of stable workers who have been employed in the warehouse for over five years. The high turnover tends to be among young male workers.

Many grievances dealt with by union delegates at both DCs are generated by interpersonal conflicts, although managers and union officials reported that a greater number is generated by misinterpretation of the industrial agreement at DCA. One delegate added that most grievances could be avoided if workers were simply more polite in their requests, and if employees thought out the reasons for their requests more clearly.

Productivity measurement

By 1990, workers' average pick-rates were monitored by managers at both DCs, even though the unions have consistently opposed the notion of performance appraisal at each DC. When it opened, the DCB managers displayed productivity charts and discussed performance with individuals each Friday. Those whose pick-rates were consistently below average were counselled and retrained, or might be dismissed or moved back to the old warehouse from which they had come. The regular discussion of pick-rates with workers has ceased, at the request of employees. Instead at DCB managers approach workers about their pick-rate if it falls much below the average rate for that employee and remains low for a few consecutive weeks. As one DCB delegate puts it: 'if a bloke's wife has their first baby he is given a few weeks to show the photos around before his rate is expected to go back to normal'. If the management see a worker's pick-rate as inadequate the shift supervisor may ask a delegate to speak with the worker to find out whether the aberrant rate is caused by personal problems. If so, such workers are given some time to readjust their rate before action is taken. In general workers are not sacked due to low productivity; rather they are counselled to improve.

At DCA the NUW does not accept the notion of a 'pick-rate'. Because of the opposition from the union and workers to measurement of individual productivity levels, managers have convened a 'productivity group' in an endeavour to improve productivity throughout the warehouse as a whole. The NUW supports this group and its delegates attend the meetings. In spite of its productivity failings and in keeping with the prevailing custom, managers at DCA have never discussed pick-rates or work targets with individual employees, on the grounds that officials of the NUW would consider such action to warrant a work stoppage.

The post-1987 'second tier' and award restructuring negotiations

Industrial relations at DCB were strained after the 1987 national wage case decision and during the consequential 1987–88 second-tier negotiations. Morale fell, as workers felt that managers were being too hard. In view of the enterprise-based nature of the negotiations, workers saw the negotiations as too 'personal', rather than being between external agencies as had generally been the custom hitherto. After a long and tedious process, the offsets conceded by the union for the 4 per cent wage rise were:

- standardisation of normal hours for each shift across FoodCo warehouses in Queensland;
- the extension of normal hours to include Saturday;
- electronic funds transfer payments on a weekly basis;
- the insertion into the award of a new disputes-settlement procedure;
- increased flexibility of meal breaks;
- provisions to enable the movement of workers between warehouses, with twenty-one days notice.

The major change for employees was a change in shift starting and finishing times. This and the introduction of electronic funds transfers (EFT) were opposed by DCB employees.

Given that FoodCo had previously paid an over-award 17.5 per cent leave loading to workers on the afternoon shifts at DCB, workers were particularly resentful that FoodCo reverted to the minimum award rate. This did not happen after any negotiations but was a decision taken unilaterally by FoodCo managers who claimed that the extra payments had resulted initially from a clerical error.

The workers felt that this should have been included as part of the second-tier negotiations. While there were no strikes during the negotiations, there were periodic union meetings from which employees 'failed to return to work'. The lack of official strikes was explained by a delegate as due to the apparent threat of fines which might be imposed for striking in so-called 'essential services' in Queensland.[2]

At DCA the second-tier negotiations resulted in shift changes, so that the day shift was extended from between 7.00 a.m. and 5.30 p.m. to between 6.00 a.m. and 6.00 p.m. A formal disciplinary procedure was also introduced such that three formal warnings were required before a weekly employee could be sacked. Warnings may be given for poor safety, absenteeism, lateness, or poor work performance. But the introduction of EFT was rejected by the union and workers.

Both parties to the industrial agreement at DCA see award restructuring as a 'farce'. After the 1988 national wage case decision, the negotiations between FoodCo and the NUW resulted in only two changes to the award: a reduction in the warning required for selective overtime from 48 hours to 24 hours, and the discontinuation of an early start on the day before a public holiday. Formerly this had meant that workers could begin and finish their shift one hour early.

According to management these changes were of 'no consequence' in comparison with some of the other nine changes which they would have liked to have seen implemented in June 1990. These were:

- an end to one-in-all-in overtime;
- an increase in the numbers of casuals;
- deletion of a provision in the award which allows employees to take one day of sick leave without a doctor's certificate;
- to enable the nurse to leave the first aid room by giving her a pager;
- the rostered day off to be a rolling one from Monday to Friday (rather than all workers there on Tuesday which is a quiet day);
- overtime on the day shift to start at 5.00 p.m. rather than 3.00 p.m.;
- managers to be allowed to operate the computers in an emergency;
- managers to be allowed to assemble orders and receive goods in an emergency and to be involved in stock taking;
- all people to be paid on Wednesdays.

For their part, the NUW argues that the managers' proposals were merely negative cost cutting. As one NUW representative puts it:

> There is nothing to restructure. All multi-skilling means is that workers do everything, but get less money for it. It eliminates jobs ... The positive aspects of restructuring: equal pay for women and juniors, better health and safety, work-based child care, the NUW (and Storemen and Packers before) have been involved in these for years. We have also got training going: insisted on first aid certificates and fork-lift certificates ... The traineeships which have been created under restructuring are simply a way of paying people less to do the same amount of work. This isn't real training; it's a con. We won't agree to it ...
>
> The problem is that in many areas, restructuring just can't be done. For example, if there are 500 employees in a warehouse, there may be scope for fifty fork-lift drivers. This is a preferred job because it is lighter and pays better. If everyone had the skills to do the job, then the employer wouldn't want to pay them all the extra money ... Employers want multi-skilling to mean that they have control over the deployment of the labour force. This means that if there is a personality conflict between a worker

and supervisor, that worker would never get the better jobs. That is why we insist on seniority. To do away with seniority for $12.50 when wages have fallen by $100 compared to inflation is just not on! For $200 we might think about it.

The management interprets the union's position as insisting that all workers should be trained and paid for acquiring new skills, irrespective of whether or not they use their new skills. As a senior manager explained:

> Award restructuring hasn't happened at DCA. The union won't accept any improvements in productivity. They simply want more money . . . they . . . haven't been willing to talk constructively about award restructuring. From them it's all rhetoric!

The company would be willing to pay higher wages if the workers cooperated in increasing productivity. Evidently there is still a considerable gap between the positions of the management and the union.

Conclusions

The following discussion reconsiders this book's key questions in the light of the FoodCo case.

To what extent do systems of conciliation and arbitration influence and shape the processes and outcomes of industrial regulation?
The industrial agreements with the SDA and NUW determine to a large extent the formal conditions of employment that prevail at DCB (with the SDA), but are less important as determinants at DCA (with the NUW), where there is more independent work group power. At DCA management says (facetiously) that 'if only we could work according to the industrial agreement we would be happy'. Despite the fact that they are constrained by the industrial agreement, they feel that just getting the employees to abide by it is a sufficiently onerous task. According to one DCA manager: 'Changing the award is out of the question'.

Some changes which resulted from second-tier offsets (the changing definitions of the shifts in the 1988 industrial agreement at DCB) resulted in changing hours of work for employees, which implies that the hours had previously restricted management. Nevertheless, by mid-1990, some of the offsets won by the DCB management under the second-tier negotiations had still not been implemented by FoodCo.

Thus, although they claimed that parts of the award were constraining their freedom to manage the warehouse, these were not in fact the real constraints. For instance, by 1991, the extension of normal hours in the 1988 agreement/award to include Saturday had still not resulted in Saturday work, in practice.

At DCA, management hires many more casuals and would hire more if they were not restricted from doing so by the agreement. The hiring of casuals is also restricted by the NUW who demands twelve months membership fees for each casual who is engaged. At DCB management are not so constrained (by the agreements) in their hiring of casual labour; there are still maximum levels of casuals specified in the award, but they do not reach this level except at peak periods of the year.

What is the nature of unionism in the warehouses? To what extent does union organisation constrain managerial decision making?
DCA managers say that union organisation is a significant constraint in two main ways: first, the union policy curtails management decision-making, and second, the union is unable to control its members, whose wishes also constrain decision-making. In relation to the second, managers contend that when they achieve an efficient operation of the warehouse and overtime rates fall, then workers start reducing their productivity so that overtime rates will rise to the accustomed levels. On the other hand, managers say that their wishes to pay people according to what they do, and to promote on the basis of merit are accepted by employees, but not by the union.

At DCB, union organisation appears to be much less of a constraint. Union delegates are seen as 'moderate' in their approach to problems by management. There is no inter-union conflict, and the unions have a flexible approach to demarcation. This contrasts with DCA, where management says that there are no demarcation problems, because the NUW is more powerful than any other unions on site and allows no storework to be done by non-NUW members.

Management and SDA full-time officials praise the SDA's shop-floor delegates as being well-informed about current agreements and as seeking to settle differences as quickly as possible. The compulsory membership agreement is favoured by the management and the unions. On their side, workplace-level managers at DCB are also well-informed about current agreements. While some supervisors at DCA were described by the union as petty and unable or unwilling to settle disputes directly with the delegates, at DCB supervisors appear to be able to settle most disputes and grievances informally.

Employees at DCB do not seem to be willing to lose pay by striking. The workforce includes a large proportion of young people repaying mortgages. There is a high turnover rate and little interest in the social club. Despite a high level of dissatisfaction generated by the second-tier negotiations, the workers did not take much collective industrial action. Many of the DCB casual workers on the afternoon shift have other jobs which they do before they start work at the warehouse (and this shift has more grievances), while the day shift has more older women who apparently 'are just interested in earning a wage'.

The relatively high number of casuals with second jobs at DCA may contribute to the high rates of disputation there. While the relationship is far from clear, it would appear likely that workers who are not dependent on one employer are more likely to be willing to lose pay by striking.

To what degree is workplace level management autonomous from its head office?

Initially workplace management at DCA suffered considerable intervention from the corporate head office. By the 1990s DCA management was more autonomous. However, decisions made elsewhere in FoodCo necessarily affected the operations of the warehouses. An example is provided by the need to reorganise the warehouses to facilitate the unloading of goods in shops.

DCB was also subject to a similar decision to reorganise. None the less, the workplace management at DCB has generally maintained a higher degree of autonomy in the day-to-day running of the warehouse.

The difficulty in assessing the efficiency of a warehouse, except by comparing costs with those of comparable warehouses, means that management is not under pressure to produce a given level of return. Its major task is to maintain the supplies to the retail outlets. As such, industrial relations are seen by even the senior managers as a very important part of their job, not least because industrial relations is an important variable when explaining the different productivity between DCA and DCB.

What is the nature, extent, and impact of recent attempts by management to increase efficiency?

There have been two types of attempt by management to increase efficiency: first, those which are related to the second tier and award restructuring, and, second, those which are independent of such commission-led initiatives. At DCB, there have been few recent and explicit attempts of the second type; even these few have had little direct impact on workers. This is largely because, when the DCs opened, the latest available technology was introduced. Since then, further technological change has mainly been fine-tuning. Furthermore, management has involved workers in its planning and introduction. Before computer-produced labels were introduced, workers were taken to look at this technique at another warehouse where this technology was already operating. These workers were asked for suggestions in relation to its implementation at DCB. The second type of proposed changes (to the work processes at DCB) have not been interpreted as threatening job security, or workers' skills.

By contrast, the post-1988 second-tier negotiations have been fraught with conflict and have resulted in a decrease in morale. Attempts to increase efficiency included the advent of EFT, changed definitions of shifts, a disputes-settlement procedure, and increased flexibility of meal breaks. Management and SDA organisers agree that the offsets have not all been fully implemented and have not resulted in the productivity gains envisaged.

At DCA, attempts to increase efficiency have not even achieved the modest success that they have had at DCB. This is because of the union's opposition to the restructuring process, which is seen as reducing jobs and workers' incomes. An attempt to introduce EFT payments failed because of opposition from individual workers rather than from the union. Both management and union interviewees agreed that the opposition to EFT was probably due to an unwillingness on the part of some male employees to let their wives know how much they earn.

The changes in shift hours and the disciplinary procedure have resulted in no discernible increase in productivity. If the workers really do 'control' overtime, as management suggests, then perhaps productivity improvements are unlikely whatever changes occur to the award.

What attempts are made by management to incorporate the workforce and its organisations? Are these related to increasing efficiency and productivity or cost cutting?

Workers at both DCs are consulted about changes and are asked for their suggestions. At DCA the past difficulties encountered by management have generated renewed attempts to incorporate workers into some elements of the management process. As well as the health and safety committee, there is a committee to discuss ways of raising productivity. This group approach can be seen as a response to the constraints which prevent management from dealing with productivity on an individual basis, as occurs at DCB.

As one manager observed, 'we're in front as long as our costs are less than the company's gross profit'. Profit is not generated directly by warehouse operations and it is difficult to measure their efficiency. The efficiency measures used are related closely to cost cutting: warehouse costs and pick-rates are the main indicators for comparing the efficiency of warehouses. Pick-rates relate to costs; since labour represents a large proportion of cost; higher pick-rates mean that fewer workers are required.

Changes which have improved productivity include the introduction of computer-printed labels at DCB. This appears to be seen as a positive change by the employees at DCB, though they were sceptical when the change was first mooted. The greatest impact of the change, however, would be felt in the shops where the labels have increased the speed of deploying goods that arrive at the shop. The change may be seen as increasing efficiency and/or as cost cutting.

DCB managers claim that they practise a modern approach to human resource management. But the SDA counters this claim by arguing that the managers do not place enough emphasis on training and career structures. The union argues that the managerial focus on penalty rates and hours indicates a cost-cutting mentality, rather than a way of trying to increase productivity or introducing real workplace reform.

The SDA and the Australian Workers Union (AWU) have proposed an extended career structure for warehouse workers in Queensland. The proposal is to extend the structure from three to four grades. The new structure culminates in a 'Stores Administrative Officer' grade. At the highest level, workers in the warehouse would be expected to implement quality control and be responsible for a whole warehouse, or at least a large section. A stores administrative officer would be required to exercise a high level of interpersonal skills in the supervision of other employees. Management, in contrast, claims that there is little scope for introducing new career structures or extended training programs and that DCB is as good or better than other DCs in respect of training and career structures.

In the early 1990s, the DCA management was aiming to introduce new training packages for all categories of workers. The management hopes to improve the performance of first-line supervisors in particular. However the management confronted considerable difficulties in trying to introduce these training programs. Unlike the SDA, the NUW was not convinced that training (multi-skilling) is appropriate for warehouse workers.

Towards an explanation of the contrast

The key differences which explain FoodCo's contrasting experiences with DCA and DCB include management strategy, tactics and style, as well as the different industrial relations experiences. The case demonstrates the importance of established practices and styles in determining the outcome of managers' strategies. DCB was successful because it began with a strong leader and a technically competent management team, in addition to a more tractable industrial context. DCB managers' strategy included careful selection, induction, and training for all of the workforce, especially the supervisors. Hence, employees at all levels of DCB have felt confident of their ability to work with the new technology. Management has achieved a relatively high-trust relationship between the workgroups, supervisors, and all levels of management, which has been further reinforced by the apparent success of DCB. All concerned have been keen to take some of the credit.

The potential for a high-trust relationship was influenced by the characteristics of the workers, as well as by management. The lack of collective militancy suggests that workers may retreat from the demands of work as individuals (e.g. by absenteeism) rather than in groups (cf. Hyman 1989). Even during second-tier negotiations and when workers were dissatisfied with the way in which managers were handling the process of award restructuring, workers took individual action such as failing to return to work, rather than engaging in collective action such as a strike.

At DCA, by contrast, there has been an adversarial pattern of relationships between workers and supervisors, and between the supervisors and the various levels of managers (local, state, and national) with mutual recriminations and scapegoating. This tendency was exacerbated by the low-trust relationship between the company and the union, as well as by the poor profitability in DCA's region of FoodCo in the 1980s. Managerial vacillation and confusion about the lines of authority and responsibility for DCA created a lower-trust ethos at DCA at the outset, which had not been overcome by the early 1990s.

The major changes which have occurred in DCA's management style did not easily induce significant changes to other aspects of DCA. In response to the failure of the early authoritarian style of management and the subsequent sub-contracting, the DCA managers adopted a more conciliatory style. Managers say that this change of style has not yet been reciprocated by the union leadership, nor has it succeeded in reducing the number of disputes at DCA. Nevertheless, the managers are optimistic that relationships are improving, albeit slowly. In other contexts, several scholars have analysed the differences between the two patterns of high-trust and low-trust relations.[3] One major question is whether and how employing organisations can make the fundamental change from a low-trust to a high-trust syndrome. For some companies, a crisis and a need for mutual survival can help to unfreeze entrenched attitudes and provide the catalyst for change.[4] It has been extremely difficult for the DCA managers and workers to break out of the vicious circle of low trust to create a higher-trust employment relationship. Increased surveillance and the threat of dismissals by DCA managers in the early period merely reinforced the low-trust syndrome. Later attempts to enhance the social and work environment by prescriptions of a human relations type came too late to break entrenched patterns. It seemed that only a crisis could provide the catalyst for change.

A crisis did provide a potential catalyst at DCA in 1985. As one FoodCo manager put it: 'the company was bleeding to death'. The surgeons, TruckCo, appeared to succeed by taking advantage of the feeling of crisis. Because DCB was organised by a different union, the SDA, while all the other TruckCo workers were organised by the Transport Workers' Union (TWU), the NUW was worried that TruckCo would displace it in favour of another union at DCA and at any other warehouses which were taken over. Therefore, the NUW had a strong incentive to cooperate with TruckCo. The workers also faced a crisis. They worried about job security. Management had contingency plans to supply DCA's stores from other warehouses, including DCB. If TruckCo failed at DCA, it could be closed, either permanently or at least temporarily. Even in the latter case, they feared that Mr Truck would not re-hire the same workers, but would rather recruit members of other unions with industrial agreements or awards with lower pay rates than the NUW.

The productivity improvements wrought by TruckCo were short-lived, however. Some of its deals were not honoured and some changes were not sustained, such as the reduction of casual employment.

If DCB's champion were moved to DCA on a longer-term basis, could he have easily solved the problems at DCA? It is unlikely, for the industrial and organisational culture of DCB was very different. Subsequent attempts by managers at DCA to change the culture of employee relations were, at best, only partially successful. The most senior manager at DCA could discuss personal matters with order assemblers informally, which did not seem possible in earlier periods. But stoppages continued. A longer-term solution requires a more significant change than simply imposing yet other managers on the employees. The new FoodCo managers, despite taking a more conciliatory approach, and establishing better relations with the NUW, have been unable to reduce the levels of stoppages or to raise productivity. These managers say their hands are, in effect, tied by the union's intransigence, which seems unlikely to change unless perhaps there is another crisis.

In some ways the analysis of the FoodCo case echoes the approach of the analysts of 'socio-technical system', from Durham coal mines to Indian textile mills. The technical system tends to put '. . . limits on the type of work organization possible, but a work organization has social and psychological properties of its own that are independent of technology'.[5] Socio-technical analysts and subsequent writers rightly emphasise that, even with a given technology, there is usually scope for decision-makers to adopt quite different strategic choices. These will be shaped by the values and power of 'dominant coalitions' and social, economic, and political contingencies. In spite of all the discussion about the effects of different technologies, the technological factors have been less crucial in determining patterns of workplace behaviour in the DCs discussed here, than the choices which have been made about the management strategies and style, work organisation and the industrial relations constraints. These choices and constraints have affected the ability of managers to use the technology, rather than the other way around. Unlike DCA, DCB fully used the new technology from its opening. Its productivity levels rose steadily in the first few years, and it has maintained the high levels.

The FoodCo study also tends to confirm Woodward's original finding that the capabilities of new technology alone do not determine the outcomes of change.[6] Rather, the capabilities of new technology enable and constrain managers' choices when introducing new systems relative to other contingent factors. Instead of portraying technical and social variables as competing with each other, the FoodCo study demonstrates that these may be seen as complementary elements in explanations of the outcomes of technological change, as found by Rose *et al.*[7]

Many critics of Australia's industrial relations argue that it is excessively centralised, and that there is far too much regulation by the federal and state industrial commissions. Against such arguments, the

FoodCo case shows that, in practice, the parties have considerable scope for determining their own industrial destiny, though their context and the force of tradition are both important. Collectively, the key players at DCA should not and do not blame the commission or 'the system' for their problems. Rather they blame each other.

Similarly, those at DCB should take credit for the success story there. At DCB and especially at DCA, the centralised system of industrial relations appears to have only a marginal impact on the actual behaviour of the parties at the workplace.

Authors' note

We acknowledge that this chapter builds on earlier research conducted with Russell Lansbury. One of us conducted the initial interviews, observation and analysis of documents at each DC in 1983. Therefore this study has a longitudinal basis. The most recent phase of this project was made possible by the inter-university grant from the Australian Research Council (chief investigators Joe Isaac and Russell Lansbury). We thank the managers and other employees at the two DCs, and officials of the SDA and NUW for their patience in answering our questions.

Part III:
Conclusions

8 Lessons from the workplace

Never before in Australia has there been so much interest in industrial relations at the workplace level. Policy-makers of virtually all ideological persuasions have focused on microeconomic reform as crucial to Australia's economic future, and significant changes to workplace industrial relations are seen as integral to that reform. Researchers have responded to this new focus of interest. In particular, the Commonwealth Department of Industrial Relations has conducted the Australian Workplace Industrial Relations Survey (AWIRS). This survey provides extremely useful data on the structure and processes of industrial relations at the workplace (see Callus *et al.* 1991). This book complements the AWIRS survey in that it provides a set of detailed case studies, all based to a certain extent on the AWIRS format, but with ample scope for the exploration of issues thrown up by the particular circumstances of each case.

The case studies seek to answer a range of important questions identified by the researchers. These include:

- To what extent do systems of conciliation and arbitration influence and shape the processes and outcomes of industrial regulation at the workplace?
- To what extent does head office control industrial relations at the workplace level, and how much autonomy is enjoyed by local management?
- To what extent are attempts made by management to 'incorporate' the workforce and its organisations? Is this related to the degree to which productivity growth rather than cost minimisation is emphasised as a major goal?
- What is the nature of unionism at the plant level and to what extent do unions constrain managerial decision-making at the workplace?

- What is the nature, extent, and impact of recent attempts by management to increase efficiency in the workplace? To what degree are such attempts related to National Wage decisions (including the second-tier negotiations and award restructuring), or are they independent of them?

The impact of arbitration systems on the workplace

It is useful to set the broader context of the way arbitration influences workplace industrial relations, drawing upon the survey material contained in the AWIRS survey (Callus *et al.* 1991). How do our case studies fit into this broader picture? Unfortunately, the AWIRS survey tells us little about the immediate impact of arbitration at workplaces. It does not give information about whether, or how often, arbitrators visit workplaces. However, it does tell us of an indirect influence: that arbitrators make awards or certify agreements which apply in almost all workplaces. Further, these awards do not generally determine actual earnings, except in the public sector (p. 241). Workplace managers spend little time preparing for tribunal hearings (an average of 3 per cent of time in all workplaces), although such activities are marginally more important in very large firms (p. 264). Most industrial relations managers did not see awards as a significant constraint on the conduct of their job (pp. 270 and 340) perhaps signifying again that the hand of the tribunals is light and remote. These, and other shreds of evidence, suggest that tribunals are not a powerful influence on the workplace, except in loose and minimal ways (such as award determination). However, the guiding influence of awards should not be dismissed too readily. Many workplaces possess a grievance procedure because it is required by an award (p. 343), or are engaged in productivity bargaining in a climate set by tribunals (p. 198).

The case studies demonstrate that the influence of the conciliation and arbitration system varies considerably between different workplaces. With one exception, all of the workplaces are subject to awards of the Australian Industrial Relations Commission. In the Food-Co case, each distribution centre is covered by a different state award. The state tribunals, in general, have wider powers to deal with industrial relations matters at the workplace level than does the federal tribunal. However, compared with other factors, this did not emerge as significant in the case studies.

When considering the influence of the arbitration system on the workplace, it is important to distinguish between two types of issues.

First, there are domestic problems and disputes which arise in the workplace and are almost always settled there: for example, a dispute related to the quality of food served in a factory canteen. Many of these disputes are not award-related, and industrial tribunals have almost no perceptible influence on the settlement of such matters. Second, there are issues which originate outside the workplace, either through National Wage Case decisions or through general union campaigns; for example, reduced working hours. Tribunals clearly have a role in responding to these matters and therefore can have a major influence, especially if a particular plant is regarded as a pace-setter in award conditions. This can be illustrated with reference to the Melbourne plant of Automakers, where pressure is often exerted by the unions to raise standards of pay and other matters which then flow on to other enterprises in related industries.

Tensions sometimes arise between the Australian Industrial Relations Commission and an individual enterprise. There are occasions when management makes concessions at the local or plant level which the Commission is reluctant to approve, since it would create an unwelcome precedent. Nevertheless, the Commission's approval is usually sought because the parties require an agreement which has legal status; for example, through a consent award. Furthermore, individual workplaces may be involved in major stoppages arising from union campaigns which seek a breakthrough in establishing new standards; for example, in superannuation benefits. If unions are sufficiently powerful, the formal powers of the Commission may not be enough to prevent the recurrence of industrial action. This has led critics of the Australian industrial relations system to complain that, rather than exercising too much influence within the workplace, the Commission appears to be either unwilling or unable to enforce its own decisions. In fact, the Commission legally has no enforcement powers and it is up to the complaining parties (either union or employer) to seek to have the awards and orders of the Commission enforced in the courts.

Recent innovations, such as second-tier agreements and award restructuring, have provided the Commission with greater influence in helping to shape the pattern of industrial relations at the workplace. But these developments have also allowed more scope for the parties to determine details of agreements and the means by which they are to be implemented. In some cases there have been almost unprecedented levels of workplace bargaining. However, it has generally been bargaining within a framework of Commission guidelines. This contrasts with the sharply divisive campaigns of the early to mid-1980s over issues such as the 35-hour week and superannuation, when the Commission had substantially less influence over final outcomes. In the Automakers case, the Commission has taken a strong line against any moves which might breach the paid rates award in that industry. However, in the PaintCo case, the authors warn against exaggerating the role of the tribunal in determining industrial relations at the workplace level. While the Commission can provide the framework for introducing a more productivity-oriented approach, for example, the onus remains on both management and unions to negotiate and implement new arrangements within the workplace.

The Hotel International case, by contrast, shows how management can use the arbitration system to achieve changes by taking the initiative in negotiations over award restructuring. Even though the management of Hotel International complained that awards represented a significant constraint on their ability to achieve greater wage flexibility (for example, through the imposition of penalty rates by the Commission), the company played a key role in the industry-level negotiations on award restructuring. This was mainly to ensure that the company retained control over changes at the workplace level.

Management has often proved adept in working with and around awards. Again, Hotel International upgraded a number of jobs to staff positions in order to take the occupants of these jobs outside the constraints imposed by the award system. Furthermore, although the award specifies the base conditions and salary levels for each position, the company negotiated above-award payments directly with staff whose services it wished to retain. Thus, the company has introduced a number of measures that have had the effect of reducing the impact of the award on day-to-day patterns of industrial relations at Hotel International, at least in some areas of its operation.

The retail distribution case provides a clear example of how the influence of state tribunals (in NSW and Queensland) varies in accordance with the strength of the unions. Although FoodCo owns the distribution centres in each state, and head office promulgates policy guidelines in regard to industrial relations, the relationship between management and employees varies considerably between the two centres. At the Queensland site, where the Shop, Distributive and Allied Employees' Association (SDA) has coverage of most distribution centre employees, industrial relations are relatively harmonious, and management has considerable latitude in setting both the formal and informal conditions of employment. By contrast, members of the more powerful and militant National Union of Workers have a history of adversarial relations with management at the Sydney Distribution Centre. Even though management feels constrained by some of the conditions laid down in the industrial agreement (or award), they argued that 'if only we could work according to the industrial agreement we would be happy'. In other words, it is not so much the rules set by the tribunal which constitute a problem, as the difficulty of gaining agreement about their interpretation by employees at the Sydney Distribution Centre.

In summary, the cases suggest that the influence of arbitration systems on the workplace is neither as extensive nor as inhibiting as argued by some commentators. Certainly the tribunals (at both the state and federal levels) play an important role in establishing the general framework of workplace rules. Yet the federal commission does not have any formal powers of enforcement and the application of many of its decisions depends upon the cooperation of the parties involved. Also the significance of arbitration's 'updraft' effect as proposed by Niland (1976, 1978 and 1989) must be questioned as there are many local workplace issues over which the tribunals have little or no influence because the management, employees, and their unions prefer to resolve their differences informally and independently. Thus the view of the Australian system as a hybrid of 'arbitrated bargaining' (Yerbury and Isaac 1971; Isaac 1979 and 1989) seems to be a more accurate picture than the more extreme view advanced by Niland and others, who see arbitration as dominating most aspects of Australian industrial relations. Furthermore, it seems arbitration has not inhibited the development of institutions and processes, at the workplace level, to the extent claimed by Fisher (1972), Fells (1987) and Niland (1976, 1978 and 1989). Indeed, recent trends towards 'managed decentralism' (McDonald and Rimmer 1989) has seen a lowering of the 'centre of gravity' (see Niland 1976), with a greater number of issues being resolved between the relevant parties at the workplace level, albeit often within a framework established through decisions of the Commission. Furthermore, if enterprise level bargaining continues to become more widely established, the parties may refer fewer workplace matters to the Commission, and the constraining influence of the Commission on the workplace may further decline.

Management control of industrial relations at the workplace

AWIRS contextual material may again be used to set a general framework within which our case study findings can be located. Callus *et al.* (1991) have much to say on relations between head office and local management. First, they confirm that the vast majority of large workplaces, with twenty or more employees, belong to a wider organisation (p. 25). Second, they demonstrate that major decisions impacting on the workplace tend to be made 'high up' in the organisation (p. 76). Industrial relations matters tend to be settled lower down, although workplaces vary in this regard (p. 78). There is decision-making power in the hands of workplace managers on issues such as overtime distribution, recruitment, and dismissals, showing the devolution of some personnel and industrial relations matters. However, key negotiable issues such as pay and working hours are generally decided by head office management. Finally, devolution in industrial relations decision-making is much greater in the private sector than the public sector (p. 257).

In order for our cases to shed light on the debate about the degree of control exercised by management at the workplace level, the following questions were asked: To what degree does corporate management direct and control the industrial relations at the workplace level? Is there any divergence between official management policy and the practical realities? What determines the extent to which plant-level management is autonomous of its head office counterpart? All of the workplaces in our study were a part of large conglomerates. In some cases corporate policy reflected a high level of centralised decision-making (as in the case of Automakers) while in others official policy decreed a high degree of independence to management at the workplace level. However, as in other aspects of workplace industrial relations, practice often diverged from formal policy.

In the case of Receptacles, broad industrial relations strategy is set by head office but implemented by local management. Thus, the influence of corporate level management is rather subtle and the general approach is based upon consent rather than coercion. It would appear that the devolved system of management at the plant level will continue to be supported by head office while the results continue to be positive. As noted in the case study: 'the parties at Receptacles enjoyed considerable autonomy in the management of industrial relations ... indeed usually management was able to achieve the outcomes that it preferred'. An apparent willingness of head office to grant autonomy to local management only as long as stable industrial relations prevail, and to intervene as soon as the situation changed, is illustrated by the differences between the two distribution centres at FoodCo where two contrasting policies operated simultaneously. The Brisbane centre, with its record of industrial peace, has continued to enjoy considerable autonomy. By contrast, the more turbulent climate at the Sydney centre has been associated with continuing intervention by head office.

PaintCo provides an example which illustrates the complex and dynamic relationship between the individual plant and head office. In terms of formal policy, PaintCo has a highly decentralised approach. Yet, paradoxically, intervention by head office has been required to install genuine autonomy at the level of the individual plants. The operation of this strategy has created some interesting problems. Traditionally, the plant enjoyed considerable independence from head office in regard to industrial relations. Concessions made by local management were often inconsistent with formal undertakings and practices at other plants. Given the presence of a strong union, the plant became a pace-setter in wages and conditions. Clearly the new devolution aims to change this position, but it is difficult to reverse the plant's leading role without intervention by head office. There has also been considerable turnover among management since the new policies were introduced, thus reducing the number of experienced managers at the plant level. Hence, there exists the strong possibility that devolution may leave relatively inexperienced plant management exposed to strong unions, ultimately requiring centralised controls to be reimposed by corporate headquarters.

Illustrations of varying degrees of centralisation are provided by three of the other cases. Hotel International demonstrates how corporate head office may intervene by setting the broad financial parameters and business goals and, within that framework, encourage individual hotels to act autonomously. This approach applies equally to matters of industrial relations and to commercial decisions. A stricter form of centralised control over industrial relations applies in both Comel and Automakers. In the former case, both the management and the union require that all negotiations on award matters are handled centrally so that all staff in the wider corporation have common standards of pay and conditions. In the latter case, Automakers' management maintains a centralised approach to industrial relations to ensure that wages are kept to an industry average and that unions are not able to play one company (or plant) off against another. At both Comel and Automakers, however, scope exists for local negotiations on non-award matters. The Automakers case also illustrates that geographic proximity may not be a significant factor in determining the relative degree of head office control. Despite its distance from head office, the Sydney plant enjoys less autonomy than the Melbourne plant, which shares the same site as the head office.

In summary, none of the cases exhibit either totally centralised or decentralised forms of management control at the workplace level. Although the desirability of greater devolution of authority to management in the workplace is frequently espoused, head office often intervenes in order to achieve desired outcomes. One example is when a workplace comes under pressure from unions and appears as though it may become a pace-setter for wage increases. Head office intervention may also reflect lack of experience with decentralisation of authority. However, the influence of corporate management on the workplace may also be rather subtle. Although plant-level management is formally responsible for day-to-day decision-making, strategy is set by head office and the performance of local management is closely monitored to ensure that it keeps within the guidelines. The findings from these cases support the rejection by Marginson *et al.* (1988) of the traditional dichotomy whereby 'strategic' decisions were the concern of head office while 'operational' decisions were made at plant level. As in the Marginson *et al.* study, the extent of head office involvement in non-strategic matters in these cases was often surprisingly high. The case studies also support the findings in the literature that successful organisations may maintain a loose-tight relationship between head office and individual plants so that they can respond quickly to changed circumstances (see Peters and Waterman 1982 and Edwards 1987).

Incorporation of employees by management

What can AWIRS tell us about the general pattern of employee incorporation in Australia? The evidence is inconclusive. Consistent with establishing a participative environment and open management style, most managers claim to adopt an approach or philosophy of either communication, teamwork–consultation, personal approach, or open-door approach (p. 269). Few admitted to being either strictly pragmatic or confrontationist. However, management consistently exaggerates the degree of harmony in the workplace, relative to the view of union delegates (p. 293). As to the specific and varied forms of employee incorporation, AWIRS offers some evidence. Profit sharing and share ownership schemes are not widespread (p. 46), although they extend to almost a quarter of larger firms with 200 or more employees (p. 244). A minority of firms, mainly large ones, employ a range of incorporation devices such as suggestion schemes (41 per cent of firms with 500 or more employees), quality circles or productivity improvement groups (23 per cent), employee board members (14 per cent), and various informal and formal communication or consultation techniques (p. 304). These proportions, however, are not trivial. Employee incorporation is present in a significant minority of both public and private sector workplaces.

The concept of 'cultural change' at corporate and workplace levels has assumed prominence in many Australian organisations in recent years. Often this is associated with the introduction of various techniques or programs which aim to strengthen the identification of employees with the organisation and its activities. Sometimes, titles such as 'Future Vision' are used in programs or campaigns to capture the interest and imagination of employees. Complementary schemes are often introduced to strengthen the relationships between employees and an organisation's clients. Financial incentives, such as bonus or share schemes may be used in order to increase the motivation of individual employees to work more effectively for the organisation. The intention is that the workers will thereby become more incorporated into the organisation and share its values and objectives.

Hotel International provides one of the most comprehensive attempts by management to ensure that employees will identify with the corporate philosophy. There is an elaborate induction program for all new employees which promotes the hotel's corporate image and objectives; there are incentives for employees who achieve high levels of performance, and awards for excellence in terms of corporate objectives; there are campaigns such as 'excellence of service' which reinforce the corporate image; and there is an emphasis on communications with staff, through the staff magazine and forums with senior management (even though the flow of information tends to be top-down rather than two-way). This approach appears to have worked well for Hotel International as measured by improved performance and profitability, yet the driving force behind the current campaign to initiate the new corporate philosophy rests heavily with the General Manager and the Director of Human Resources. It remains to be seen whether the approach could be sustained without their continuing support.

Receptacles has introduced a number of schemes to create and maintain a 'participative milieu' within the company. The most important of these is the Common Interest Programme (CIP). This is a 'value-added bonus scheme' which was first introduced in 1982 to improve productivity at the workplace level. The CIP scheme provided a substantial boost to incomes of workers at the plant, to the extent that by 1989 there was a large increase in CIP bonuses. This caused management to renegotiate the basis of the bonus payments. The CIP does have a participative dimension through the monthly representatives' meeting, although it is anticipated that this aspect will be absorbed within a plant consultative committee. Considerable effort and resources have also been invested in an employee communications program to 'educate' the workforce in regard to the company's competitive market position and to promote a 'sense of commitment to the organisation'. While Receptacles has enjoyed increasing levels of productivity, suggesting success for CIP, the introduction of such schemes is not without contradictions. As pointed out in the case study: 'these mechanisms have also provoked a bargaining awareness among union representatives, so much so that the dynamics of these domestic institutions have moved them more towards a bargaining role and away from the intended consultative role, around which they were conceived.' Hence, it is concluded that the 'incorporation' of employees through these schemes has, at best, been only 'partial and spasmodic' and that there have been some unanticipated consequences.

Automakers has mounted a very comprehensive program to change the industrial relations climate at both plant and corporate levels. Known as the Employee Involvement (EI) scheme, it aims to 'unlock the creative potential of employees by involving them in decisions affecting their work'. The EI scheme uses work groups, established on a voluntary basis, to improve the work environment, productivity and product quality at the workplace level. It has been operating since 1982, with the support of the unions which cover the largest number of workers in the industry, and has been hailed by Automakers as an important ingredient in the achievement of more harmonious industrial relations and higher productivity. Yet the participation rate in EI by eligible employees throughout the company is still only 30 per cent and there remains a good deal of scepticism among those who had chosen not to become involved. There is also disappointment among management that long-term problems of high absenteeism and labour turnover remain despite the considerable resources invested in the EI scheme. Hence, it is difficult to argue that full incorporation of the majority of the workforce has been achieved at Automakers.

Other organisations in the study also have highly developed employee involvement programs. PaintCo has three schemes: a Customer First program, an employee share ownership plan, and a health and safety bonus scheme, all of which are aimed ostensibly at strengthening employee identification with the company and raising productivity. The Customer First program elicits suggestions from work teams which are almost invariably costed in terms of savings in time, materials, etc., although the bonus payments which flow from this are based on an aggregate productivity measure for the whole workplace (such as the speed and accuracy of deliveries to customers). The health and safety bonus rests on a visible and significant cost saving to the company in terms of accident-free days. In reality, cost minimisation rather than productivity enhancement appears to be the most immediate objective of these schemes (see Curtin and Mathews 1990). The employee share ownership scheme is qualitatively different, seeking to establish closer employer-employee bonds. However, since the scheme is a corporate one, and not confined to the workplace, it is difficult to see how it can breed a strong sense of common interest at the workplace level.

The impact of these schemes on the workplace culture at PaintCo is difficult to determine. Certainly the performance of the share scheme depends only very slightly on workplace performance. Although the introduction of the Customer First and employee share ownership plans coincided with a decline in industrial disputation, no causal role can be attributed to these initiatives. While the industrial relations climate at PaintCo has improved considerably in recent years, this has also been a national trend. Hence, wider factors such as the Accord and associated wages polices must also be considered. It appears unlikely that these schemes have resulted in total incorporation of the employees, let alone the union delegates. Although PaintCo has enjoyed a period of industrial tranquility, it is likely that the workforce and their unions would combat vigorously any attempt by management to dilute their wages or conditions.

The two remaining cases did not achieve as much progress in these areas. FoodCo has made attempts to involve employees at both distribution centres in discussions about productivity. While some success has been achieved in Brisbane, both the workers and their unions in Sydney refused to be involved in discussions about productivity based on individual performance. The employees in the distribution centre in Brisbane were involved in discussions with management about the introduction of computer-printed labels in order to increase the speed of deploying goods when they arrived at the shop, and this resulted in greater efficiency. Yet the union representing the employees complained that the company is not doing enough to improve training and career structures. It is somewhat surprising that FoodCo has not sought to take a more active role in seeking to incorporate its employees at the Brisbane Distribution Centre, given a generally positive industrial relations climate.

By contrast, at Comel, there has been an attempt to change the corporate culture at headquarters level and in some other parts of the organisation, yet this has been unsuccessful at the workplace level. This may be due to management's fear that it could have unintended consequences and re-ignite the previously inflammatory industrial relations situation. Ironically, senior management has sought to strengthen the allegiance of the supervisors towards the organisation, but this has simply led to increased tension within managerial ranks.

In summary, while most of the organisations in the study have sought to incorporate their employees through a range of programs, it is difficult to assess their success. This is largely because the objectives of many of the schemes are couched in vague language such as 'changing the corporate culture'. In some cases, it is possible to demonstrate that the introduction of an employee participation program has been accompanied by higher levels of productivity or profitability, but it is difficult to establish a causal relationship. In general, there is little overt resistance by the unions or employees to these schemes, except where they are seen as posing a threat to wages or conditions of work. For the most part, incorporation schemes operate independently of the existing industrial relations system and aim to strengthen the identification of the employees with their employer or encourage greater labour-management cooperation. Employees, for the most part, tend to tolerate rather than be enthusiastic about these schemes, and it is not possible to predict their likely long-term effects with any certainty. However, employees appear to accept such managerial initiatives when they can see direct benefits accruing from them. Thus, incorporation attempts appear to sit more comfortably with 'productivity enhancement' rather than 'cost minimisation' programs (see Curtain and Mathews 1990). However, while most incorporation attempts involve varying degrees of employee participation in decision-making, it seems that, as found by Gardner *et al.* (1986) and Lansbury and Davis (1990), management was not interested in genuine power sharing. Employee involvement in decision-making was encouraged through a variety of mechanisms, but not to the extent of weakening managerial control. Indeed, the incorporation attempts observed in these cases may provide support for the claim by Ramsay (1986) that such mechanisms, by giving employees a sense of 'belonging', actually strengthen management's position by increasing deference to 'control from above' (p. 53).

The role of the unions at the workplace

AWIRS tells us a great deal about the general picture of workplace union organisation. Without summarising all the findings, a few key points can be drawn out. Callus *et al.* (1990) do not paint a rosy picture. Workplace union delegates are found in 66 per cent of unionised workplaces, but their incidence varies with workplace size, and the average ratio of delegate to union members is low (only 1:38). Union delegates tend to put little time into the job, and lack experience and training: 80 per cent of delegates spend less than three hours a week on their union duties, 50 per cent have less than two years experience (p. 277), and 61 per cent have had no training (p. 282). These and other indices suggest that the duties of delegates are often trivial, and that they do not often have a say in major issues in the workplace. While these generalisations may suggest that union workplace organisation and action tends to be weak, caution should be exercised. Callus *et al.* distinguish 'active bargainers' as those plants where union presence is a significant restraint upon management, and these are very common among large workplaces. Most of our case studies would fulfil the criteria for 'active bargainers', the exceptions being Comel and Hotel International.

It might reasonably be expected that unionism would exert a powerful influence in all of the workplaces represented by our case studies. The level of unionisation varies from 80 to 100 per cent and some of the largest unions in Australia are prominently represented. The number of elected union delegates, however, differs markedly between workplaces, as does the ratio of delegates to employees. Furthermore, while some of the workplaces have a history of militancy, most have experienced only a low to medium level of industrial conflict in the past few years.

One of the most active bargainers is PaintCo, where the two dominant unions are the Federated Miscellaneous Workers' Union, and the National Union of Workers. The blue-collar workforce is covered by a *de facto* closed shop. The workforce has been periodically militant with a known capacity to sustain long strikes. The workers place heavy demands on both management and union delegates. Relationships with the external union organisers are not always close, but the delegates understand how to harness the power of the shop floor and are able to use their union's resources to advantage in dealing with management. Yet despite the considerable power and influence which the delegates are able to exercise at PaintCo, management has introduced a number of significant changes such as new equipment, plant reorganisation, and the construction of a new warehouse, without encountering any significant shop-floor resistance. This is because the delegates and the members tend to take an instrumental approach to their employment situation. Their primary concerns appear to be focused on wages, job security, and working conditions. Interest in management decision-making is correspondingly incidental to these other purposes. Notable examples where union delegates seek to constrain management are in regard to the hiring of temporary workers, contract workers and the contracting-out of canteen services, all of which touch upon workers' sense of job security. Other influences exercised by delegates are more subtle, and management is constrained by custom and practice or informal rules which operate within the workplace.

Union organisation at Receptacles also appears to be strong. Workers are employed under a post-entry closed shop and one union, the Federation of Industrial, Manufacturing and Engineering Employees (FIMEE), covers 90 per cent of the workforce. There are seven union delegates for a workforce of just over 100 and the local organiser regularly visits the plant. Yet this appearance of strong unionism is somewhat misleading. The company operates a number of consultative mechanisms within the plant, and the union does not seem to exercise much constraint on managerial decision-making at the workplace level.

A similar pattern of rather dormant unionism is evident at the Brisbane Distribution Centre of FoodCo, where the SDA has about 95 per cent coverage, as well as at the Sydney plant of Automakers, where the Vehicle Builders Employees Federation (VBEF) has a closed shop. The Hotel International is the clearest example of a marginalised union, in that the Federated Liquor and Allied Industries Employees' Union covers approximately 80 per cent of the employees, but has only one elected delegate and a small non-elected committee servicing almost 600 members. At Comel, the largest union covers 60 per cent of the employees and there is an overall union density of 90 per cent. Yet, despite this high density rate, the previously active Combined Union Shop Committee is now semi-moribund. Furthermore, although the plant was formerly a hotbed of unionism, there is now a high turnover of shop stewards and there are difficulties in finding replacements.

One should be cautious, however, in concluding that workplace unionism is dormant or compliant in all cases. In two of the companies studied, FoodCo and Automakers, there are sharp internal contrasts. In FoodCo's Sydney Distribution Centre, where the National Union of Workers has almost total coverage, the union delegates are relatively militant and have been willing to strike even in defiance of their own officials. A similar pattern of independent delegate activity exists within the Melbourne assembly plant of Automakers. By contrast, FoodCo's Brisbane Distribution Centre and Automaker's Sydney assembly plant both appear to be 'models' of industrial harmony.

In summary, given the high level of unionisation and the presence of large well-organised unions in all of the case studies, it could be reasonably assumed that unionism would be influential at the workplace level. However, while some plants had a reputation for shop-floor militancy in the past, all have relatively low levels of industrial disputation at the present time. Part of the explanation for this situation may be that the general economic circumstances and the operations of the Accord between the government and the ACTU have had a dampening effect on union activity. Yet shop steward organisation appears to be patchy and industrial conflict is spasmodic. The unions tend to concentrate on traditional issues such as wages, job security, and working conditions and, for the most part, management ensures that these basic requirements are met. Some managers complain about restrictions imposed on their freedom of operation as a result of union policies and award conditions. Yet it appears that the unions, especially at the workplace level, allow management considerable latitude to introduce new forms of work organisation, equipment, and technology. Most of the Australian literature on workplace unionism considers only the question of union impact on management in a rather incidental fashion. Frenkel and Coolican (1984) who did address it directly in respect of two relatively militant unions, found that the workplace representatives were not even consulted by management on a range of important issues. This finding is generally supported by our case studies. Only on few occasions did the extent of steward or delegate involvement match that found by Benson (1991) in respect of the Victorian power industry.

Workplace union organisations observed in our case studies were found, even in their more developed forms, to be interested only in a very limited range of issues. The only occasion on which unions appear to move strongly against management are when employees' earnings or job security are threatened; for example, by the introduction of contract labour. The evidence presented by these case studies generally supports an 'economistic' or 'instrumentalist' perception of Australian trade unions (see, for example, Martin 1975): their concerns at the workplace rarely extend beyond earnings and a limited range of working conditions. Unfortunately, little evidence emerged to either support or refute the Freeman and Medoff (1984) contention that active unionism can lead to productivity improvements. Perhaps this is a further indication of the relatively low levels of workplace union activity.

Improving efficiency in the workplace

AWIRS provides some general evidence about the effects of workplace bargaining on improved efficiency, especially with respect to the second-tier negotiations during 1987 and 1988. The survey was conducted too early, however, to capture changes arising from award restructuring. Evidence and views upon this can be gleaned from Sloan and Wooden (1990), Rimmer and Verevis (1990), and the 1991 National Wage Case decision. Broadly, AWIRS captures the dynamics of workplace reform and hints at rapid, extensive, and varied change (p. 198). It is less adept at attributing these changes to the influence of tribunals, government policy, and particular wage fixing principles. Neither is it clear what role unions are playing in all this. However, it does seem that many managers wish to make far more extensive reforms, but are blocked by barriers, of which financial resources and management organisation or policy are usually more significant than union resistance. In short, management (and their financial resources) seem to be the main impediment to efficiency gains, rather than unions (p. 204).

There is increasing emphasis on the need for reform at the workplace level in order to achieve greater efficiency and higher productivity. In some cases, these efforts have been initiated by management within the enterprise as part of a program to change the workplace culture. In other cases, reforms have been negotiated between management and unions. Often these have been processed through the conciliation and arbitration system, as in the second-tier negotiations and award restructuring. These approaches are not necessarily mutually exclusive and some organisations have sought to pursue each simultaneously.

In Automakers, for example, management has a two-strand approach to improving efficiency in the workplace. One strand involves taking a leading role in developing a common approach among the automobile manufacturers to negotiating agreements with the unions on structural efficiency and award restructuring. This means giving a prominent role to the unions, especially the VBEF, as negotiating partners. The second strand, illustrated by the Employee Involvement (EI) program, is an attempt to forge more direct links and stronger loyalties between individual employees and the company. While the unions are not excluded from this process, and most give it their formal support, the EI program has been initiated and guided by management as part of its drive to improve product quality and productivity at the workplace level. Neither management nor union representatives at Automakers are enthusiastic about changes which have been achieved through the second-tier negotiations. In fact, the union representatives report considerable antagonism among their members towards concessions made by union negotiators in order to achieve the 4 per cent wage increase under the second-tier agreement, as well as towards award restructuring. By contrast, the EI program receives general support from both unions and management, even though its scope is rather limited. Indeed, improvements in efficiency and quality at Automakers are ascribed by both sides to a combination of approaches rather than a single strategy.

There is a similar two-strand approach at PaintCo. One approach is to seek improved efficiency through incorporation schemes, such as the Customer First program and the health and safety bonus scheme. The other approach is through negotiations over changes in awards. The second-tier negotiations were not a great success. The employees at PaintCo had to be pressed by union organisers to accept the concessions which had been made in return for wage increases. Subsequently, very few of the offsets were adhered to in a way that realised their full value in terms of savings. Management hoped, nevertheless, that gains in areas such as reduced demarcation problems might be obtained through on-going award restructuring negotiations. By contrast, the incorporation schemes (although limited in scope) seemed to have a better pay-off in terms of improving efficiency. There are three possible explanations for these outcomes at PaintCo. First, it may be that the issues raised in the second-tier negotiations appeared to be more threatening to worker interests than were the interests addressed in incorporation schemes. Second, the latter schemes gave employees more immediate scope to contribute their ideas and knowledge rather than having solutions by others imposed on them. Third, there is a continuous financial incentive underpinning involvement in the incorporation schemes rather than a one-off wage increase under the second tier agreement. One of the important points which emerges in the PaintCo case is that while agreement may be achieved in principle to improved efficiency (as in the second-tier negotiations) employees must be fully committed to changes to ensure that implementation will be successful.

At Hotel International, a range of trade-offs were negotiated between management and the union in exchange for the 4 per cent wage increase under the second-tier decision. While most of the concessions granted by the union were fairly minor, the local union representative felt that the negotiations diminished the level of trust between the employees and management. The more significant initiatives to achieve greater efficiency, however, have been undertaken independently by the new owner of Hotel International, even though the local management claims that the new industrial relations climate associated with the second-tier negotiations have facilitated many of the changes. An alternative interpretation is that the prevailing industrial relations situation has meant that the unions have been in a weaker position to resist changes sought by management. It should also be noted that Hotel International management took a leading role in industry-level negotiations on award restructuring. These negotiations were regarded as an opportunity both to gain more flexibility at the workplace level and to reduce the constraints imposed by the award. It is also pertinent that management recently changed its interpretation of the union membership agreement at Hotel International. While it will continue to collect dues on behalf of the union, it will no longer require employees to fill in a blue card (the membership form) as a condition of employment. Clearly, the new corporate culture at the Hotel International, which emphasises excellence in service as part of the management's drive to achieve greater efficiency, perceives a diminished role for unions.

At Receptacles, a sustained period of high demand for their products and consequent strong profitability has enabled the company to improve wages and introduce significant changes to achieve a high level of technological 'know-how' and productive efficiency. Receptacles has embarked on a wide range of incorporation measures, including a Common Interest Programme, which has enabled the company to share some of the financial gains from increased productivity with the employees. The second-tier agreement is seen by neither management nor the unions as a source of significant change in itself. However, it does set in place structures and preconditions for future changes. It also enhances the role played by local delegates in the negotiation process and gives greater prominence to the consultative committee within the plant. More extensive changes have been introduced as a result of the award restructuring process. These were negotiated over an extended period and include a reduction in job classifications, payment for skills achieved, scope for more flexibility and variation in work, and broadbanding of wages. The achievement of greater productive efficiency at Receptacles, however, is not without complications. In many ways the company is ahead of the national trends towards a greater emphasis on efficiency and flexibility at the workplace level. Yet the high wages at the plant are built upon the assumption that strong demand for the company's products will continue. Should an economic recession result in lower levels of earnings, especially through the Common Interest program, considerable industrial relations tensions could emerge.

At Comel, negotiations over structural efficiency and award restructuring were conducted by corporate headquarters and national union officials with little reference to the plant. The outcomes of these negotiations were communicated to the rank and file and to the delegates. Of greater significance is the restructuring of the corporation as a whole which has resulted in decentralisation of operational responsibility and the requirement that management achieve greater efficiency at the workplace level. As virtually all of the output from the plant has, until recently, been absorbed by the various divisions of the parent enterprise, the necessity to achieve high levels of efficiency in order to survive in the market-place is not yet a feature of the local corporate culture. Nevertheless, the corporation has set financial targets and the plant will have to increasingly compete with external companies in order to sell its products to the parent body in the future. This will be a major challenge for the plant.

At FoodCo, attempts by management to achieve increased efficiency through the second-tier negotiations have been fraught with conflict. Even at the Brisbane Distribution Centre, where a high level of industrial harmony normally prevails, the employees view management as having been 'too hard' in negotiations. While there were no official strikes, there were frequent union meetings from which employees failed to return to work. Ultimately, the SDA conceded a number of offsets in return for the 4 per cent wage increase, despite opposition from many of its members. It is significant, therefore, that management has failed to fully implement the changes and has not achieved many of the productivity gains which it had envisaged. Management has been even less successful at FoodCo's Sydney Distribution Centre. Extensive negotiations yielded only two minor changes to the award and both sides regarded the results as disappointing. The changes in shift hours and the introduction of a disciplinary procedure, sought by management, have yielded no discernible increase in productivity.

An ironical aspect of discussions about productivity and efficiency at FoodCo is that the two distribution centres, when they were built in the 1980s, incorporated some of the latest applications of automated storage and retrieval at the time. The efficiencies which were expected to flow from the highly computerised approach to warehousing and distribution have failed to be achieved in the Sydney Centre largely as a result of poor management and industrial relations. Even in Brisbane, where management has been more competent and a more positive industrial relations climate has prevailed, the SDA claims that management has focused narrowly on cost-cutting measures. FoodCo management admits that its main indicators for comparing the efficiency of distribution centres are warehouse costs and pick-rates rather than direct competitive comparisons of market performance. Since labour represents a large proportion of costs, and higher pick-rates mean that fewer workers are required, efficiency tends to be seen in terms of workforce reduction rather than investing in human resources development. Unfortunately it seems the cost minimisation model has prevailed over the productivity enhancement approach (See Curtin and Mathews 1990) in this instance.

In summary, attempts by management to achieve greater efficiency at the workplace level through the formal industrial relations system, such as the second-tier negotiations and award restructuring, met with mixed success. As was found by Rimmer and Verevis (1990) with respect to award restructuring, most of the unions and employers expressed disappointment with the outcomes, although some felt that the system needed more time to yield results. Changes achieved through the conciliation and arbitration process were regarded by most employees as distant and beyond their immediate control. By contrast, many of the management initiatives, such as employee involvement schemes, were received more positively. Often these appeared to be more concerned with the immediate realities of the workplace compared with changes achieved through the industrial tribunals. Unfortunately, most changes associated with the attempt to increase efficiency have not been in place long enough to provide evidence in respect of the post-Fordism/neo-Fordism debate (see Macdonald 1989; Bramble and Fieldes 1990). However, workforce reductions and increased labour intensity were observed in several of the cases and a reduced role for unionism seems likely in at least one other.

Conclusions

The case studies presented in this book do not provide answers to all the questions which have been raised, but they do shed light on a range of factors which influence the nature of industrial relations at the workplace. There emerge at least two faces of workplace industrial relations: one which is strongly influenced by the formal structures and processes of conciliation and arbitration; and another more informal system which operates with a high degree of independence from decisions of the industrial tribunals. The two faces, however, are not mutually exclusive and there is considerable interaction between the formal and informal aspects of workplace industrial relations. None of the workplaces examined in the study could be regarded as typical of all situations. However, they do provide the opportunity to observe the dynamics of industrial relations within relatively large multi-plant organisations which have well-established unions covering their workforce and are subject to the awards of federal and/or state industrial commissions.

The unions were not as influential as might have been expected in such highly unionised workplaces. They tended to focus their efforts on traditional issues such as pursuing improved wages and conditions through the tribunals. With some minor exceptions, neither union organisers nor delegates played a dominant role within the workplace. Despite some sporadic industrial action, most of the unions were quiescent and sought improvements through the conciliation and arbitration process rather than by direct action.

In the AWIRS report, Callus *et al.* (1991) developed a schema for the classification of workplaces. Depending on the level and activity of workplace unionism, the nature of management structures and procedures, and the type of bargaining present, workplaces were categorised as 'informal', 'unstructured inactive', 'structured inactive', 'reactive bargainers' or 'active bargainers'. As noted previously, most of our case studies fulfilled the criteria for active bargainers in that there was an active union presence in the workplace and management had a set of formal procedures and structures to handle industrial relations. However, when examined in closer detail, union power in many of the case studies turned out to be weak, and management took the initiative on most matters. These findings raise questions about the ability of many union delegates in the workplaces covered by the case studies to effectively engage in bargaining, particularly if the trend towards an enterprise-level focus continues and the role of workplace representatives is consequently enlarged. Many of the delegates in the case studies appeared to be ill-equipped and uncertain about their roles in a changing industrial relations environment. This mirrored the findings of the AWIRS report.

Despite complaints by some managers about restrictions imposed by the unions and award provisions, employers encountered little resistance at the workplace level to changes which they introduced, especially when these did not affect award conditions. A wide range of activities was initiated by management to induce changes in the workplace culture, usually with the view to strengthening employer–employee relationships. While there was some passive resistance or non-cooperation exhibited by a minority of employees, most acquiesced in the changes, especially when financial or other benefits were provided by employers as an incentive. Indeed, many of the changes induced through these methods were welcomed by employees. It was therefore surprising that management did not seek to introduce more far-reaching changes at the workplace level. Part of the explanation may be that while most organisations espoused devolved and decentralised approaches to industrial relations, there was a reluctance to move very far or fast in that direction. Managers at the workplace level were often hesitant about exercising their authority without reference to the corporate head office.

The formal industrial relations system, as represented by the conciliation and arbitration tribunals, did not emerge as a major impediment to changes at the workplace level. Despite some disappointment expressed about the outcomes of negotiations over structural efficiency and award restructuring, there was little apparent discontent about the system overall. Both management and the unions were concerned to retain access to the industrial relations commissions on award matters, even though some preferred to resolve disputes over local or domestic issues through direct negotiations. As indicated by the AWIRS report, most parties wanted to retain a role for the tribunals, but not as a dominant force. The case studies confirmed the findings of the AWIRS report that 'many of the industrial relations decisions that are made by management beyond the workplace never involve the industrial relations tribunals nor concern issues that are the subject of conciliation and arbitration' (Callus *et al.* 1991). Thus, it is clear that a complete explanation of workplace industrial relations requires an analysis of the impact of decisions made by a variety of parties, such as corporate management, union leaders and government officials who are 'beyond the workplace' (see Marginson *et al.* 1988).

The general picture of workplace industrial relations in Australia which emerges from the case studies is one of cautious pragmatism on the part of both unions and management. It suggests that the BCA's preoccupation with union structures and arbitration processes as significant barriers to change may be misplaced. Neither management nor union representatives at the workplace level in most of our case studies perceived the existing system as a major barrier to change. Unions were generally forced into a defensive position when management focused exclusively on cost minimisation methods of introducing change. Yet, in the cases where management pursued a clear strategy to achieve greater efficiency, they rarely encountered strong resistance from the unions. Indeed, where management sought to actively involve the employees and the local union representatives in 'productivity enhancing' activities, their initiatives were generally well received.

Notes

Chapter 1

[1] See *Arbitration in Contempt* (1986), the Proceedings of the inaugural meeting of the H. R. Nicholls Society; for a critique and further information on the New Right and Industrial Relations see Dabscheck (1987).

[2] In the September 1990 issue of *The Journal of Industrial Relations* the BCA Report is defended against the criticisms of Frenkel and Peetz who reply with a rejoinder.

[3] The membership of the original Workplace research group, as reported by Callus and Lansbury (1988) was John Benson, Ron Callus, Steve Frenkel, Gerry Griffin, Joe Isaac, Russell Lansbury, Ray Markey, David Peetz, Malcolm Rimmer, Vic Taylor and Jon Zappala.

[4] The December 1976 issue of the *Journal of Industrial Relations* was entirely devoted to the topic.

[5] The oil industry has long exhibited characteristics that make it conducive to successful collective bargaining. These include its cohesiveness and the strength of the union organisation (see Riach and Howard 1973).

[6] Lumley provides a useful summary of the debate within the Australian literature up to that time.

[7] In Australia some of the important writings on the subject include Lumley (1983), Macdonald (1985), Bray and Taylor (1986), Deery and Purcell (1989) and Bramble (1989).

[8] It appears that a large proportion of Australian workplaces are part of multi-establishment companies, especially those engaged in manufacturing. Frenkel (1987) reported that 73 per cent of the plants he surveyed in the Australian engineering industry were part of multi-plant companies (p. 42). When he disaggregated in terms of size the significance of multi-plant companies became more apparent in that 95 per cent of companies employing 500 or more persons belonged to this category.

[9] The finding is also supported by the recently published report of the Confederation of Australian Industry (CAI 1991).

[10] Award restructuring, which post-dated Rimmer's study, would be similarly supportive of workplace unionism.

[11] This period saw the introduction, by the Whitlam government, of the Trade Union Training Authority.

[12] The extent to which workers and their organisations are able to constrain the 'right to manage' is used as an indicator of shop steward strength in some British studies (e.g. Terry 1986). Terry, while admitting the difficulties of definition and measurement, lists 'job controls' as a third 'substantive indice' of steward power.

[13] It is recognised that there is a variety of such arrangements and that they differ according to whether they apply pre- or post-entry, to their degree of formality and to the means by which they are regulated (see Zappala 1991b).

Chapter 2

[1] In 1990 the general manager (human resources) was appointed to the board and his position renamed director of human resources.

[2] The first of these was the Commonwealth Government's Policy on Employee Participation released in June 1978. Later items were produced by the National Employee Participation Steering Committee, and included *Employee Participation—A Broad View* (AGPS, 1979); and *Employee Participation—Ways and Means*, (AGPS, 1980).

Chapter 3

[1] The Paintco Panel carries on several functions of the Board of Directors which existed when the company was an independent legal entity. The Board was wound up and replaced by the Panel after Paintco became a wholly-owned subsidiary.

[2] Since the case study was completed there has been a reduction in the number of trade unions at Paintco, and therefore redistribution of members between trade unions. We describe the position before these changes. There have also been major changes among the job delegates.

[3] The effectiveness of safety policy and procedure is evident in the decline of medically treated injuries from 29.1 per million manhours in 1985 to 5.3 in 1988.

[4] The Commission prohibited productivity bargaining over standard hours in April 1981, but shortly afterwards abandoned centralised wages fixing. A general movement towards 38 hours began later that year. The Commission generally refused to adjust working hours below 38 hours per week. See Australian Conciliation and Arbitration Commission, *Inquiry into wage fixing principles*, 7 April 1981.

Chapter 4

[1] This dispute commenced in August 1989 and resulted in a mass resignation of pilots. Only a limited internal air service was available for the remainder of 1989 and even by June 1990 the airline industry had not completely returned to normal.

[2] For ABS statistical purposes.

[3] As defined by the Australian Bureau of Statistics.

[4] Additional changes to the award, under the auspices of award restructuring, led to the award being renamed in 1990 as The Hotels, Resorts and Hospitality Industry Award. As these changes occurred after the completion of the case study they are not referred to in this chapter.

[5] This was the case with the second-tier, 4 per cent negotiations.

[6] The award restructuring exercise, which resulted in changes to the spread of hours and career progression, has further provided an opportunity for management to make the workplace more flexible and to reduce the impact of some of the perceived award constraints.

Chapter 6

[1] This is calculated by the sum of direct and indirect labour costs (including salaried

employees) as a percentage of manufacturing costs (excluding material costs).

[2] One such incident in 1942 concerned a dispute over women doing welding work; this was heard in the Commission.

[3] The only strikes that have occurred in the last twenty years appear to have been in support of state-wide or national issues and such instances have been rare (see section on industrial action). In 1988 there was a 24-hour stoppage in support of the union's campaign over the second tier wage increases and during the period of our research there was another 24-hour strike which was part of the state-wide 'day of outrage' with changes to worker's compensation being the focus of attention for VBEF members.

[4] Management rated the relationship similarly, pointing to indicators such as the high level of participation by delegates in the EI program and the general attitude of positive cooperation in the plant.

[5] In paid rates or going rates awards, 'the rates prescribed are the actual wages paid, that is, no over-award payments apply' (Sheehan and Worland 1985).

[6] Only limited information was provided to employees on issues such as marketing and investment plans, corporate strategy, and performance against budget.

[7] It should be noted, however, that this remoteness of the Sydney plant from the main Victorian plant does have certain advantages for management. It is very difficult, for example, for any influences from the rather more militant workforce in Victoria to permeate the Sydney plant. Also, management is more easily able to promote and benefit from the more cooperative atmosphere and positive workforce attitudes at the Sydney plant than would be the case if it were geographically closer to the Victorian operation.

Chapter 7

[1] Source: Metal Trades Industry Association.

[2] The Essential Services Act 1979 was repealed in 1990. It had never actually been used to impose such fines, but perhaps it had had a deterrent effect. An Essential Services Act was introduced in NSW in 1988. For discussion of such legislation see Bamber and Watson 1991.

[3] Fox, A. *Man Mismanagement* 2nd. ed. London, Hutchinson, 1986; but also see Walton R. and McKersie, R. *Behavioral Theory of Labor Negotiations* New York, McGraw-Hill, 1965.

[4] Purcell, J. *Good industrial relations: Theory and practice* London, Macmillan, 1981; Trevor, M. *Toshiba's New British Company: Competitiveness through Innovation in Industry* London: Policy Studies Institute, 1988.

[5] Trist, E. L., Higgin, G. W., Murray, H. and Pollock, A. B. *Organizational Choice* London: Tavistock, 1963.

[6] Woodward, J. *Industrial organization : Theory and Practice* Oxford, Oxford University Press, 1965.

[7] Rose, H., McLoughlin, I., King, R. and Clark, J. 'Opening the black box: The relation between technology and work' *New Technology, Work and Employment* 1, 1, 1986: 18–26.

Bibliography

Australian Bureau of Statistics. *Hotels & Bars and Accommodation Industries Australia.* Cat. No. 8656.0. Canberra, 1986–87.

Australian Bureau of Statistics. *Tourist Accommodation Australia.* June quarter, Cat. No. 8635.0. Canberra, 1989.

Australian Bureau of Statistics. *Tourist Accommodation Victoria.* June quarter, Cat. No. 8635.2. Canberra, 1989.

Australian Conciliation and Arbitration Commission. *Hotel and Retail Liquor Industry Award.* 1983.

Australian Conciliation and Arbitration Commission. *Hotel and Retail Liquor Industry Award.* Print No. H3480, 8 July, 1988.

Australian Conciliation and Arbitration Commission. *Hotel and Retail Liquor Industry Award.* Print No. H6670, 28 February, 1989.

Australian Council of Trade Unions/Trade Development Council. *Australia Reconstructed.* Canberra: AGPS, 1987.

Badham, R. and Mathews, J. 'The New Production Systems Debate.' *Labour and Industry* 2 (2) (June 1989): 194–246.

Bamber, G. and Lansbury, R. *New Technology: International Perspectives on Human Resources and Industrial Relations.* London, Sydney and Boston: Allen and Unwin, 1989.

Bamber, G. and Watson, K. 'The Prevention and Settlement of Industrial Disputes in Australian Essential Services.' *Working Paper* Geneva/Brisbane: International Labour Organisation/Graduate School of Management, The University of Queensland, 1991.

Beer, M. and Spector, B. eds *Readings in Human Resource Management*, New York: The Free Press, 1985.

Benson, J. 'Workplace Union Organisation in Australia.' *Labour and Industry* 1 (3) (October 1988): 407–30.

Benson, J. *Unions at the Workplace: Shop Steward Leadership and Ideology.* Melbourne: Oxford University Press, 1991.

Blain, N. *Pilots and Management.* London: Allen and Unwin, 1972.

Blain, N. and Plowman, D. 'The Australian Industrial Relations Literature, 1970–1986.' *The Journal of Industrial Relations* 29 (3) (September 1987): 295–320.

Blandy, R., Dawkins, P., Gannicott, K., Kain, P., Kasper, W. and Kriegler, R. *Structured Chaos: The Process of Productivity Advance.* Melbourne: Oxford University Press, 1985.

Bramble, T. 'Political Economy and Management Strategy in the Metal and Engineering Industry.' *The Journal of Industrial Relations* 31 (1 March 1989).

Bramble, T. and Fieldes, D. '"Post-Fordism": Utopian Fantasy or Historical Break?' *Industrial Relations Working Papers*, School of Industrial Relations and Organisational Behaviour, The University of New South Wales, (April 1990).

Bray, M. and Taylor, V. eds. *Managing Labour? Essays in the Political Economy of Australian Industrial Relations*, Sydney: McGraw-Hill, 1986.

Brown, M., Wilson, K. and Worland, D. 'The Role of Internal and External Influences upon the Industrial Relations Practice of Organisations.' Report for the Committee of Review into Australian Industrial Relations Law and Systems, Department of Applied Economics, Footscray Institute of Technology, 1985.

Brown, R. K. 'Approaches to Workplace Behaviour.' In Parker, S. R. *et al.* eds *The Sociology of Industry*. London: George Allen and Unwin, 1973.

Brown, W. J. and Rowe, L. G. 'Employers and the Push for Decentralised Wage Setting.' In Niland, J. ed. *Wage Fixation in Australia*. Sydney: Allen and Unwin, 1986, 124–44.

Buchanan, D. A. and Huczynski, A. A. *Organisational Behaviour*. London: Prentice-Hall, 1983.

Burawoy, M. *The Politics of Production*. London: Verso, 1985.

Business Council of Australia (BCA). *Enterprise-Based Bargaining Units—A Better Way of Working—Report to the Business Council of Australia by the Industrial Relations Study Commission,* Melbourne: BCA, 1989.

Callus, R. and Lansbury, R. 'Workplace Industrial Relations—A Conference Report.' *Labour and Industry* 1 (2) (June 1988): 364–72.

Callus, R., Morehead, A., Cully, M. and Buchanan, J. *Industrial Relations at Work: The Australian Workplace Industrial Relations Survey*. Canberra: Commonwealth Department of Industrial Relations, Australian Government Publishing Service, 1991.

Champagne, P. and McAfee, R. *Motivating Strategies for Performance and Productivity: A Guide to Human Resource Development*. Quorum Books, 1989.

Charlesworth, S. *Employment in the Hospitality Industry*. Melbourne: FLAIEU, 1983.

Child, J. *Unionism and the Labour Movement*. Melbourne: Macmillan, 1971.

Child, J. 'Managerial Strategies, New Technology and the Labour Process.' In Knights, D. *et al.* eds *Job Redesign*. Aldershot: Gower, 1985.

Clark, J. *The Process of Technological Change: New Technology and Social Choice in the Workplace*. Cambridge: Cambridge University Press, 1988.

Confederation of Australian Industry. *The Training Needs of Managers in Australia's Changing Industrial Relations Environment*. Report by the Confederation of Australian Industry for the National Labour Consultative Council, 1991.

Crombie, A. 'The Case Study Method and the Theory of Organisation', *The Australian and New Zealand Journal of Sociology* 5 (2) (1969): 111–20.

Curtain, R. and Mathews, J. 'Two Models of Award Restructuring in Australia', *Labour and Industry* 3 (1) March (1990): 58–75.

Cutcher-Gershenfeld, J., Kochan, T. and Verma, A. 'Recent Developments in US Employee Involvement Initiatives: Erosion or Diffusion.' *Pacific Rim Labor Policy Conference*. Washington D.C.: Asia Pacific Business Institute/Bureau of National Affairs, 1987.

Dabscheck, B. 'New Right or Old Wrong? Ideology and Industrial Relations.' *The Journal of Industrial Relations* 29 (4) (December 1987): 425–49.

Dabscheck, B. 'The BCA's Plan to Americanise Australian Industrial Relations.' *Journal of Australian Political Economy* (27 November 1990): 1–15.

Davis, E. M. and Lansbury, R. D. eds. *Democracy and Control in the Workplace*. Melbourne: Longman Cheshire, 1986.

Deery, S. 'Industrial Relations on the Australian Waterfront: A Policy of Laissez-Faire.' *The Journal of Industrial Relations* 19 (1) (March 1977): 93–7.

Deery, S. 'The Impact of the National Stevedoring Industry Conference (1965–67) on Industrial Relations on the Australian Waterfront.' *The Journal of Industrial Relations* 20 (2) (June 1978): 202–22.

Deery, S. and Purcell, J. 'Strategic Choices in Industrial Relations Management in Large Organisations.' *The Journal of Industrial Relations* 31 (4) (December 1989): 459–77.

Derber, M. 'Changing Union–Management Relations at the Plant Level in Australian Metal Working.' *The Journal of Industrial Relations* 19 (1) (March 1977): 1–23.

de Vyver, F. T. 'The Melbourne Building Industry Agreement.' *The Journal of Industrial Relations* 1 (1) (March 1959): 7–19.

de Vyver, F. T. 'The Melbourne Building Industry Agreement: A Re-Examination.' *The Journal of Industrial Relations* 12 (2) (July 1970).

Dufty, N. *Industrial Relations in the Public Sector: The Firemen.* St Lucia: University of Queensland Press, 1979.

Dufty, N. and Fells, R. *Dynamics of Industrial Relations in Australia.* Sydney: Prentice Hall, 1989.

Dunphy, D. C. (with R. Dick). *Organisational Change by Choice.* Sydney: McGraw-Hill, 1981.

Edwards, P. K. *Managing the Factory—A Survey of General Managers.* Oxford: Blackwell, 1987.

Edwards, P. K and Scullion, H. *The Social Organisation of Industrial Conflict: Control and Resistance in the Workplace.* Oxford: Blackwell, 1982.

Employee Involvement: Sydney Assembly Plant Booklet (anon).

Fells, R. 'Industrial Relations at the Plant Level: A Case Study.' *The Journal of Industrial Relations.* 29 (3) (September 1987): 350–64.

Fisher, W. K. 'Plant Level Relationships: The Role of the Tribunal.' *The Journal of Industrial Relations* 14 (3) (September 1972): 264–71.

Foenander, O. de R. 'The Achievement and Significance of Industrial Regulation in Australia.' *International Labour Review* LXXV (2) (February 1957): 104–18.

Fox, A. *Man Mismanagement* (2nd edn). London: Hutchinson, 1986.

Freeman, R. and Medoff, J. *What do Unions do?* New York: Basic Books, 1984.

Frenkel, S. 'Theory and Research Strategy.' In Frenkel, S. ed. *Industrial Action: Patterns of Labour Conflict.* Sydney: George Allen and Unwin, 1980.

Frenkel, S. 'Managing Through the Recession: An Analysis of Workplace Industrial Relations in the Australian Engineering Industry.' *Labour and Industry* 1 (1) (October 1987): 39–60.

Frenkel, S. and Coolican, A. *Unions Against Capitalism? A Sociological Comparison of the Australian Building and Metal Workers' Union.* Sydney: George Allen and Unwin Australia, 1984.

Frenkel, S. and Peetz, D. 'Enterprise Bargaining: The BCA's Report on Industrial Relations Reform.' *The Journal of Industrial Relations* 32 (1) (March 1990): 69–99.

Gardner, M., Littler, C., Quinlan, M. and Palmer, G. 'Management and Industrial Democracy: Structure and Strategies.' In Ford, B. and Tilley, L. eds *Diversity, Change and Tradition: The Environment for Industrial Democracy in Australia.* Summary of research for the Policy Discussion Paper on Industrial Democracy and Employee Participation (Department of Employment and Industrial Relations) Canberra: AGPS, 1986.

Gill, F. and Zappala, J. *The Closed Shop Revisited: An Essay on Method.* Australian Centre for Industrial Relations Research and Teaching Working Paper No. 6, Sydney: University of Sydney, 1990.

Gilmour, P. and Lansbury, R. D. 'The Changing Role of the Supervisor: Implications for Industrial Relations.' *The Journal of Industrial Relations* 19 (3) (1977): 225–40.

Gilmour, P. and Lansbury, R. D. *Marginal Manager: The Changing Role of Supervisors in Australia.* St Lucia: University of Queensland Press, 1984.

Goldthorpe, J. H. *et al. The Affluent Worker: Industrial Attitudes and Behaviour.* Cambridge: Cambridge University Press, 1968.

Guille, H. 'A Tale of Two States: The Hanger and Niland Reports.' *Labour and Industry* 2 (3) (October 1989): 453–69.

Hancock, K. 'Economics and the Reform of Industrial Relations.' In Ford, G. W., Hearn, J. M. and Lansbury, R. D. eds *Australian Labour Relations: Readings* (4th edn)

South Melbourne: Macmillan, 1987.

Hill, S. *Competition and Control at Work: The New Industrial Sociology.* London: Heinemann Educational, 1981.

Hotchkiss, W. E. 'The Broken Hills Mines Agreement—A Study of Some Objective Factors in Industrial Negotiations.' *The Journal of Industrial Relations* 12 (1) (March 1970): 9–19.

Howard, W. A. *Making Industrial Relations Work: A Study of Six Isolated Mines.* Industrial Relations Monographs, Kensington: IRRC, 1985.

Howard, W. A. and Fox, C. *Industrial Relations Reform—A Policy for Australia.* Melbourne: Longman Cheshire, 1988.

Hyman, R. *Strikes.* (4th edn) London: Macmillan, 1989.

Isaac, J. E. 'The Prospects for Collective Bargaining in Australia.' *Economic Record* 34 (69) (December 1958): 347–61.

Isaac, J. E. 'Professor Niland on Collective Bargaining and Compulsory Arbitration in Australia.' *The Journal of Industrial Relations* 21 (4) (December 1979): 466–76.

Isaac, J. E. 'Directions for Research.' In Sutcliffe, P. and Ralston, D. eds *Trends in Australasian Industrial Relations.* Brisbane: Proceedings of biennial conference of Association of Industrial Relations Academics of Australia and New Zealand, 1985.

Isaac, J. E. 'The Arbitration Commission: Prime Mover or Facilitator?' *The Journal of Industrial Relations* 31 (3) (September 1989): 407–27.

Isaac, J. E. and Ford, G. E. *Australian Labour Relations: Readings.* (2nd edn) Melbourne: Sun Books, 1971.

Kelly, D. *Defining the 'Workplace' in Workplace Industrial Relations.* ACIRRT Working Paper No. 4, July, Sydney: Australian Centre for Industrial Relations Research and Teaching, University of Sydney, 1990.

Kinnie, N. 'Human Resource Management and Changes in Management Control Systems.' In J. Storey ed. *New Perspectives on Human Resource Management.* London: Routledge, 1989.

Knights, D. and Collinson, D. 'Redesigning Work on the Shopfloor: A Question of Control or Consent?' In D. Knights, H. Willmott, and D. Collinson eds *Job Design: Critical Perspectives on the Labour Process.* London: Gower, 1984.

Laffer, K. 'The ACTU Arbitration Proposals.' *Public Administration* (Australia) XV (1) (March 1958).

Lansbury, R. D. and Davis, E. M. 'Employee Involvement and Workers' Participation in Management: The Australian Experience.' *Advances in Industrial and Labour Relations* 5, (1990): 33–57.

Lansbury, R. D. and Gilmour, P. *Organisations: An Australian Perspective.* Melbourne: Longman Cheshire, 1982.

Lansbury, R. D. and Spillane, R. *Organisational Behaviour: The Australian Context* (2nd edn) Sydney: Longman Cheshire, 1991.

Littler, C., Quinlan, M. and Kitay, J. 'Australian Workplace Industrial Relations: Towards a Conceptual Framework.' *The Journal of Industrial Relations* 31 (4) (December 1989): 500–25.

Lumley, R. 'Control over the Organisation and Conduct of Work: Evidence for Some Australian Workplaces.' *The Journal of Industrial Relations* 25 (3) (September 1983): 301–16.

Macdonald, D. K. 'The Employer and the Labour Process in New South Wales Government Organisations.' Ph. D. thesis Sydney: University of New South Wales, 1985a.

Macdonald, D. K. 'The Role of Management in Industrial Relations and Some Views on its Conceptualisation and Analysis.' *The Journal of Management Studies* 22 (5) (September 1985b): 523–46.

Macdonald, D. K. 'Labour Flexibility, Industrial Relations and Productivity.' *Labour Economics and Productivity* 1 (1) (March 1989): 22–41.

McDonald, T. and Rimmer, M. 'Award Restructuring and Wages Policy.' *Growth 37* CEDA, (1989): 111–34.

Marginson, P., Edwards, P. K., Martin, R., Purcell, J. and Sisson, K. *Beyond the Workplace: Managing Industrial Relations in the Multi-Establishment Enterprise.* Oxford: Blackwell, 1988.

Martin, R. M. *Trade Unions in Australia.* Ringwood: Pelican Books, 1975.

Mathews J. *Tools of Change—New Technology and the Democratisation of Work.* Sydney: Pluto Press, 1989.

Mitchell, J. 'Case and Situation Analysis.' *Sociological Review* 31 (2) (May 1983): 187–211.

Niland, J. 'The Case for More Collective Bargaining in Australia.' *The Journal of Industrial Relations* 18 (4) (December 1976): 365–90.

Niland, J. *Collective Bargaining and Compulsory Arbitration in Australia,* Kensington: New South Wales University Press, 1978.

Niland, J. *Transforming Industrial Relations in New South Wales: A Green Paper Volume 1,* Commissioned by the NSW Department of Industrial Relations and Employment. Sydney: Government Printer, 1989.

Perlman, M. 'An Industrial Problem, Australia's Longshoremen.' *Labor Law Journal* 4 (July 1953).

Peters, T. J. and Waterman, R. H. *In Search of Excellence: Lessons from America's Best-Run Companies.* New York: Harper and Row, 1982.

Piore, M. and Sabel, C. *The Second Industrial Divide—Possibilities for Prosperity.* New York: Basic Books, 1984.

Purcell, J. *Good Industrial Relations: Theory and Practice.* London: Macmillan, 1981.

Queen, S. 'Round Table on the Case Study in Sociological Research.' *Publications of the American Sociological Review* 22, (1928).

Quinlan, M. and Rimmer, M. 'Workplace Industrial Reform and Legislative Change: Hancock, Hanger, Niland and the Business Council of Australia.' *Labour and Industry* 2 (3) (October 1989): 434–52.

Ramsay, H. 'Industrial Democracy and the Question of Control.' In Davis, E. and Lansbury. R. eds *Democracy and Control in the Workplace.* Melbourne: Longman Cheshire, 1986.

Riach, P. A. and Howard, W. A. *Productivity Agreements and Australian Wage Determination.* Sydney: John Wiley, 1973.

Rimmer, M. 'Work Place Unionism.' In Ford, B. and Plowman, D. eds *Australian Unions: An Industrial Relations Perspective.* (2nd edn) South Melbourne: Macmillan, 1989.

Rimmer, M. and Verevis, C. *Progress of Award Restructuring: Case Studies.* Report commissioned by the Business Council of Australia from the National Key Centre of Industrial Relations, Monash University, Clayton, and the Industrial Relations Research Centre, University of New South Wales, Kensington: September, 1990.

Rimmer, M. and Zappala, J. 'Labour Market Flexibility and the Second Tier.' *Australian Bulletin of Labour* 14 (4) (September 1988): 564–91.

Rose, H., McLoughlin, I., King, R. and Clark, J. 'Opening the Black Box: The Relation Between Technology and Work.' *New Technology, Work and Employment* 1 (1), (1986): 18–26.

Sheehan, B. and Worland, D. *Glossary of Industrial Relations Terms.* Preston: The Industrial Relations Society of Victoria and the Department of Applied Economics and Industrial Relations, Preston Institute of Technology, 1985.

Stouffer, S. *Social Research to Test Ideas.* New York: The Free Press of Glencoe, 1962.

Sutcliffe, J. T. *A History of Trade Unionism in Australia.* Melbourne: Macmillan, 1967.

Terry, M. 'How Do We Know If Shop Stewards Are Getting Weaker?' *British Journal of Industrial Relations* 24 (2) (July 1986): 169–79.

Townley, B. 'Employee Communication Programmes.' In K. Sisson ed. *Personnel Management in Britain.* Oxford: Blackwell, 1989.

Trevor, M. *Toshiba's New British Company: Competitiveness Through Innovation in Industry*. London: Policy Studies Institute, 1988.

Trist, E. L., Higgin, G. W., Murray, H. and Pollock, A. B. *Organisational Choice*. London: Tavistock, 1963.

Walker, K. F. *Australian Industrial Relations Systems*. Cambridge, Mass.: Harvard University Press, 1970.

Walton, R. 'Advantages and Attributes of the Case Study.' *The Journal of Applied Behavioural Science* 8 (1) (Jan–Feb 1972): 73–8.

Walton, R. and McKersie R. *Behavioral Theory of Labor Negotiations*. New York: McGraw-Hill, 1965.

Wilkinson, B. *The Shopfloor Politics of New Technology*. London: Heinemann, 1983.

Woodward, J. *Industrial Organization: Theory and Practice*. Oxford: Oxford University Press, 1965.

Worland, D. and Wilson, K. 'Employment and Labour Costs in the Hospitality Industry: Evidence from Victoria, Australia.' *International Journal of Hospitality Management* Vol.7 No. 4 (1988): 363–77.

Yerbury, D. and Isaac, J. 'Recent Trends in Collective Bargaining in Australia.' *International Labour Review* 103 (May 1971): 421–52.

Zappala, G. *Workplace Industrial Relations in Australia—An Annotated and Selected Bibliography* (2nd edn) Sydney: Australian Centre for Industrial Relations Research and Teaching, University of Sydney, 1991a.

Zappala, G. *The Closed Shop: Help or Hindrance for the Union Movement*. ACIRRT Working Paper No. 9, Sydney: Australian Centre for Industrial Relations Research and Teaching, University of Sydney, 1991b.

Notes on contributors

GREG J. BAMBER is Reader in the Graduate School of Management at the University of Queensland. He is currently conducting research on the transferability of Japanese management styles to 'western' enterprises. He has published numerous articles and books including *Militant Managers?*, *International and Comparative Industrial Relations* and *New Technology: International Perspectives on Human Resources and Industrial Relations*; the last two with Russell Lansbury.

JOHN BENSON is Senior Lecturer in the Department of Economics and Deputy Director of the Centre for Industrial Relations and Labour Studies at the University of Melbourne. His major research focus over the past ten years has been on industrial relations at the workplace. Oxford University Press recently published his book *Unions at the Workplace: Shop Steward Leadership and Ideology*. Dr Benson's current research is a three country study of the relationship between workplace labour relations and productivity.

GERARD GRIFFIN is Senior Lecturer in Industrial Relations at the University of Melbourne. His current research interest is the character, structure and changing membership of trade unions, an area in which he has published the book, *White-Collar Union Militancy*, and several journal articles.

J.E. ISAAC was Professor of Economics at the University of Melbourne and then at Monash University until his appointment to the Australian Conciliation and Arbitration Commission in 1974. He retired from that position in 1989 and has since been associated with the two industrial relations centres at the above universities.

RUSSELL LANSBURY is Professor and Head of the Department of Industrial Relations at the University of Sydney. He was the Foundation Director of the Australian Centre for Industrial Relations Research and Teaching (ACIRRT). He holds a Ph.D. from the London School of

Economics and has been a Senior Fulbright Fellow at MIT and Harvard University. He has published on technological change, industrial democracy and the role of management in industrial relations.

DUNCAN MACDONALD is Senior Lecturer in Industrial Relations in the Department of Economics at Newcastle University. His research interests include the public sector, workplace industrial relations and award restructuring. Dr Macdonald is also Director of the Workplace Change Course in the Hunter Region.

MALCOLM RIMMER is Professor and Director of the National Key Centre in Industrial Relations at Monash University. He is the co-author (with Mark Bray) of *Delivering the Goods: A History of the Transport Workers' Union in New South Wales, 1888–1986*, and (with Chrissie Verevis) of *Award Restructuring: Progress at the Workplace*.

CLAIRE RUNCIMAN is the Executive Director of the Survey Research and Consultancy Unit at the University of Queensland. She is also a director of Bookoola Research Pty Ltd, a company which provides research services for Aboriginal groups. As well as consultancy reports, Dr Runciman has published articles on job tenure in the retail industry and trends in the labour market.

VIC TAYLOR is Principal Lecturer in the Department of Business and Management at the City Polytechnic of Hong Kong. In recent years he has written on the politics of Australian industrial relations and the changing perceptions of industrial relations in management education. In 1991 he jointly edited, with Mark Bray, the collection entitled *The Other Side of Flexibility*. He has just commenced a study of business power and labour management in Asia.

ELSA UNDERHILL is Lecturer in Industrial Relations at the Victoria University of Technology. She is the author of a chapter on contract labour in the building industry in *The Other Side of Flexibility* and has recently written (with Malcolm Rimmer) 'Can and Should Unions Charge for Services?' in *What Can Unions Do*?

DAVID WORLAND is Principal Lecturer, Victoria University of Technology. He has published in the fields of hospitality, human resources and employee information and is currently involved in research into overaward payments.

Index